THE HARDCORE TRUTH

THE BOB HOLLY STORY

BOB HOLLY WITH **ROSS WILLIAMS**

ECW PRESS

Published by ECW Press
2120 Queen Street East, Suite 200, Toronto, Ontario, Canada M4E 1E2
416-694-3348 / info@ecwpress.com

LIBRARY AND ARCHIVES CANADA CATALOGUING IN PUBLICATION
Holly, Bob, 1963–
The hardcore truth : the Bob Holly story / Bob Holly.

ISBN 978-1-77041-109-8
ALSO ISSUED AS: 978-1-77090-378-4 (PDF), 978-1-77090-379-1 (EPUB)

1. Holly, Bob, 1963–. 2. Wrestlers—United States—Biography.

1. Title.

GV1196.H65A3 2013   796.812092   C2012-907529-9

Editor for the press: Michael Holmes
Cover images: George Napolitano
Interior images: Courtesy Bob Holly, unless
otherwise indicated.

PRINTED AND BOUND IN CANADA

PREFACE

"What the fuck are you doing?"

Bob's steely glare bored into me as I asked myself exactly the same thing. . . . There I was, a not entirely athletic 31-year-old who had made his pro wrestling debut just four months earlier, in the ring with "Hardcore" Holly — and he looked pissed off. Even the referee was giving us a wide berth. With no more than a foot between us, I was certainly within clouting distance. The question was just how hard and how prolonged the clouting was going to be. Time seemed to stand still while neither of us did a thing. The audience buzzed, anticipating the forthcoming violence, and all I could think about was how embarrassing it would be to be carted off to the hospital whilst wearing altogether too much spandex.

I was *supposed* to be finished for the evening. I'd opened the show, winning a 12-minute contest that was, at that point, the best match of my career. I had been looking forward to watching the main event that would see Bob Holly and Jake McCluskey pitted against the UK Kid and Leon Shah. But, as Leon hobbled back into the locker room after his first bout of the evening, I began to feel uneasy. The unease quickly turned into full-blown panic as Leon explained to promoter Tom (the UK Kid) that he couldn't put any real weight on his leg. "No worries," said Tom. "We'll just use Ross instead."

Oh shit.

It was brown trousers time for sure. Still, I manned up and didn't let on.

"So, what are we going to do?" I enquired as casually as I could manage.

"Dunno. We'll call it in the ring," replied the UK Kid, a 12-year veteran. Five-year pro McCluskey looked on in amusement.

"But Tom," I whispered, "I've never done a tag match before. Can we at least lay out a couple of spots?"

Tom gave me a devilish smirk. "Well, if you want to go and discuss your ideas with Bob, feel free . . ."

I looked at Bob, taking nanoseconds to decide that approaching him would not be a clever move. Apparently, nanoseconds were too long. Bob caught me staring in his direction and thundered, "What the fuck're you lookin' at?" across the locker room.

I averted my gaze, changed my underwear, and got warmed up for the match.

Ten minutes later, as I was jogging up and down a corridor, Tom's voice rang out. "Ross, are you coming or not?" Tom was in his gear, ready to go. Bob and Jake were ready too, standing halfway down the corridor. Mustering all my bravado, I tried something along the lines of a confident swagger: "Yeah, I thought I might give it a go." Passing Jake and Bob, I offered a nod and a simple "see you out there." Bob's voice, quiet but full of menace, followed me down the corridor: "You've got a fuckin' attitude problem."

As I passed Rob Holte, whose often stoic expression now showed something approaching sympathy, I said, "Tell my mother I love her." Rob was my favorite opponent and had always looked after me but, even so, I would often leave the ring a little worse for wear after our matches. I knew *that* was nothing compared to what I was about to experience.

I approached the ring on jelly-legs, running on a mixture of adrenaline and terror, and awaited my fate. As Bob's music blared over the speakers, Tom approached and said, "Don't worry, I'll work most of the match. Just follow my lead, you'll be fine."

Breathing a sigh of relief, I took up a position on the apron — a

did actually help me believe the other stuff! The more you get to know Bob, the more you realize he is just not into bullshit and he will call a spade a spade. If you suck, he'll tell you. If you're good at something, he'll put you over for it. In short, he'll tell you what you *need* to hear and not what you *want* to hear. I wouldn't have it any other way.

Up until our match, Bob and I had had something of an up-and-down relationship. In training sessions and at shows, I felt he was starting to warm to my promo ability and my drive to improve in-ring, but he didn't seem to feel that I was tough enough. During our match, he took it upon himself to test me. Bob gave me an opportunity to earn his respect — an opportunity that I took with both hands. After earning his respect, I've got to know Robert Howard the man, as well as Bob Holly the wrestler. I've had the chance to learn about his career, his background, his trials and tribulations, and to better understand the circumstances behind certain situations for which he has often been vilified by the wrestling media. Above all else, I've had the chance to get to know an unfailingly honest, down-to-earth, caring, and downright decent human being.

Now, I have the privilege of sharing *The Hardcore Truth* with the world. After the story has been told, I believe even Bob's most staunch detractors will have a different answer to his long-time catchphrase, "How do you like me now?"

— *Ross Williams*

Ever the British gent, I believe I instinctively replied, "That's quite all right," before he clobbered me again, saving the stiffest shot for last.

After my brutalization and his apology, the rest of the match went smoothly (save for my nose being cut open — my mistake there, I caught my face on something Jake was wearing), and my input was limited to some basic holds, plenty of cheating, and being sent sailing over the top rope to the unpadded floor. I can't take any credit for the quality of the match, since everyone else was just working around me, but it remains my best match — and my favorite, for that matter.

Back in the locker room, after having a picture taken in which I proudly displayed my bloody nose and red-raw chest, I wandered over to Bob to thank him for the match. He shook my hand, thanked *me*, and said, "You really impressed me out there. You were in the right place at the right time and you took your beating like a man. You did great." He also told me that my bloodied chest would hurt like hell when I showered. He was definitely not wrong. It was unquestionably the most painful shower I have taken in my life.

Still, long after the wounds on my chest had healed and as my eardrum slowly repaired itself, I had a memory to cherish and one heck of a story to tell — and video footage to back it up! About 10 weeks later, around the time my eardrum had finally healed, I was surprised to receive an email from Bob — and the content was even more surprising. In the email, Bob reiterated that he had "nothing but respect for me" and apologized for any times he'd treated me badly. (For the record, I don't feel he ever had.) He finished by writing, "I hope you accept my apology." Since then, we've kept in touch, leading to this project. He's filled me in on a few things: that he pushed for me to replace Leon for that match in Southampton and that, months before that, when he first heard me cut a promo in training, he pushed hard for Tom to use me regularly on shows. Bob really gets behind the people who he believes work hard to improve and he is extremely supportive while remaining honest to a fault. During my training and wrestling "career," he informed me repeatedly (and accurately!) that I struggle with the athletic side of things but also told me that I had good timing, took a fantastic bump, and could cut a damn fine promo. The fact that he's so blunt in observing my lack of athletic acumen position I expected to maintain for most of the match. Roughly 18 seconds later, after two or three quick bumps, Tom scurried over to tag me in.

I dropped off the apron, refusing his hand, assuming I should play the cowardly heel.

Tom whispered, "Get between us."

By this, he meant that I should sneak into the ring, lure Bob into our corner, and let Tom jump him from behind. Having never been in a tag match before and not yet being aware of all the wrestling lingo, I thought Tom meant that I should *physically* get between them. So I slid into the ring and marched up to Bob with my arms outstretched as if to say, "Whaddya think *you're* doing, tough guy?"

Under my breath, I asked, "Do you want to hit me?"

This is where we came in.

"What the fuck are you doing?"

My options seemed to be: A) run away and have Bob catch me and beat the everlasting crap out of me for being a pussy; B) back away and have Bob grab me and beat the everlasting crap out of me for being a pussy; or C) shove him and see what happened.

I went with C and gave him a respectful shove.

Bob "Hardcore" Holly then respectfully smacked me upside my head, bursting my eardrum. As he reached down to hoist me off the canvas, I realized I couldn't hear a damn thing out of my right ear. What if he tried to call some moves to me, I didn't catch them, and I blew a spot? He'd think I was fucking with him and would absolutely destroy me! These fears were quickly dismissed when his plans became evident. He backed me up into the corner and pulled my shirt over my head, exposing my chest.

Bob's chops are notorious for hurting like hell. Up until that point, I could only speculate. Two minutes later, having been on the receiving end of about a dozen of Bob's finest, I could confirm that yes, they do indeed hurt like hell. My chest, which was now bleeding, seconded the opinion. The crowd had popped for each chop with increasing fervor but, by the last, they were wincing in pain along with me.

Then something happened that changed my view of Bob entirely.

Propping me up in the corner and pulling my shirt over my face once more, he leaned in and whispered in my ear, "Sorry, man."

CHAPTER 1

BREAD, GRAVY, AND BABY FOOD

I've never been a fan of bullies.

I know; it's ironic, given the way a lot of wrestling fans ended up seeing me later in my career, but the fact remains that I encountered bullying at a young age and I learned to stand up to it pretty fast.

My brother was always up to no good. We never really had a brotherly relationship when we were kids. Even though he's only a year and a half older than me, we rarely played together. He and his friends constantly picked on me. One of them in particular liked to help him torment me. They were always together and always trying to get to me. They genuinely scared me.

If I was playing in the yard by myself, they would sneak up behind me with a gallon bucket of water and dump it over my head. It wasn't a practical joke between brothers. It was a couple of mean-spirited little shits trying to make themselves feel big by picking on someone younger and weaker. It wasn't a one-time thing, either. They did this again and again — more times than I care to remember.

One day, after this had gone on for quite a while, I saw my brother's friend walking down the street with his mom. At that point I'd just had enough and had to do something. I ran over to them and asked the kid, "Where's your bucket of water now?" He started saying a bunch of mean

1

things, so I drilled him in the mouth, right in front of his mom. I knocked him down and started kicking him. I still remember his mother screaming at me, saying that she was going to call the police and have me arrested for beating up her kid.

I was six. I guess you could say I've been hardcore since then.

I figured that if nobody else was going to stand up for me, I was going to have to do it myself. Maybe I could have handled it in a less violent way but I'll say this — after I stood my ground, those bullies quit coming near me. I didn't have anyone to help me fight my battles when I was young. You hear stories where the oldest kid in the family stands up for the younger ones — that never happened for me. My brother was half the problem. As we got older, we didn't fight much but we didn't hang out or do anything together. The day after he graduated, he went off to join the Marines. I was glad to see him gone.

You could probably say I was unlucky with my dad too. My mom and dad divorced when I was young, so I didn't really know him. I know he was a street fighter, always getting into trouble with bikers and stuff like that. He was a real jackass; he didn't pay child support or anything.

I've been blessed with a great mom, though. My relationship with her has always been good. She's very goofy, very silly, and one of the kindest people you'll ever meet — she doesn't have an enemy in this world. I love her to death.

She taught me all about hard work. After my dad left and my brother started school, she would take me to work with her because she couldn't afford a babysitter. We couldn't afford a car either, so she and I would walk to her workplace. I'd sit on the floor for eight hours each day as she soldered wires on boards. It wasn't an ideal childhood, but she did her best for me and my brother. Every single day, we walked three miles there, she worked, and then we walked three miles back home. I remember trying to keep up with her; she walked so damn fast. I managed, but it sure was tough.

When we got home, all we had to eat were bread, gravy, and baby food. It was all we could afford and what we had for dinner every night. But Mom did everything she could to feed us. She always did the best she could with what she had. Was I unhappy? I didn't know any better. I was

just a little kid and I had my mom, so as far as I was concerned, that was all I needed.

I did sometimes wish my dad was around, though. Recently, my mom told me that sometimes he would call to say he would come by but would rarely show up. I don't remember that but it obviously affected me. Mom told me she found me in the closet one day — she heard me talking to somebody. "Bobby, what are you doing?" she asked. "Who are you talking to?"

I said, "I'm talking to my dad." I was so disappointed that he hadn't shown up that day that I had this make-believe conversation, pretending he was with me. I still loved my dad — or at least felt a need for a father figure.

I didn't see him regularly and nothing he did back then created a lasting impact. Honestly, to this day, I don't even remember what he looks like. There were a handful of times when he did come to visit me at the apartment in Glendale, California. I don't recall too much about those visits. He'd turn up, spend a while with me, and leave. He wouldn't pay any child support and his visits became rarer as time went on. As I got older, he vanished from my life completely.

The last time I saw him, I was 16. We'd moved to a different state and I hadn't heard from him in years. Then, out of the blue, he decided to come up and visit his old family — with his new family. He was remarried with two kids. It was kind of awkward since we couldn't spend any quality time together. There was no chance for it to be a father-and-son sort of thing — for either me or my brother — because we were always in a group of people. I hadn't seen him for nine years and I really didn't know him. He was a stranger to me, but he was still my dad. I would have liked to have had a little one-on-one time with him. I didn't get it — they hung out for about an hour, then left to go camping. The next day, we went to their camp site, we all had a picnic, and then they headed back to California. That was the last time I saw him or even spoke to him.

He tried to get in touch with me after I started to appear on TV with the WWF in the mid '90s, and that just hurt. He hadn't been there for me when I was growing up and needed a dad, but now that I'd attained a level of notoriety, he wanted back in? I didn't want to talk to him so I didn't take his calls. I'd always wanted a relationship with my father, but not one that was motivated by my achieving some sort of fame. As time has gone on, I've found myself wanting to find out more about him and to see if we could form any sort of bond. So, I started doing some research to track him down. I found him in the end — but too late. He died in 2008. I wish I'd reached out sooner. Despite his not being there for me when I was a kid, I do regret not getting to know him.

A few years after my parents separated, Mom met a guy named Gary through my aunt Elaine, and he ended up becoming my stepdad. Gary was a racing enthusiast who helped my uncle Don work on his race car, so that was how he knew my aunt. He was basically a workaholic. During the week, he worked in maintenance for the county school district. On the weekends, he was a janitor at a wood mill. He was a hard worker, I'll give him that, but he was a horrible male role model. He wasn't a father figure to me; he was just a guy my mom was married to. I know why she did it. She was struggling to keep a roof over our heads and could barely feed us, so when she found somebody that she could tolerate, they got married. We moved from Glendale to Ventura, California, to live with him, so at least we had a roof over our heads and food on the table. They're not together anymore — right after I graduated high school, they divorced. I don't know if that was her plan all along or if it was because there had been some infidelity on his part.

He wasn't bad to us but he wasn't good. He was very strict. When my brother and I got home from school, we weren't allowed to play, watch TV, or eat; we were given work to do around the house and that's all we did. I don't want to say Gary was like a drill sergeant because that would be too much of a compliment to him. He was always on us for no reason. For example, every weekend we had to cut the grass. If he felt we hadn't cut the grass correctly, he'd make us cut the entire yard again until we'd done it the way he wanted it. If we missed one weed when we were pulling them, we had to start over. It felt like we'd been put on the earth to serve him. Every Saturday morning: "get up, cut the grass, rake the leaves, chop the wood" . . . and whatever else he could find for us to do. Even during school vacations, it was the same. I had a summer job, but since that didn't start until 3 p.m., I had to get up at 7 to start working around the house.

If we wanted to play high school sports, we had to buy our own gear. We got no help financially. We got no support of any kind. Our mountain of chores came first and then we had to get ourselves to and from practice. As far as I'm concerned, parents should help their kids to succeed, whether in sports or education. You push them, but you support them and say, "Whatever you need, I'm here for you. All you have to do is ask." I didn't have that. If I wanted to succeed, everything was on me. My mother tried, but you need the whole team behind you. Gary had the financial means to help, and without his support it was damn near impossible for me to do anything in high school. The only things Gary taught me were how to cut grass, chop wood, pull weeds, and wash dishes — stuff like that. I learned everything else on my own.

Gary was definitely hands off. I don't get why he was like that — he knew what he signed up for when he married my mother. She had two boys, so we were part of the deal. Maybe he just saw the marriage as a good way to get some cheap labor. That wouldn't surprise me — Gary was a real tightwad. It wasn't just sports gear I had to pay for; I had to buy my own school clothes. He bought us two pairs of jeans, a pair of tennis shoes, and some white T-shirts, and that's all we got for the year. If we wanted anything else, we had to work a regular job to earn the money. Once I started working, the bastard made me pay rent. Here I was, still in high school and I was paying 50 dollars a month to my stepfather. That was a lot of damn money to a 17 year old, especially back in 1980! I understand paying rent to your folks if you're living at home after you've graduated — but not when you're still a minor.

My brother and I were nervous wrecks whenever he was around. It was horrible. He never laid a hand on us, but he made us uncomfortable all the time. He didn't care if we were upset, if we were hurt, if we had any problems; all that mattered to him was that we were able to work around the yard and the house. I'm sure my mom wasn't too happy, but what could she do? She was as dependent on him as we were, if not more so. She was just trying to keep the peace. Aunt Elaine told me that my mother *did* stand up for us behind closed doors, but in the end, she had to follow Gary's lead and say, "Well, you gotta work."

It was too bad that we had to work so much, because I could have been really good at football. Whenever we played it in PE, I played wide receiver. I was small but fast, and I had great hands. If I could touch the ball, I'd catch it. The Grants Pass High School Football coach was also my PE teacher, and he told me that if I played for him in my senior year, he was sure I would get a college scholarship — a full ride. I had to tell him I couldn't because my parents were making me work. It was a damn shame that I didn't get to play college football.

Still, for all of the negative thoughts about Gary I had during my teenage years, I did develop a very strong work ethic because of him. I'm very particular — the engine bay of each of my vehicles has to be spotless, for example. Everything has to be in a pristine condition; everything has to look good. All of my tools are in a certain order. Nice and neat — everything clean. I pay attention to detail. This work ethic was reflected in my time as a wrestler. I always strove for the perfect match. You never get it, but you always strive for it. You're constantly working to have better matches. I am a perfectionist and my own worst critic. I may never reach perfection but as long as I'm striving for it, I'll always do the best I can.

Despite how it might sound, and even though Gary made me feel like a slave a lot of the time, I didn't grow up unhappy. He and I didn't have much in common, but we both liked auto racing and we both liked wrestling.

CHAPTER 2

THE OPENING BELL

One of the good things about moving in with Gary was that he had a TV. This was new to us because we had never been able to afford one. I discovered roller derby pretty quickly and thought it was great. If you look at it now, it's obviously a work, but back then I thought it was real. Later, when I was in fourth grade, my stepdad's parents and siblings moved from California to Oregon so we moved too. I can still remember flipping through *TV Guide* and finding *Big Time Wrestling*.

I tuned in and I was hooked right away. I'd never seen anything like it. Pat Patterson, Pepper Gomez, Rocky Johnson, Peter Maivia, Mr. Saito . . . it was the greatest thing on the planet. I couldn't wait for the next Saturday so I could see some more. Pat Patterson was the big babyface. It's mind-boggling to think that I ended up working alongside Pat, and that about 25 years after I first saw him wrestle, I cussed him out in front of the entire WWE locker room.

A while after we got to Oregon, I found out that there were other wrestling groups, including Portland Wrestling. I was in heaven! I still remember the guys who made the biggest first impression on me. There was Jesse "The Body" Ventura, Jimmy "Superfly" Snuka, and, of course, "Rowdy" Roddy Piper. Those guys were great, but the guy I liked the most was "Playboy" Buddy Rose. His interviews were good, he was a great

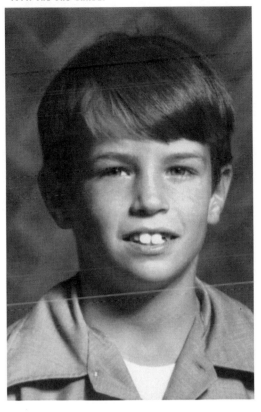

worker, and he made everything so believable. Even now, I still think that he was one of the greatest workers who ever lived. Buddy Rose never got the respect he deserved. He was such an awesome heel. I had my other favorites — Mr. Saito, Bob Roop, Ricky Hunter, Rocky Johnson, Patterson, Ray Stevens, Kenji Shibuya, and Peter Maivia, but in my opinion, Buddy Rose was *the man*. He didn't get a shot when he joined the wwf because the owner, Vince McMahon, just didn't like most fat guys. People remember Buddy Rose as the fat guy in Vince's stupid blow-away diet ads and as a wrestler who lost to everybody. I remember him as my first real wrestling hero.

Gary and I tuned in every Saturday like clockwork for *Big Time Wrestling* at 3:30 and then *Portland Wrestling*. It wasn't a family thing. Mom never watched and my brother didn't like it either — he was more into *Star Trek*. He and his friends picked on me sometimes because of the wrestling thing but I didn't give a damn. Come on, seriously, which is nerdier — wrestling or Mr. Spock? Hey, if people like *Star Trek*, good for them. Just don't tell me I'm a nerd for being into wrestling!

Even though my brother didn't care much for it, some of my friends got into wrestling with me. Whenever Gary couldn't watch with me, Mike Brown would come over and we'd watch the shows together. Inevitably, some of my friends and I would end up wrestling each other. When I was in junior high, my friend Scott Clause and I would take a roll of aluminum foil from the kitchen cupboard. We'd start with a little ball and make something the size of a basketball. Then we'd take it outside and beat it down until it was as compact and hard as we could make it. Then we'd have a wrestling match — an "Aluminum Foil Ball Match." Whoever got to the ball first could use it on his opponent. The problem was, back then, we still thought wrestling was real. We beat the holy hell out of each other. Everybody on TV bled from the forehead, so I'd pound his face with the aluminum ball to try and split his head wide open — until he'd start crying. He gave as good as he got, though: he would get the ball from me, crack me upside the head, and try his damnedest to make *me* bleed. But no matter how hard we tried, neither of us ever managed to get the job done.

When Dutch Savage and "Playboy" Buddy Rose went on TV and had a coal miner's glove match . . . well, that wasn't going to end well for us after we saw that. In that match, there was a pole on the corner post of the ring with a glove hanging from it. The "coal miner's glove" was a welding glove with a piece of steel flat bar attached to it. The first wrestler to get up the pole and get the glove could use it. So, thinking this was probably the best idea of all time, I got myself a glove from the shed at home, found a piece of flat bar lying around, and duct-taped the metal to the glove so we could have our own coal miner's glove match. My friend and I would lay out some garden hose to outline the wrestling ring, stick a pole in the ground, and put the glove on top of it. Then we'd fucking kill each other. We ended up with bloody noses, busted lips, and a few headaches here and there. Our parents never knew. If I got a fat lip or a scraped face, they would ask what happened. "Oh, we were just outside playing," I'd say, and they bought it.

Later, when I was in high school, I'd end up pretending to fight with another friend, Randy Rudy, in the front yard. We were doing it to see if we could get people on the highway to slow down and watch us (and they did), so I guess that was my first taste of fighting to entertain other people! We didn't hold back on each other because we still hadn't quite figured out that the wrestling on TV wasn't real. Back then, wrestlers protected the business more than anything, and the way everything was done was so much more realistic than nowadays. When I was a kid, I guess I always had it in my mind that it *might* be a work, but I also had that doubt, that little something that tells you it just might be real. It was sort of like believing in Santa — you question it but you also really want to believe in it. Then you're kind of disappointed when you figure it out.

We couldn't afford to go to a show when I was a kid, but by the time I was a senior in high school, I had a job and a little money left over after I'd paid rent. When I found out that *Portland Wrestling* was on tour and coming to Grants Pass, I asked for the night off but my bosses wouldn't give it to me. I was furious. I decided I was going to go to work, do everything I could as quickly as I could, and then haul ass out of there to go straight to the show. I thought I might get fired but I didn't care. It was a regular house show and a lot of my favorites were there, including "Playboy" Buddy Rose. The next day, I didn't get fired but I definitely got in trouble. It was absolutely worth it.

I loved wrestling. Even back then, I knew I wanted to do it for a living. It just never occurred to me that I actually *could* . . .

CHAPTER 3

NEED FOR SPEED

I've had a number of concussions. This shouldn't surprise anyone, especially after they learn that my childhood friends and I beat on each other with steel-plated gloves for fun, but my first concussion actually happened before those childhood wrestling matches. I was five.

I remember getting a tricycle for my fifth birthday, back when we lived in the second story of an apartment block in Glendale. Mom was asleep. Unsurprisingly, my brother didn't care to help me get this tricycle down to the ground level so I decided I'd ride the damn thing down the stairs. Well, I got to the bottom but I sure wasn't on my trike anymore . . . I slammed my head on the concrete and my mom woke up to the sound of me screaming my lungs out. Within seconds, I had a bump the size of a big egg on my head. Off we went to the hospital — which wasn't an easy task back then.

Everything we needed was about three miles from our apartment. Mom's work, the stores, and, of course, the hospital. We didn't have a car so she had to play human ambulance with me — she carried me in her arms all the way there and back. That wasn't the only time we had to make that trip. Far from it, because I always seemed to get myself into some sort of trouble. In my defense, there were always plenty of things around to injure myself on. I was playing in a nearby field one day when I stepped right on a four-inch nail sticking out of a discarded board. That nail went clean through my foot. Back to the hospital we went. I was hard work for my mother . . .

My daredevil streak led to bike riding. By the age of 16, I'd gotten into dirt bikes. It was something I kept up with until recently. Even when I was with WWE, I was on a dirt bike every chance I got. Whenever I had a day off, I would come home, load up, and go riding somewhere. In my WWE days, after I'd had a couple of decent earning years, I decided to buy a custom-built CR500 built by Service Honda out of Indiana. It was the best bike on the market. A CR500 put in a 250 aluminum frame — that thing was a damn rocket ship. Back when I was 16, though, I couldn't afford anything like *that*. I was working at a golf course as a range picker and, after I'd bought what I needed for school, I was able to afford my first dirt bike. It was a Yamaha YZ125, and I loved that thing. Around the time I graduated, I bought a Suzuki RM250 and started doing hill climbs.

If you don't know much about dirt bike racing, I can tell you that a hill climb is usually on the side of a mountain or a massive hill, which is at a 45-degree angle or more, and you've got to get up the ridge as quickly as you can. The flag drops, the timer starts, and you just twist that throttle, hope you go straight, and hang on for dear life. One of the guys in our group lived in a house on the edge of a big mountain, so we'd practice there. The hill was pretty steep, so it was ideal. Rain or shine, we rode those dirt bikes. Sometimes this wasn't the smartest move. One time, when we were about to do our final run of the day, it started to rain pretty hard. It was my turn, so I twisted the throttle, dumped the clutch, and shot up that hill like a cat with its ass on fire. All of a sudden the bike did a 180 because the ground was slick with rain. I shot back down with the throttle wide open. I didn't have time to think or be scared. I plowed straight into some trees, which stopped the bike dead. I was thrown forward, against the handlebars, and I just hung there. After a few seconds, I started moving around. I was shaken up but thought I was okay. When I took my helmet off, the pain hit me like a bolt of lightning. It was so intense that I thought I was going to die right then and there. I'd gone from wide open to a dead stop in a split second. My head was killing me from the whiplash, and I'd smacked my right leg so hard on the handlebars that I thought I'd broken the bone. My bike was pinned between two of the trees. Even with four guys pulling, they couldn't get it out. In the end, they had to get a chainsaw to cut that bike free. I was amazed to find that the rims, forks, and handlebars were not damaged — the crash felt like it damn near killed me and the bike hardly got a scratch!

I could barely move, but I was so stubborn that I decided I was going to get back on and go up that damn hill one more time. I couldn't throw my leg over the bike, so my friends helped me. I started going back up the hill but everything hurt so much, I couldn't stay on. I just laid it down, got off, and dropped down there with it. My friends came up the hill, got the bike, got me, loaded us both onto the truck, and headed off. I struggled to walk for about a month after that. I had such a bad contusion on my leg that it was as useless as if I'd broken it. By that point, I was working at Gold River Distributing, the beer warehouse, and a lot of my job was driving a forklift. My leg really wasn't in good enough shape to do that, but I couldn't afford to take time off. I had to earn money, so I forced myself to carry on through the pain.

As upset as I was, it wasn't long before I felt the need to get back on the bike. About four months later, I threw my leg back over that thing and kicked it. I wasn't going to let something like a crash stop me for long.

By 1983, *the* bike to own was a water-cooled dirt bike with a radiator. Since I had a pretty good-paying job, I was the first one of my friends to get one. I was the talk of the town. Everywhere we went, everybody wanted to look at my bike. Man, that thing was fast too — really fast. That's when I got into motocross. I thought it was awesome. A track with ruts and big jumps and whoop-de-doos, where you pin the throttle and haul ass — where could I sign up? I started entering motocross races, but I wasn't really good enough to compete. I did it for fun, but some of the other guys rode every single day. Racing was their job, and it was all they ever did. I would have loved to do that but, number one, I wasn't fast enough and, number two, I didn't have the support needed to be successful.

It's always something I come back to for fun. Whenever I was off from WWE with an injury, I traveled to Delbarton, West Virginia. The town holds hillclimb races every month during the summer and people come from all around the country for them. At one point, the hill gets up to something like a 70-degree gradient. It's a fucking big hill. I managed to get over it once and they timed me at about 16 seconds. I was happy with that.

So from the age of 16 all the way through until the end of my WWE run, I always had a dirt bike. I don't have one now because my CR500 was stolen in 2009. One Sunday, I'd been washing down the bike outside my workshop, along with a Rincon 680 four-wheeler that I'd just got. As it was getting late, I left them outside and went in for the night. I lived out in the country in Mobile, Alabama, where there were very few other homes, so you could leave everything unlocked. Or so I thought. When I woke at 6 a.m., I looked out the kitchen window. Something didn't look right. I thought, "Wait a second . . . my pressure washer is sitting there, my dirt bike stand is sitting there, but my dirt bike is gone . . ." I started second-guessing myself, so I went to see if I'd put the bike back in the shop. That's when I noticed the four-wheeler was gone too.

My property sat about three hundred yards off the main road, and I could see where the four-wheeler and the dirt bike had been pushed through the grass down the hill to the access road. I called the police and filed a report. The next day, I got to thinking that the guys who had stolen my vehicles had probably looked in my workshop too. I had a lot of things in there — all my tools, shop equipment, a welding machine, and burning rigs. I figured, if they'd seen all of that, they would probably come back and try to take more. Sure enough, three o'clock in the morning, when I woke up to get some water and looked out of the kitchen window, I saw headlights. The car was moving slowly and stopped at the bottom of the hill by the pond. I stood and watched, wondering what this was all about. A truck turned up and parked at the bottom of the hill. Then another one. And a third truck and a second car. They all sat at the bottom of the hill with their parking lights on. *This is pretty frickin' interesting*, I thought to myself . . . so I went to my bedroom, got my 9mm Smith & Wesson, and loaded it. I went outside, hid in the dark where they wouldn't see me, and waited. I stood barefoot in just my boxer shorts, holding my 9mm with a full clip, ready to unload if they came onto my property.

After about 10 minutes, they cranked up their vehicles and pulled away really slowly. I was damned if I was going to let this one slide, since I figured they'd stolen my dirt bike and four-wheeler, so I ran back in and grabbed my truck keys, still barefoot and in boxers. There was a little gas station/convenience store at the end of my road where I thought they might stop to plan what to do next. I drove to the store but they weren't there, so I ended up driving all around the area, searching. I couldn't find them anywhere, which is probably for the best given how crazily I was acting. I got home and sat there, hoping they'd return. For several nights, I didn't sleep — I just kept looking outside and waiting for someone to come back. They never did. I'd always taken great care of my bikes; after each ride, I'd spend two or three hours, sometimes up to half a day, making sure they were spotless. If you'd seen them, you'd have wondered if I ever rode them at all. They looked like they just came off the showroom floor. I'd invested about $14,000 in that dirt bike and the four-wheeler had cost me about $10,000. It still makes me mad.

CHAPTER 4
GROWING UP IN THE FAST LANE

Her name was Linda Kievet and she was a senior.

I'd noticed her in the hallway at school and, even though I was still a junior, I just had to get to know her better. She had options — a lot of the other guys were after her — but she became *my* high school sweetheart.

She had already enlisted in the Air Force, so she was going to leave right after she graduated. We both knew this. Until then, though, we were pretty much attached at the hip; we spent all of our time together. On Saturdays, I would drive to Linda's house to pick her up and we'd either go out with our friends or go back to my house to watch wrestling. By now, my parents were away square dancing every Saturday evening, so sometimes the television wouldn't be switched on at all when she was at my house . . . that's all I'll say about that!

She would hang out with me at the golf course where I worked, when I was picking the driving range or cleaning carts. Sometimes she would work alongside me during tournaments. We went to the prom together. I was crazy about her. I wasn't the only one — everyone loved Linda. My parents thought she was the greatest thing God ever put on this earth. Her mom and dad liked me a lot too. Her dad loved the outdoors and was a real man's man. He loved to go out on the ocean in his fishing boat, and he had his own shop where he would restore cars and fix stuff. He could fix anything. He was amazing, a truly great man.

Linda's parents had a vacation spot out in Brookings, Oregon. Just before she left for the Air Force, they invited me to go to Brookings with them for the weekend. That meant a lot to me. It meant even more that her dad let me drive his Jeep around the town. He didn't let *anybody* drive that thing and there he was, letting a 17 year old borrow it to take his daughter out. That's how much he trusted me. It was an unbelievable weekend, hanging out on the beach, driving around town in her dad's Jeep, Bob Seger playing on the radio. That weekend made it even harder to see her go into the Air Force.

She graduated from high school and that was it: time for her to leave. It broke my heart. She was stationed in Texas — and Texas is a whole world away when you're a teenager. We kept in touch through letters and phone calls and she came back home a couple of times to visit. On one hand, it was great to see her, but on the other I absolutely hated it because I knew she would just have to leave again. The last time I saw her was the summer of 1981. We lost touch after that summer. Over the years, I often thought of her and was heartbroken every time I'd hear a Bob Seger song on the radio.

After Linda left, I still had another year of school to go. I just got on with it, went to school, watched my wrestling, and worked at the beer warehouse. The job paid well but was pretty boring. Filling orders, loading them up, shipping them out — a lot of hard work, which I was fine with. I just didn't like that I had to work by myself most nights. I got paid for eight hours flat. No overtime — but they expected me to get all the work done. With no help, there was just no way I could make that happen, so sometimes I would end up working three or four hours a night for free. Whenever a holiday made for a four day work week and a three day weekend, the orders would double and I'd end up working 13 hours or more a night but only getting paid for eight. That sucked.

As much as I missed Linda, I was a young guy with some money coming in, so I did my best to enjoy myself. I was going up to a motocross race in Albany, Oregon, with a friend of mine and he knew this girl who had a friend . . . so he asked me if I wanted to meet her. I said, "Sure, whatever." We ended up dating. She was pregnant within six months. It

was completely unexpected and unplanned. I hadn't seen a future with her before that. I'd always thought it was just going to be a fling, and then on to the next one. And the next one, and the next one . . . I was just a young guy, laying pipe. Now I was going to be a dad with big responsibilities. Well, I'd graduated, I had a decent job, and I worked hard, so I figured it would be fine. We moved in together but then her family decided they were going to Alabama — and that she was going with them. I was told, "You're welcome to come with us if you'd like. But if you don't, that's fine too." I wasn't too crazy about moving to Alabama but I didn't want to be away from my daughter, Stephanie. I did what I had to do to keep her in my life, so I packed up and moved with them. I didn't want my child growing up without her dad around, which is kind of ironic — that ended up happening anyway because of what I would eventually do for a living.

The relationship was okay. It wasn't the greatest thing in the world, but it was all right. Stephanie's mom didn't really understand that she needed to change after Stephanie was born. We were both probably too young to have a child (she was a couple of years younger than me), but I always thought that if you have a child, you grow up real quick. I did; she didn't. There was a lot of arguing. As soon as I got home from work, she would want to go out and party with her friends. I would work a long day and end up at home watching Stephanie by myself while Steph's mom was out having a good time. It put so much strain on our relationship. I felt like I was being mentally abused, and when I called her on it, she wouldn't accept responsibility for anything. Everything was put back on me, everything was always my fault.

We had one car so I would either walk to work or get her to drop me off so that she could have the car in case she had to take Steph somewhere. If I asked her to pick me up afterwards, she'd usually say she couldn't because she was cooking dinner. But there never was any dinner when I got home! Even when it was pouring rain and I called for a ride, I'd get "I'm cooking dinner." After a 10-hour work day, I'd walk 25 minutes in the rain, get home, and discover her sitting on the couch, watching TV. "I was getting ready to start dinner but then this came on . . ." After a few years, I couldn't take it anymore. I had to move on.

When we separated, we agreed that I would be able to see Stephanie any time I wanted. It wasn't one of those arrangements where the dad only gets to see his daughter on the weekends. That's one thing I'll say for Steph's mother; she never tried to withhold Stephanie from me. She just wasn't the greatest at doing right by our daughter. She made a lot of promises to that kid — and then broke every one of them. After we went our separate ways, she got married and had a few more kids. Stephanie ended up spending entire summers babysitting because her mom wanted to go out. Stephanie wasn't even a teenager. She should have had her whole summer to enjoy, but there she was stuck at home, babysitting. Her mother was supposed to pay her and never did. Well, even though her mom said she didn't have any money, she still managed to go out and get a tit job and new furniture. That's the kind of mother she was. It pissed me off.

It pissed Stephanie off too. When she was 12, she told me she didn't want to live with her mom anymore. Her mother treated her like a live-in babysitter, so she couldn't enjoy being a child. They didn't get along at all. Since Stephanie wanted to come and live with me, I saw an attorney and got custody of her. Her mother didn't fight it; I got the papers drawn up and she signed them, giving me custody of Stephanie. It worked out well. A few years ago, I was over at Stephanie's house when her mother turned up. We talked a bit and she actually apologized for the way she had treated me all those years. I accepted her apology. I thought her gesture was very kind.

Writing this has reminded me of how hard it was in those early days — the lengths I went to in order to put food on the table and keep a roof over our heads. You hear a lot of guys talking about how they would fight tooth and nail for their family, but I *literally* fought for mine.

CHAPTER 5
FIGHTING FOR FOOD AND DIAPERS

When we first moved to Alabama, I was hopeful for the future. I knew it was going to be tough, but I was more than happy to work hard. Always have been. I got a job as a mechanic working for Meineke, an auto shop in Mobile, and was able to scrape together enough money to rent us a place. It was all off the sweat of my brow — Stephanie's mom didn't do much to help us financially. She did get a job at Kentucky Fried Chicken, which lasted about a month. Then she started working at Colonel Dixie, a fast-food restaurant that only had locations in the South. That lasted about a month too. After Stephanie was born, it got even tougher because of the extra mouth to feed. The job at the auto shop just wasn't covering our bills, but what else could I do? I only had experience from the golf range and the warehouse. College wasn't an option. I had a child to raise, I had to work, and bills were piling up.

Sometimes I talked to the guys at work about how I was finding things tough financially. One day, one of my friends there told me about a tough-man contest with a cash prize he'd seen advertised at a nearby bar. He knew that I liked wrestling and that I'd gotten into a fight or two in my life, so he figured I might be interested in making some extra money bar-fighting. You're damn right I was interested! I wasn't really working out or

training at that point, but I knew I was tough because I had a lot of heart and determination. Heart and determination will get a man a long way.

When the next Friday rolled around, I discovered I would have to get through three fights in order to win any money. It was an elimination deal. Two guys, no matter how big or small either was, would go at it; the best man would win and then it was on to the next fight. We had to wear these big 16oz gloves — they were like frickin' pillows. It was hard to do anything with those on, but you just had to hit as hard as you could and hope for the best. No kicking or grappling or anything like that, just straight up bar-fighting.

I won my first fight. I couldn't knock the guy out because of those things on my hands, but I pummelled him hard enough to make him cower down and cover up, so they stopped the fight. The second guy was tougher and we went to a decision after three two-minute rounds — I won because I'd outpunched him. Then, in the final, in spite of those gloves, I knocked the guy out cold. Winning those three fights earned me one hundred bucks. That was a lot of money back in the early '80s. It was definitely a lot of money to me, about what I made at my regular job in two or three days. Even though I was happy about winning the money, I was worn out. People don't realize that in a fight, you're swinging, you're going, and it takes it out of you. Fighting three times was tough. I was spent. I got home, beaten and bruised, but Stephanie's mother didn't care. She was pissed at me because I'd been out late at a bar.

The next weekend, there was a fight night at a different bar, so I figured I'd go and see if I could win some more money. I did — another hundred bucks. She was still mad. She didn't ever want me going to the bars because of the women there. She wasn't worried about my health, she was just worried about other women hitting on me and taking away her meal ticket. A few girls did throw themselves at me, but I didn't take them up on anything. One woman was trouble enough, so why would I want more?! I was at those bars for one reason and one reason only. I've never been a bar-type person. I'm not a big drinker — never was. I've been drunk a few times in my life but I've never been one to party. I only went to bars back then to enter these tough-man contests, to try to keep a roof over our heads and food on the table. I don't think Stephanie's mother ever truly appreciated what I was doing to provide for our family.

I fought for about six months, two or three weekends a month, going from bar to bar. I probably made a couple grand out of it. We needed that money. She didn't seem to understand that and it caused a lot of problems at home. I went undefeated for a long time. I only lost once, actually. It was at the bar where I'd started fighting, and I'd got through my first match of the night just fine. Getting ready for my second fight, I stepped into the ring, put my gloves on, and looked across at the guy I was going to fight. You poor bastard, I thought. I knew this guy and this was a sure thing. He and I were the same size, but I could clearly see how out of shape he was. I don't know what possessed him to get in the ring in the first place. I figured I'd get this match over quickly and save my energy for the final. I was fixing to clean his fucking clock.

When we were just about ready to start, the ref said, "Hold on . . ." My opponent got out of the ring and this other guy got in. I looked at my corner where my friend, Stoney, was and said, "Something's not right. You need to find out what the hell's going on here." He asked the ref what was happening and was told that the original guy didn't want to fight me, so they were subbing him with this guy. I could either fight him or go home. Stoney was pissed. I didn't care; I figured I'd just clean *that* guy's clock instead. It didn't quite work out that way. Turns out this other guy was a Golden Gloves boxer and the Alabama state champion. That bastard worked on my kidneys for three solid rounds. He beat my kidneys black and blue, and I lost on points. No exaggeration, I could barely move for a few days after that fight. I pissed blood for several days. That guy knew what he was doing. There weren't supposed to be any amateur or professional boxers there, just people off the street. It was the only bar fight I lost. I took a beating that night and didn't make any money because I only got paid if I won.

A few weeks after that fight, I was waiting at a bar between matches when a guy came up to me. He said, "Just so you know, you were set up." It turns out this guy was the trainer of the boxer who'd pounded me. The trainer explained that word had got around town that I was beating everyone, and this bar didn't want to pay me anymore. The boxer was a friend of the bar's owner, so he came to take me out and win the tournament. He did it as a favor, so they didn't need to pay him. Even though I'd lost, the trainer said he was impressed with me and that I had good technique. If I had proper training, he thought I could go a long way. He said he'd train me for free. I wasn't interested in being a boxer though. I still wanted to wrestle.

Soon after, I quit the bar-fighting scene. I was bored. I had to get there by seven or eight o' clock to sign up and then wait, because the fights didn't get started until midnight. I was sitting there for that whole time with my thumb up my ass. It got old real quick. It was a lot different from my later wrestling days because, even though I had to turn up early and wait around a lot for WWE, it wasn't a bar environment and I could always find something to do. It was a job — I was paid to be there at a certain time and wrestle. Even if they didn't use me, they would still pay me. With the bar fights, it wasn't work. I *could* win money, but there was no guarantee. I could spend an evening there but if I lost, I walked away with nothing.

I don't regret bar-fighting. It was necessary to pay for baby food and diapers. Sure, it didn't help my relationship, but that was doomed to begin with. I didn't go fighting in order to take out my homefront frustrations, I did it for the money and because I pure, flat-out enjoyed it. Nobody got hurt on my account and no one held grudges after fights. No one liked being humiliated in front of a drunken crowd of people hooting and hollering and calling them a pussy, but they didn't hold a grudge.

I always liked to fight. Still do, although I don't go looking for them. I've never cared if I lose. If I get my ass whipped, that's fine. I enjoy the challenge of a good fight. As a younger man, I got in my share of fights that weren't part of tough-man contests. I remember getting into a fight with a football player from the University of Alabama who was at the bar with his buddies. They were getting kind of unruly and being asked to leave by the bouncer, who happened to be one of my friends. Joey kept asking them to leave but they weren't listening, so I went over and said something to them. The football player grabbed me, lifted me off the ground, and slammed me against the wall. Then he made the mistake of letting me go. As soon as he put me down, I drilled him and got him off his feet. I jumped on him and we struggled for a bit — he ended up on top of me. He was trying to hit me, so as soon as I got my hand free, my finger went straight in his eye. He got off me fast and started screaming. I didn't pop that eye all the way out but it was almost fixing to hang out of the socket. Another time, some friends and I were hanging out, shooting pool when this guy started acting like a dick and mouthing off. He turned to me and tried to start a fight, telling me he was going to whip my ass. I asked him what made him think that. He kept mouthing off and getting up in my face, and he didn't know I had a pool cue behind my back. I took that stick and cracked him right on the bridge of his nose, split it wide open. He dropped like a ton of bricks. Hey — there's no fair in fighting. If they're going to jump me, I'm going to fight them and I'm not going to fight fair.

Some time after I'd quit the tough-man contests, a bouncer friend of mine told me that the owner of the bar where he worked had been trying to come up with different ideas to draw a crowd. What he'd come up with was to bring in a bear and see if anyone could take it down. I'd never been to a zoo and I sure hadn't seen a bear in person before, so I figured, why not? I'll go wrestle a bear. The worst that could happen was the bear killing me. I'd split up with Stephanie's mother by this point, so I was thinking, "I'll do what I want, thank you." I suppose it was a manly pride thing — or a stupid pride thing — but, seriously, how many people can say they've wrestled a bear?! Only three guys did that night at the bar. I thought it would be fun.

They brought the bear out and it was pretty impressive. It was about 6'4" and must have weighed a little over 300 pounds and, let me tell you, that motherfucker was *strong*. It would probably have taken Mark Henry and tossed him around like a rag doll. I didn't think I could take the bear, I just thought it would be a good story, something entertaining. It sure was   and all at my expense.

I know it sounds ridiculous but I was afraid I might hurt the bear and then I'd feel terrible. Now, I'm not saying that I'm a monster who can whip the shit out of anything, but I didn't know how much I could do without hurting the bear. I knew that it could rip my head off if it wanted to and I also knew that when you play rough, somebody always gets hurt. And that somebody was probably going to be me, so I kind of danced around with it and took it easy. I tried to muscle it down. Needless to say, that didn't go well. I was no match for a bear. I wasn't going to punch the bear — punching it would probably just have pissed it off, and if it got too excited, there was not a damn thing anybody was going to do about it. They had a big long chain on the bear but that wasn't going to do any good. I would have been the sacrificial lamb.

I've still got the video of that fight. For the first few moments, it looks like I'm doing okay. Then that fucking bear bit me on top of my fucking head and that was it — the beginning of me going bald. I had a full head of hair until that point! The bear got me down and ended up on top of me, putting me in an extremely compromised position. Basically, it looked like the bear was sexually assaulting me. That pretty much ended my bear-wrestling career. Believe it or not, my friend actually took the bear down. He stepped into the ring after my turn was over, and he had learned what not to do by watching me. Obviously I weakened the bear for him, so I'm going to claim the assist on that one . . . !

After I'd finished bar-fighting, enjoyed my brief bear-wrestling career, and split up from Stephanie's mom, I started thinking more about what I wanted to do with my life. I now knew I could hold my own in a fight and that I was pretty tough, and I thought about wrestling more and more. A respected boxing trainer had seen something tough enough in me to offer to train me for free, so I knew I had some potential. I just didn't know how or where to get into wrestling. The business was all hush-hush back then and you had to know somebody who knew somebody to find a trainer. It wasn't like nowadays, with everything out in the open and all these nobodies who have never done anything in the business running training schools. I had a fortunate break. When the manager of the auto shop where I worked found out I liked wrestling, he introduced me to a girl who was friends with a local wrestler. She and I got talking, and that's how I met Marcel Pringle.

CHAPTER 6

CHASING DOWN A DREAM

I'd worked as a mechanic for about three years and had no idea what was in my future. I was paying the bills, doing my best to be a good dad to Steph, and just getting on with my life. I wasn't on the fast track anywhere but I was okay with that. I knew that if the opportunity came along to do something better, I'd take it — but there was nothing I really *wanted* to do as a job, so I had nothing to pursue. I still thought that maybe I could wrestle, but I had no idea how to get started. Back then, you had to know someone in the business to get in the door.

Even so, the weekends were still the best part of my week because of the wrestling — the only thing that had changed from my childhood was which promotions I had access to. I didn't get *Portland Wrestling* anymore; Mobile's main wrestling TV show was called *Gulf Coast Wrestling*, which became my new favorite thing to watch. There was "Bullet" Bob Armstrong, Mike "The Hippy" Boyette, "Cowboy" Bob Kelly, and, of course, "Marvellous" Marcel Pringle. Those were the top guys and they were pretty big names locally. It wasn't the only wrestling show, mind you. I had access to so much more wrestling than ever before, including WCCW out of Texas with the Von Erichs, Continental Championship Wrestling out of Birmingham with the Fullers, and Florida Championship Wrestling with Dusty Rhodes. There was so much wrestling on TV, I was in hog — or wrestling — heaven down there in Alabama. I was so wrapped up in wrestling that I'd spend a lot of work time talking about it with the others. The manager there was a wrestling fan too, so he ended up bringing a TV in and we'd both work Saturdays and watch wrestling when we weren't busy.

The National Wrestling Alliance show — that would end up being WCW — was starting to get exposure on TBS, and the World Wrestling Federation was expanding nationwide from its New York base. Hulk Hogan was starting to come through and get hot. The territories were great and I loved those shows, and it became obvious that the WWF was going to get big. I thought it was the greatest thing in the world. The amount of talent there was unbelievable. Many of those wrestlers were monsters too — these huge, powerful guys who would turn your head if you saw them in the street. In the NWA, I liked the Road Warriors and the Barbarian because they were big, rugged guys. They intrigued me. I liked their style, their look, the way they wrestled — just full on and in your face. But in the WWF, I loved Bret Hart as soon as I saw the Hart Foundation. Even though Bret is not a small guy by any means, he was small compared with some of the others. He was cool and he was just so realistic. His wrestling was incredible, even way back then. As time went on, he would get even better. Everything he did made sense and nothing was just to do something — everything he did had a reason and led to something else. He was a great storyteller.

Still, as much as I liked all the new guys I saw, "Playboy" Buddy Rose was my favorite, bar none. It was a shame that, because I didn't get *Portland Wrestling,* I couldn't watch him anymore. I was excited when he joined the WWF in 1989; he'd done some stuff with the WWF before and I figured he was finally going to be a top guy in the business because he had everything it took. He had so much talent, as much as anybody could ever have in wrestling. He had charisma, cut great promos, knew how to tell a story; he could be a babyface, he was a fucking great heel — but he fell flat on his face in the WWF. Honestly, I thought he easily could have been the WWF's top guy but Vince didn't like fat guys. That was Buddy Rose's gimmick. Back in Portland, he wasn't obese; he was just a bigger guy who didn't work out and lift weights but still looked like a wrestler and could move. The WWF was becoming all about physique. Sure, some fat guys got pushed, including King Kong Bundy, Earthquake, and Yokozuna, but Vince blew hot and cold with them all. For instance, when Yokozuna came in, Vince put a big sumo-style diaper on him as a rib. He wound up getting over, so Vince ended up pushing him anyway. No such luck with Buddy Rose — he probably got told to put on weight and get fatter, and then Vince gave him a terrible gimmick, the "blow-away diet," and had him lose to everybody. It was such a waste of one of the most talented men to ever lace up a pair of boots.

Every Saturday, as I watched all that wrestling at work, I still held the dream that maybe somehow I could be a wrestler. Back then, there wasn't really anywhere to learn. Finding a wrestling trainer back then was almost impossible, because the internet didn't exist and wrestling schools weren't listed in the Yellow Pages. It was all word of mouth and you had to know the right people. If you were able to get trained, then you would learn your craft and perfect all your moves in the territorial promotions before you went to the big time of the WWF or the NWA, but getting in the door was hard unless you knew somebody.

Although I didn't know anybody, my manager did. One Saturday, we were working and watching wrestling and he came out and said, "I know this girl who knows one of these guys. . . ." So knowing what a big fan I was and how much I wanted to wrestle, he said he'd call her and see if she could get me to meet this guy. I thought this was going to be my only chance to get into the business, so I bugged my boss and his friend to death for this guy to get in touch with me.

Marcel Pringle, when he was not on TV being "Marvellous," worked a regular job as a welder at a cryogenic plant called Taylor Wharton. One day, after he got off work, he came by and I finally got to meet him. I asked him if he could train me. He told me he couldn't. I asked if he could put me in touch with a trainer. He told me he couldn't do that either, that there weren't people around there who could train a guy like me. Like I said, everything was really closed-shop back then. He thought I was just another guy who said he wanted to be a wrestler because he'd seen it on TV. I managed to get his phone number — which he reluctantly gave to me — and was persistent, calling him and asking him if he'd train me. He kept putting me off and putting me off and then one day, out of nowhere, he told me that there was this place in Pensacola, Florida, that was opening a training school. He told me years later that this was his way of getting rid of me since I was bugging the hell out of him all the time!

I didn't need telling twice. I got in my car, drove about an hour and twenty minutes down to the Border Street Arena in Pensacola, and signed up. The guys who were running the school were Bob Sweetan and Rip Tyler. I'd seen both of them on TV and I knew they were rough, intimidating guys. They didn't work out like the guys who were in the WWF. Instead, they were just tough guys who could beat your ass in a second. Sweetan was about 5'10" and 280 pounds. Tyler was 6' and 250 pounds. Neither were muscled, they were just big and powerful — Sweetan, in particular. He was a hard-nosed Texan and came across on TV like a flat-out evil bastard. As a heel on the shows, he would cause all sorts of mayhem, so when I first met him, it was like "oh shit . . ." — he was intimidating as hell. I didn't know they were characters back then.

They were charging $3,000 to train, which I didn't have, but they gave the option of making payments along the way. I had to scrape together every penny I could for those payments plus gas money to get me down there. They didn't care what sort of condition you were in when you signed up. They didn't smarten you up to the fact that it was a work either, that's for damn sure. I got the crap kicked out of me by Sweetan several times. He kept trying to get me to quit. They both absolutely tortured me, using old-school wrestling stuff to stretch me. Everything was so hush-hush back then that they wanted to make believers out of us all. They were so rough with me, it's a wonder that I even kept wrestling. But that's how bad I wanted it. That's what they wanted to test. They didn't want to waste their time on somebody who wasn't going to be able to take the hardships of the business. Sweetan fucked with us physically and mentally because wrestling is a tough business. It takes a certain mentality to survive, and he wanted to see if we had it. Most of the guys just flat-out didn't have it. Our class had about 20 people in the beginning. By the end, there were only three of us left.

To start with, they taught us the basics, not the fancy stuff — how to fall and how to take bumps without killing ourselves. We took one bump after another. Sweetan ran our asses into the ground: bump — get up — bump

— get up — bump — get up . . . over and over again. He constantly made us run stairs to improve our conditioning and go for runs by the arena while he rode his bike behind us. We'd run in a group and if any of us slowed down, he'd make us start over. Even if we'd run two miles, if one of us slowed down, he made us run the two miles back to the arena and start all over. It was absolutely brutal. A lot of the guys just couldn't take it. It got even worse in the summer because it gets humid as hell in Florida. The arena didn't have air conditioning, so that place was like an oven.

As brutal as it was, I was excited. I drove over there every weekday after work and trained. By the time I'd get home, it'd be midnight and I'd have to be up by 6 a.m. to get ready to go to work. I did that for God knows how long. When I'd been training a while, I called Marcel and invited him to come with me. He still thought I was somebody who was just wasting his time, but I finally got him to come. Seeing me in the ring, he realized that I did have some talent and was actually serious about being a wrestler. He started to warm to me and have more to do with me. Lenny (Marcel's real name) and I became pretty good friends. He even got me a job at Taylor Wharton. They needed a pipe-cutter and, while it wasn't a complicated or great job, it was a foot in the door at a great place to work. He looked after me once I was there. Later on, Lenny asked me if I wanted to learn to weld, since he was friends with the welding instructor. I knew that if I learned, I'd be able to make more money, so hell yeah! I would stay about an hour after work to learn how to weld, then get in the car, go to Pensacola to train, drive all the way back, grab a few hours' sleep, then do it all again. I was exhausted. After a few months, I took a welding test and passed, so I got promoted to flux core welder. It's the dirtiest job in welding — dirty and hot — and it's where everyone starts out. I was paying my dues in both the wrestling and the welding industries. No wonder I was so run down! I wanted to learn to TIG weld, because that was a better job with more money, so I started to practice that after work until I passed my TIG test. You've got to be really good, because you're welding stainless pipe and that stuff has to be X-rayed to make sure there are no breaches in the weld whatsoever. It was government stuff for the big cryogenic tanks with different sized pipes running in and out and around it — that was the next job I got.

Through all of that, I kept wrestling. After eight months or so of training, I "graduated" from the wrestling school along with just two other guys. They even gave me a "wrestling license" as a kind of diploma. I've still got that card somewhere. . . .

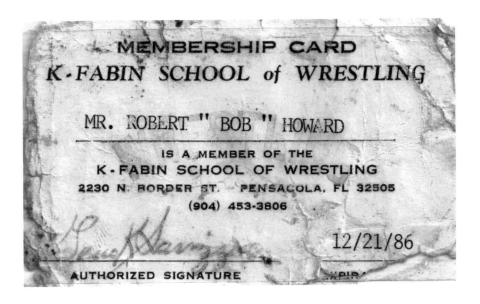

MEMBERSHIP CARD
K-FABIN SCHOOL of WRESTLING

MR. ROBERT " BOB " HOWARD

IS A MEMBER OF THE
K-FABIN SCHOOL OF WRESTLING
2230 N. BORDER ST. PENSACOLA, FL 32505
(904) 453-3806

12/21/86

AUTHORIZED SIGNATURE

My first match ever was in front of about 30 people, against a fat guy whose name I can't even remember — it was Tim something. We were absolutely horrible. There was no pace, no story, and no reaction from the audience — it was just a bunch of moves. Of course, at the time, I was so excited to be in the ring in front of a crowd that I thought the match was great. I've got a tape of that match somewhere — and *nobody* is seeing it!

I started out as "Hollywood" Bob Holly. Rip gave me that name — I was a white-meat babyface, so the "Hollywood" part wasn't really a gimmick; it was just a nickname designed to give me some sort of flavor because I had none. I had a pair of trunks, a pair of boots, and some kneepads. I was just a plain babyface, but that was how people always started in those days. You learned to wrestle as a babyface and you started in front of the crowds as a babyface because the heel called the match, dictating what we did in the ring and the pace of the match. The heel told the babyface when to go to certain moves or spots, and had to know how to get heat (meaning how to get the crowd to boo him and root for the babyface to beat his ass) and how to get that babyface over. You had to have experience to call a match, so until you had enough experience, you worked as a babyface. They turned you into a heel once you understood how to tell a story in the ring and how to control the pace of a match in order to get a reaction from the audience. The heels had the gimmicks, the flashy robes, and the characters. The babyfaces had a nothing nickname and a pair of trunks. Even if you were an experienced babyface and had got over — which means the crowd reacted to you like you were a star — the heel still called the match. Wrestling has changed since then. It evolved in the '90s to a point where the most experienced guy tended to call the match, whether he was a heel or a babyface. If you were the less experienced wrestler, you might make suggestions depending on how well you knew the guy you were working with. If you knew him well enough, you might throw a few ideas in here and there, but if you were working with a guy you just met, you didn't say a fucking word and you let the senior guy call the whole match. You have to build up trust in the other wrestlers by proving that you know what you're doing and that you understand how a match works before you start suggesting things.

After I'd been working on independent shows for a while, Rip Tyler set up a deal with a Japanese star who went by the name Mr. Ito. Since the school was going well, Tyler and Sweetan thought it would be a good idea to get a TV show going too. It cost money to run TV and Mr. Ito was going to be the main sponsor, which is how World Organization Wrestling TV got underway. They used me and Lenny, of course. Tyler and Sweetan both wrestled, and they also called in talent from around the area — we ended up using "Mr. Olympia" Jerry Stubbs, Ron Starr, and even the Rock 'n' Roll Express a couple of times. There was a lot of talent on hand and it turned out to be a good TV show that ran for two years. There aren't many clips of it out there, but I know Lenny has got all the shows recorded on Betamax.

He and I were still both working at Taylor Wharton, so on Wednesday nights we'd load up the car and drive down to Pensacola to tape two hour–long shows. It wasn't just a two-hour deal though, since we had to do promos too. The wrestling part of the show was taped in front of about 40 people, and that was fine. The promos took the longest time to get done.

BOB HAD THIS PICTURE TAKEN IN 1986 AND SENT A DUPLICATE ALONG WITH A LETTER TO CONTINENTAL CHAMPIONSHIP WRESTLING OUT OF BIRMINGHAM, ALABAMA. IN HIS LETTER HE STATED HE WOULD DO ANYTHING TO GET HIRED. HE NEVER HEARD BACK!

Back then, you had to cut a two-minute promo and you had up to 15 guys all recording them. Fifteen guys each doing a two-minute promo should equal half an hour, right? Wrong! Everybody screwed up, over and over. If you screwed up, you had to start again. It took forever. You'd get to the last 15 seconds of the promo and they'd count you down so that you could end the promo right on time. If you missed the mark, back you went to start all over. We'd be there until 4 a.m. sometimes, with work the next day and over an hour's drive in front of us too. You had to *really* want it. I wanted it but Bob Sweetan had his doubts about me. About two months into wrestling with wow, my career nearly ended before it even started. Sweetan called me into his office and came close to firing me. I was so burned out from both wrestling and working a full-time job, but Sweetan didn't care. He told me to step it up or he'd have to let me go. There were plenty of others who wanted to wrestle. I was tired but I kept on going.

After a while, wow started running house shows (non-televised events) too, which drew 300 to 400 people per show. It grew until we were getting 700 to 1,000 people at our weekend shows at high schools or armories. Though I was getting paid at this point, I was lucky to get 40 dollars for a house show. A year after we started running the weekend shows, Tyler and Sweetan were doing such good business that they decided to start doing house shows during the week as well. They wanted both me and Lenny to quit our jobs and move to Pensacola to make sure we were at all the shows. At 40 bucks a night minus travel costs, we weren't going to make any money, so we both refused. We enjoyed our jobs and we were making good money. They tried to tell us that we'd make more as wrestlers, but that was bullshit and we knew it. We figured out a way to do the shows and keep our jobs too. A regular day for us went like this: we'd get off work at 3:30 p.m., drive to the house show, wrestle, drive back, and get in about 2 a.m. We started work again the next day at 7 a.m. It got even harder whenever we had to do mandatory overtime. We'd have to work two extra hours and then haul ass to whatever town we were wrestling in. I was burning the candle at both ends to say the least, but I was young and I could handle it. It gave me a whole lot of experience, which was the most important part of getting into the big leagues. I needed to hone my craft and get used to working an audience.

I also needed to get used to other common practices in wrestling, such as making myself bleed. Most people nowadays seem to know how this is done; you cut off a corner of a razor blade, wrap it up in tape so that only a bit of the edge is exposed, and then cover that with tape too until the time comes to cut yourself. Then you hide the blade somewhere on your body. Some guys put it in their trunks or under their wrist tape. I always kept it in my mouth. It was much easier and more convincing. I didn't have to dig around for it; I'd just get hit, put my hands up to my face in order to sell that hit, spit the blade out into my hands, and, boom, away I went. People ask me how I managed not to swallow the blade — it's simple; you just don't, unless you want to have a major problem later!

I did about 15 or so bladejobs with wow. It was part of the business and had been forever. A heel would beat down a babyface and make him bleed, and then you'd want to pay to see the babyface get his revenge. Simple and effective booking. My first bladejob was by far the worst — or best, depending how you look at it — of my career. The booker came up to me backstage at the Waterfront Arena in Pensacola and said, "You're getting color tonight," and that was that. I just thought, "Well, that's part of the business, I might as well get used to it" and went about making my blade. I was wrestling Pat Rose that night. The match was going fine and then it came time to get color. The problem was that I dropped the blade. The bigger problem was that he found it first and said, "Here, I'll do it" and gigged me. That's a big no-no in wrestling; you never blade a guy unless he asks you to do it for him. He went too deep and cut an artery in my forehead. As soon as I sat up, blood shot out of my forehead like a spigot had been opened. Every time my heart pumped, more blood shot across the ring. It was a mess. After we finished the match, they had to take a mop and bucket to clean the mat and the floor. We didn't have trainers or medical people backstage at those shows, and rather than going to the hospital, I taped it up myself. It took forever to stop bleeding. Later on, when I took the bandage off, I saw the cut was about an inch long and about half an inch wide. It was awful, so I figured *then* that I should probably go to the ER. It's a good thing I did: I needed stitches, and when they were stitching me up, it started to bleed again. It took ages for the blood to stop. In the end, they gave me 18 stitches — 10 on the outside and eight on the inside. I didn't feel too good that night, given how much blood I'd lost.

I got paid 25 dollars for that match.

I literally put my blood, sweat, and tears into my work with that group, but World Organization Wrestling came to a close after about two years. The TV shows were really good and we were drawing good crowds at the house shows, but it turned out that someone was stealing money. Mr. Ito decided to pull the plug on it.

I was the only one from WOW who went on to the big leagues. Lenny could have if he'd wanted to — he was a good wrestler but what he excelled at was talking on the microphone and getting heat. I think he would have made it big back when having heel managers at ringside was hot. He could have been one of the very best. He taught me a lot about talking for the business and working on camera. We even had our own 30-minute show on local TV every Wednesday, *The Marvellous Marcel Pringle and Beautiful*

Bob Holly Show. You can find one episode of it on YouTube, in which an old grandma puts a pie in Marcel's face and I've got long hair and a terrible moustache. Marcel also had connections — he'd grown up with Percy Pringle, who went on to become Paul Bearer and work as one of the top managers in the WWF. Lenny could have easily got looked at for the big time, but he just didn't think he could handle the traveling that went with working for them. Some are made for it and some aren't. He had a great job at Taylor Wharton and was happy wrestling locally. Good for him, I always thought.

Once Mr. Ito pulled the plug, everything started winding down, but I wasn't ready to let that stop me. I'd worked damn hard to get that far and I was going to keep wrestling for damn sure . . .

PART 1: "IS IT FAKE?"

It doesn't bother me anymore when people describe wrestling as fake. I just tell them, "It's fake to a degree — just like watching a movie." It's an athletic soap opera. When I started out, sure, it bothered me that people called it fake, but all that did was get me into a few fights here and there. People can think what they want; everybody is entitled to an opinion.

I think that a lot of people only say it's fake because they want to see you get mad. I'm not going to do that. I won't sit here, tell you it's all real, and insult your intelligence. I am going to explain to you why we do what we do, why it hurts, and how seriously we can get hurt. Getting slammed on the floor is real. Hitting the ropes hurts — most people don't even consider that. Sometimes we end up getting hit in the face for real and all it takes is one good shot to fuck you up. If you're wrestling night after night, somebody is going to slip up and somebody is going to get hurt. How can you get hurt if it's fake?

When wrestling is called fake, nobody in the business gets too offended anymore, especially since Vince McMahon came out in the late '90s and basically admitted it was entertainment, not sports. Some people who don't like wrestling started going, "Oh, I always knew it was fake." People who like wrestling pay their money to suspend their disbelief for a few hours.

CHAPTER 7
THE WRESTLING GRAVEYARD

Now that WOW was out of business, if I wanted to keep wrestling, I was going to have to look farther away. Just like everybody else, my goal was to get into the WWF, but although I'd improved and learned a lot, I wasn't ready to try out for the big leagues. I was still trying to make a name for myself, so I was going to have to go to another territory first. Since I was living in the South, the best bet seemed to be the Southern promotions. Pat Rose made up for attempting brain surgery on me by calling around, and he got us a spot as a tag team with Mid-South Wrestling in Tennessee. That territory was run by the Jerries — Jerry Jarrett and Jerry Lawler. They had a TV show, so it would be good for exposure, and the territory had been running for a while so people knew about it. People also knew about some of their wrestlers, including Scott Steiner, the Fullers, the Moondogs, and Jeff Jarrett, the son of the promoter, who obviously was getting a pretty big push and was treated like a star. Jerry Lawler was their main attraction — they loved him in Memphis.

The promotion got a lot more coverage in the wrestling press and on TV than WOW ever did, so I thought it was going to be my ticket to the WWF. They didn't make me and Pat any promises in advance about our push or what they would pay us; they just said, "You'll make enough money here to live comfortably." I thought hard about that one and came to the

decision that if I wanted to make it in wrestling, this was something I was going to have to do. If I didn't try, I'd never know. Plus, I'd heard the territory was hot and drew good crowds, so I figured I was going to make decent money. I quit my job at Taylor Wharton, packed up all my worldly possessions into my car, and got on the road to Memphis.

Pat and I were going to come in as a heel team. I'd had some experience in wow working as a heel towards the end. They had brought in Ron Starr from Puerto Rico and we'd tagged together; I learned how to be a heel from him. I enjoyed it and I learned how to get a lot of heat, so I was comfortable starting out in Memphis as a heel. We weren't given a gimmick though; we were just a straightforward tag team who happened to be bad guys.

It all started well enough. We traveled around, wrestled six nights in a row, and were off on Sunday. I started to learn from some of the others; it was good experience to watch and work with a new bunch of wrestlers. I worked on my craft, got information about how to play out different scenarios, and was given critiques on my work here and there, what to do, what not to do. It all helped polish me. I got to wrestle at the Mid-South Coliseum, which was a hotbed for Southern wrestling. It was a piss-stained hellhole with wooden benches instead of real chairs but it was a wrestling venue. They did a lot of good business in that place, so I was just glad to be there, wrestling.

I was told we would get paid every two weeks, but when that first paycheck came, I knew something wasn't right. Jeff Jarrett came in with everybody's envelopes and handed out the checks. Everybody looked at them and, to a man, everybody looked so depressed. Jeff came back in later, all smiles, and said, "Damn, you guys are all acting like somebody died." Somebody else said, "You get the fucking paycheck we just got, you'd feel the same damn way." He didn't say anything. He knew.

Nobody was making money. The most I ever made working for Jeff's useless fucking Pappy was $189 for two weeks' work. $189 for 12 shows. That's about 15 bucks a match. You couldn't even eat and get to the shows on that. Everyone piled four or more into a car to travel. I took showers at the buildings, ate nothing but crackers and Vienna sausage, because I couldn't afford any other food, and slept in my car in rest areas. It was terrible. Meanwhile, Jarrett and Lawler were putting all the money in their own pockets. The only wrestler they paid well was Jeff. He was driving around in a nice vehicle and making a ton of money. What could any of us say to him? His dad was the promoter! Jeff was a real dickhead back then. Still is, as far as I'm concerned. He reminds me a lot of Triple H — and that's not a good thing. Jeff will stab you in the back because he's not man enough to stab you in the front. When you talk to him face to face, he's charming and he'll suck you in, make you feel you can trust him, but as soon as you're gone he'll bury you, and you'll never know it. He's the furthest thing from a man. I ended up working with him in the WWF years later and he just kept doing things that made me realize how worthless he is. . . .

But I'll get to that later.

Mid-South Wrestling wasn't working out. They'd told me I'd make enough to live comfortably but one step up from being a vagrant didn't seem too comfortable to me. After a couple of months, I couldn't take it any more so I went crawling back to Taylor Wharton in Mobile and got my old job back.

I called around looking for other places to wrestle and ended up hearing from a guy I knew, who asked if I wanted to go to Atlanta and do a couple of shots for the NWA. At that point, the NWA was the second biggest promotion in the United States, so it looked like a huge step forward on paper but it wasn't anything like that in reality. Guys who knew how to bump were needed to lose to the wrestlers the NWA were building up as stars — what, in the business, is known as a jobber or an enhancement talent. It was a nothing job where you'd go in, the superstar would throw you around and beat you, you'd get paid, and you'd go home. I was trying to get my foot in the door anywhere I could though, so I said, "Sure, let's get to Atlanta." I hoped that, if I did okay in the ring, they might look at me seriously.

The first time I was up there, I got put in a six-man tag team match, me and two other enhancement guys against Sid Vicious, Arn Anderson, and Tully Blanchard. I didn't get a chance to show anything there — I was in the ring for about 40 seconds. I got beat up a bit and tagged out before Sid hit his finishing move on one of the other jobbers. That was it. I got paid $250 for that. It would have taken me three weeks to earn that with Jerry fucking Jarrett. I thought, "Hell yeah, I'm okay with earning that sort of money for a long drive and less than a minute's work!" They called me back to do another squash match soon after that. Easy money, I figured. I drove to Atlanta, walked in the arena, and was told, "You're working with Flair."

Ric Flair was a multiple-time World Champion and, at that point, already considered one of the greatest wrestlers who ever lived. I was a nervous wreck when I found out I would be working with him. The agents — backstage managers — were matter of fact about it: "You're with Flair, just do what he says." I went up to him in the locker room and said, "Mr. Flair, I'm working with you tonight. I can pretty much do whatever you need me to." He said, "All right, just listen to me out there," and walked off. He didn't shake my hand, didn't talk about the match, nothing. This was Ric Flair, the biggest name in professional wrestling, and he acted like it too. I got so wound up before that match. I just didn't want to fuck anything up, but he hadn't talked to me about anything. I didn't even know what the finish was going to be. I had to go out there without knowing a damn thing, listen, and just do what he said. It was intimidating to say the least.

When it was time, I went out to the ring. No music, no fanfare, no reaction. I just stood in that ring, shaking like a leaf. Flair's music hit and there he was, in one of his extravagant robes, strutting to the ring for a match with me. I might have looked calm, but I was panicking on the inside. We locked up and he started calling things to me, telling me what to do. He had me bump him around at the start. I thought, "Damn, he's giving me an awful lot already. . . ." I threw him around with some tackles and clotheslines. I did a hiptoss out of the corner on him, being sure to protect him by tucking his head as he went so he got over and didn't hurt his neck. I had thought he'd just go out there, run through a couple of his moves with me, and finish me off in two or three minutes. We ended up going back and forth for about 10 minutes before he got me in the figure-four leglock and I gave up. I couldn't believe it. I was the guy they brought in for the stars to beat the piss out of, and here was the biggest star of them all giving me some offense and making me look like I stood a chance. He didn't treat me like just a job guy out there; he gave me more than he gave most other enhancement guys. It was a great experience.

Coming to the back, I waited for him by the curtain so I could thank him for the match. After he'd finished celebrating in front of the crowd, he got to the back, walked over and just kept walking. I didn't know what to do. It was common courtesy to thank your opponent after the match, or at least that's always what I'd been taught. I thought I'd better go find him. I caught up with him in the locker room, walked over, and said, "Thank you for the match."

He just said, "Yep."

I went to leave and then he said, "Hey, when you gave me the hiptoss, you held my head down. I hold my head up to get up high on that. Don't hold my head down." I apologized and that was that. He turned away

and went about his business. Back then, I didn't know much better — I thought, "Hell, he's one of the biggest stars in the business." But when I reflect back, it's wrong in so many ways.

Whenever somebody let me beat them, even when I was on TV a lot and at the highest point of my career, I still made sure to thank the guy who put me over, because he had helped make me look good. I didn't make them come looking for me. My ego was never that big that I made people track me down and thank me for beating them! What Flair did was kind of fucked up, in my opinion. I appreciated how much he gave me in the match, but the way he acted afterwards left a little to be desired. As great as he was, who was he to do that to somebody who put him over and made him look good? You can be the biggest star in the entire wrestling industry and you've still got no right to *not* thank someone. It's just courtesy.

Years later, in the 2000s, when Flair and I were both working for WWE, I told him that I'd worked with him back in the NWA and he didn't remember. That didn't surprise me because he worked so many matches. He was Ric Flair, so of course I'd remember. Who was I at that point? Not memorable enough to stand out from all the other jobbers, obviously! I didn't tell him about how he treated me after the match though. I didn't see any reason to bring it up. I've got a lot of respect for Ric, for what he's done in the business and who he became. It's just sad to see him now when he's in his 60s and still out there trying to wrestle. He's become a parody of himself. He needs to get out of the business. He needed to years ago. WWE gave him a huge send-off in 2008 at *WrestleMania XXIV*, where he had what was supposed to be his final match against Shawn Michaels. They put him in the Hall of Fame and threw him a huge retirement ceremony on the *RAW* after *'Mania*. It was the perfect way to retire. Then he signed up with TNA, a group that likes to kid themselves that they are competition for WWE, and he's still doing matches now and then as I write this book. It's really sad. His retirement was the biggest send-off WWE had ever done by a mile and him coming back to wrestle for TNA was a total slap in the face both to Shawn and to Vince McMahon.

After I'd done my match with Flair and gone back home with another $250 in my pocket, I was feeling pretty good and starting to get more confident about my wrestling. I got called back soon after and ended up working with Jackie Fulton. They were trying to push Jackie, but he was past it at that point and slowing down. We had a decent match, but he'd give me an armdrag or knock me down and I'd be up on my feet before he was. I wasn't trying to make him look bad; I was just working the way I worked and he couldn't keep up with me. I took these bumps for him and was up before he was ready to go into the next move. I spent a lot of that match waiting on him. That was my first experience of making somebody else look bad by doing my job well. I was just trying to show the agents in the back that I could wrestle, that I was fast and knew what I was doing in there: here's the guy you're pushing and I'm waiting on him! At least Jackie had the class to thank me for the match afterwards.

As soon as I walked in the dressing room after that match, Ron Simmons — who had been watching the match on a monitor with Butch Reed — looked up at me and just said, "Damn, they need to be pushing you instead of him." That was the first thing Ron ever said to me. I didn't respond. Who the hell was I to say anything? I didn't even work there, I was a hired hand who came in and did jobs. I just kept on hoping that somebody would get wind of what I could do and give me a proper shot.

As it happens, I *did* get noticed that night: Jim Cornette stopped me in the corridor as I was leaving and told me that I'd done well. Jim had been working in the office for that promotion and used to have some say in who got hired. He told me that he'd had a falling out with Dusty Rhodes (the head booker) a few weeks before and that he was off the booking team. He didn't have any stroke any more, but he said that if he had seen me wrestle a few weeks earlier, he would have made sure to get me a job and give me a push. Right place, wrong time. We talked for a little bit and he took my number. He told me that he was leaving the company because he disagreed with a lot of the things they did, and then he gave me a piece of advice: "You've got talent, so quit coming up here and doing jobs, because that is all they will ever use you for."

Two weeks later, the guy I'd been riding with to Atlanta called me and asked if I wanted to go there again for another squash payday. I took Cornette's advice and said I wasn't going to go. I never told him why; I figured it was none of his business. I just said that I had my reasons. He got pissed with me and that was the last time we ever spoke.

Several months went by and I just kept on working at Taylor Wharton. I didn't give much thought to wrestling because I didn't know if it was going to go anywhere for me. I was making good money again at my job. Out of nowhere, I got a call from Jim Cornette. He told me that he was starting a new wrestling promotion called Smoky Mountain Wrestling and he wanted me on board. I figured I'd see what it was like, so one Saturday I loaded up my '81 Camaro z28 and drove the 10 hours to South Carolina for a TV taping they were doing. We got me a flashy robe and sunglasses and I became "Hollywood" Bob Holly again — only it was more than just a nickname this time, it was a proper heel gimmick. I wrestled Reno Riggins for the first Smoky Mountain taping. He was a pretty decent worker — a short fella but a decent worker. I enjoyed it, so I started doing the TV tapings for Cornette. I had to be back at work on Mondays, so I'd do the show on Saturdays and drive home. I'd get in on Sundays around 8 a.m. and collapse, sleep through the day, and get back to work on Monday. It was tiring but fine. Then Cornette started running house shows during the week and said he wanted me full time. He was going to make me one of his main heels. It sounded good, but I wasn't sure. He was paying me around $150 for each TV taping and I'd been burned before by giving up my job. We came to the compromise that I'd arrange to work Monday to Thursday at Taylor Wharton, and I'd do his house shows on Fridays and Sundays and the tapings on Saturdays. After the Sunday house show, I'd drive back home and go straight to work on Monday morning with no sleep. It was exhausting but there was no way I was giving up my job after what happened in Memphis.

Working in SMW was great. I got lots of quality TV time and had some good matches with Robert Gibson, Tim Horner, and the Heavenly Bodies . . . Cornette has an eye for talent and one of the greatest minds in the business. He knows how to tell a story; he knows how to put on a show — unlike a lot of people who call themselves promoters but don't know their ass from a hole in the ground. I find it sad that although he's a fucking great promoter, it doesn't end well when he works for a big company because he's kind of set in his ways and stands up for what he believes in. They don't like that, so they end up pushing him out the door. It's a shame nobody listens to him. He and I have had a few issues in the past, but to this day I love Jim Cornette to death. I have nothing but good things to say about that man. He's completely the opposite of Jerry Jarrett: he makes sure his guys get paid as well as he can afford. On one weekend I did for SMW, somebody stole my luggage. Cornette gave me money out of his own pocket to go and buy new clothes and everything. I would have loved to work for Jimmy full time, but I just couldn't take the chance of giving up my job and then having nowhere to go if SMW folded. I was right to do that — SMW went out of business in 1995. I was long gone by that point. Working a four-day week and then going on the road for three days was killing me. I was always worn out and I was starting to make less money at work because of all the vacation time and sick days I was taking to go wrestle for Jim. I knew I would eventually have to choose between wrestling and my job. After about four months with SMW, I called Jimmy and told him I had to quit. He tried to talk me into staying and said that he thought I could go a long way but I told him I couldn't do it any more. I had a good job, I'd recently got the opportunity to start car racing, and I just couldn't keep burning my candle at both ends. He said he hated it, but he understood and wished me the best.

I thought that was it for me and wrestling, so I went back home and built me a race car.

CHAPTER 8

NEED FOR *MORE* SPEED

Somehow I'd managed to get into my uncle's race car. I was six, so of course I was curious. I thought I'd play in there and was having a great time, pushing stuff, grabbing things, all of that. All of a sudden, I started it up and it made the loudest noise I had ever heard in my life. I flew out of that car and inside the house like the Devil was on my heels.

I got into car racing at an early age. It was how Gary met my mom, since he was friends with my aunt Elaine's husband and used to help him with his race car over at Saugus Speedway in California. It was one of the few things I'm thankful to my stepdad for — we went to the track most Saturday nights. My mother absolutely despised it so they would argue each Saturday evening, regular as clockwork, and I'd just be hanging in the background saying, "Please, please, Mom, just go!" If I didn't get to go, it was the end of the world. One time, Mom and Gary were going to go to a party afterwards so my brother and I had to go to the babysitter — and despite being seven, I cried like a baby because I couldn't go to the track. I felt so abused!

Fast-forward to me at 30 years old and I'd wrestled for over five years, had a kid, ridden (and crashed) a few dirtbikes . . . my interest in car racing was still there and I regularly found myself at the track in Mobile. By this point, I'd finished up with SMW and left Taylor Wharton to go to work for Cowin Equipment in Mobile as a heavy equipment mechanic. That was a great company and a great job. The people were wonderful, there was no pressure — I loved working there. I ended up working as the welder and, ironically, having that job at Cowin meant that the foreman called you "Sparky." I didn't like that name so much, so I told the foreman to knock it off.

No wrestling meant I had my weekends to myself again, so I was at the racetrack every chance I got. It's where I met my first wife, Terri. She was the photographer down there and started introducing me around, so I could get to know the guys and get my foot in the door. One of Terri's best friends was married to a guy named Carl who raced there. After I got to know him a bit, I said offhand that I'd like to try his car out at the track on a practice day. Carl said, "Well, if you want to drive, why don't we build you a race car." That sounded good to me but there was no way in hell I could afford to build a race car. He said he knew a guy who would let us have a car. It was a '74 Chevelle Malibu and it was just sitting out in a field, doing nothing. Carl said we'd strip it down until it was just metal, he'd get all the parts and whatever else we needed to build the car, and I could pay him back. He had his own plumbing business and said I could work for him on the weekends, roughing in houses and laying the pipe in the ground before they put the foundation up. So that became my life — I worked as a heavy equipment mechanic during the week, I laid pipe (actual pipe!) for Carl on the weekends, and then I spent any free time I had at the races or working on building my car. Life couldn't get any better. I got so interested in racing that I stopped watching wrestling for the first time since I'd been a kid. Racing was my passion now.

We finished building my car in the middle of the racing season of '92, so it was time to get out there and see what it could do. On Thursday nights, the tracks had open practice, so we took my car down and thought we'd try it out. I was pretty nervous — I'd never been in a race car before (or, at least, not since I was six). Carl explained that I needed to get used to the feel of the car before I got it up to speed. So I made two laps and everything was going okay. I was doing about 40 mph and then, all of a sudden, the car locked up, skidded, and slid sideways. I was thinking, "What the hell just happened? The motor locked up after only two laps?" Something was definitely wrong. We got it back to the pit and quickly found out that the transmission had locked up. Why? Because the bonehead heavy equipment mechanic (me) had forgotten to put gear oil in it after we stuck the transmission in. We wrecked the transmission on Thursday, got another one and put it in on the Friday, and Saturday was my first race. I'd had two laps at 40 mph at the most and I was about to get into a race with 28 other cars. I was getting ready to have a fucking stroke.

The track opened for practice at 5, so I went to try to figure out what I was doing. All the other cars started whizzing by and scaring the shit out of me. I talked to Carl after the practice and he was asking me all this stuff like "What is your car doing?" "Is it pushing, is it loose?" — I didn't know what the fuck he was talking about! "Pushing" is when you go into the corner and the car doesn't want to turn, so it just goes straight up the track, and "loose" is when the back end wants to come around and you spin out. But I hadn't been driving the car fast enough to know what it was doing. I realized I was going to have to either go fast or go home.

6 p.m. It was time to go. We did qualifying first to set up the heat race. I was always a horrible qualifier. We got to the heat race, which was to determine the starting positions in the feature race. It was a six-lap race that would take anywhere between five to six minutes, depending on how many cautions they had. The Mobile speedway is a half-mile high-banked oval, so you could haul ass on that track. It was pretty dangerous too, because there was no wall around it except for the front straight. If you went off the banking, you were going to sail off and catch some serious air. I started at the back in the heat race, sixth out of six, so I put my foot down to see what my car could do. "This is pretty damn cool," I thought . . . and I found I wasn't scared anymore. I started passing cars. Actually, I passed almost all of the cars. The only real practice I'd ever had was earlier that day and I was in second and right on the leader's tail. I thought, "I'm fixing to win my first heat race," and got pretty excited. A bit too excited. Instead of being patient and picking the right time to get by the leader, I tried to get it all in one shot. We came off a turn where there was nothing but asphalt, grass, and dirt — I got my right side tire in that dirt and the fucking car decided to start sliding sideways. I shot straight down the back stretch, right in front of the traffic, down into the infield, and into the air.

The car bottomed out and I only just missed a big mound of dirt where a telephone pole was. I was inches away. That would have ended my racing career right there — it would have totaled the car and I wouldn't have had the money to put it back together. We managed to get the car back on the track and I finished dead last. At least everybody who finished got through to the feature race.

Before the feature, David Jones, one of the guys who had helped me build my car, came over to me and said, "Bob, look — I've been involved in racing for a while. I just want you to know that you shouldn't expect to go out there and win a race for at least two years. Go out there, learn to drive, learn to race, pay your dues, and get experience." I was cool with that. I figured it was good advice from someone who knew what he was doing, and that getting experience was the way forward. The feature was definitely good experience. There was no real drama or anything and I did pretty well for a first timer, finishing fourth overall. I was pleased with that. Bob House was the guy who won the race, who had won every race that season up until that point. Right there, I set my sights on him and his black car.

We spent the week checking everything over and working on the car. Practice on Thursday went better and I was ready the next weekend. Once again, I started last in the heat because I suck at qualifying but am better during the actual races. By the time they waved the checkered flag, I was in first and won the heat. It felt like I'd redeemed myself from my previous heat race. We got lined up for the feature and I ended up on the pole with Bob House right next to me. He'd been winning each week and I was the new guy, the underdog, and nobody was really paying attention to me. It was perfect heel versus babyface stuff. Even our cars were the right color — his black and mine white. He raced like a heel too, as far as I knew. He was on my back bumper fast in that race and I thought he was about to knock it clean off. He was beating on it through all the turns, and I didn't know what was going on. I had no idea about the way people drive dirty and try to wreck you. I managed to stay in control and was still in first after 19 of the 20 laps. He was still ramming me, trying to get around me, and I was just trying to hang on and not blow it. People had been trying all season to beat Bob House but I managed it in my second ever race.

When I got out of that car, the crowd popped like crazy. Everybody was excited, especially all the people who helped me build my car. We got our picture taken with the flag and the trophy. I was on cloud nine, thinking life couldn't get any better than that. I saw David Jones wandering around and called out, "Hey David, thought I wasn't going to win for two years!" He just looked at me and walked off. He didn't like that so much. There was some jealousy there and we developed a little heat over it.

The next week, during the heat race, they black-flagged me for the first time. That means that either something's wrong with the car or I'd broken some rule. There sure didn't seem to be anything wrong with the car. I pulled into the pits and the track official came over to tell me that I'd broken out of my time. I didn't even know what that meant! He explained that I was driving faster in the heat than I had during the qualifier, so it looked like I had been intentionally driving slow in the qualifier in order to get a better spot in the heat race. It definitely wasn't intentional; I just sucked at qualifying because I had nobody to chase and nobody on my tail. He didn't buy this and I ended up starting dead last in the feature.

After I'd had such a great start the week before, I was brought right back down. There was no way that I was going to get to the front in 20 laps. I was worried that if I tried to push through the field, I'd just end up wadding the car up. I talked to Carl, who said, "Just go out there, do the best you can, and stay out of trouble." I didn't know how the hell I was meant to stay out of trouble when, half the time, those races ended up a wreck-fest, but I told him I'd try. Well, sure enough, that race went downhill for lots of people quickly; there were cautions and people wrecking everywhere and I managed to dodge them all. By lap 16, I found myself in second right behind Bob House. How I got there, I have no idea. We were going through the turns and I thought I'd see about doing to him what he tried to do to me the week before. I started beating on his back bumper, trying to push him down the back straightaway. I couldn't manage it and he ended up winning, with me in second. I might not have won but I was still happy as hell with that. The crowd must have liked it too, because suddenly we had a rivalry, right at the end of the season. Bob House had already wrapped up the points win for the 1992 season, so the growing rivalry between me and him made it more interesting for the fans.

It was pretty similar the next week: I was terrible in the qualifier, did well in the heat, got black flagged, started at the back of the feature, ended up at the front with Bob House, and started hammering on his bumper at about 90 mph. This time though, I managed to get by him to win the race. My fourth week in that race car and I'd won twice. David Jones was not happy at all. When I got the chance, I couldn't resist calling out to him again, "Thought I wasn't going to win for two years!" I wasn't just poking the bear, I was shoving a damn arrow in there. He wouldn't talk to me after that. He ended up building his own car, but he never beat me.

The rest of the '92 season went by with Bob and me exchanging wins. It looked like the next season was going to be real interesting. Even though I was only in about half of the races, I finished fifth overall on points that year. I figured I had a good shot at winning in '93. I set about working on my car to make sure it was ready. I had been winning some money in those races and it went right back into improving the car. I got a good sponsor, Port City Marble, and was coming back to take that championship from Bob House.

In one of the last races of the '92 season, I met a guy who would end up helping me quite a bit. Something happened to my car during a heat race, and I pulled into the pit. I started yelling to the crew that my clutch was gone and this guy, who I'd never met in my life, dove in the passenger side, got underneath the dash where the pedals were, and put the rod back in the slave cylinder. Incredible — just like that, I had my clutch back. He got out and I got back on the track and finished the heat. Afterwards, he introduced himself and said he wanted to help me on my car, if that was all right by me. That is how I met Jimbo Walker.

CHAPTER 9

A POLITICAL RACE

I rebuilt my car over the winter, getting it ready and in great shape for the new season. I was in the zone and ready to go — and despite getting in a crash in the first race, I won. A car spun right in front of me and I T-boned him, right into the driver side door. It pushed my hood up and wrinkled the whole front end of my car, but I never went into the pits; I just kept on racing. My hood kept popping up and blocking my vision — the officials in the tower were probably thinking about black-flagging me — but it wasn't affecting my driving. I kept on going all the way to first place. Bob House didn't place. He didn't even *race* — he'd given up. I'd been looking forward to showing him who the new guy in town was and he had skipped out on me. Maybe he didn't like the competition. I guess I must have run him out of town . . .

Competition showed up anyway in the form of Rod Merrill. It was either me or him each week. If I didn't win, he did. If he didn't win, I did. We were evenly matched but there was a discrepancy as far as the track being against me; Rod's father was the flag man and it sometimes seemed like they made decisions that favored Rod. He raced dirty too — on the second week, coming off a corner, he got up underneath me, got his front fender underneath my left rear quarter panel, and spun me out. He won that week and I came in second. I got him back the next week by doing the exact same thing. I spun him out and won the race — a little payback. He didn't like that so much. The next week, when we ended up in the same heat race, he hit me pretty hard. That pissed me off, so I spun him out again. The officials didn't take a liking to that and made me start at the back of the field in the feature. That made me even madder, so when I'd managed to work my way up to second place, I made a point of spinning Rod out again. This went back and forth for several weeks, tit for tat. It was getting out of hand. Eventually, the officials pulled us both aside and told us to knock it off or they were going to park both of us for the rest of the year. We made an agreement to lay off each other and shook hands — we said we'd just race for points from then on. It didn't quite work that way.

After a few weeks of fair racing, I was leading Rod overall by 10 points. Coming off a turn in a heat race, he was passing but hit me on the way. It wasn't an accident. He pushed me down the back straightaway and I had to do everything I could to keep control of my car. I managed to get it back on track and got a good run on him. This wasn't intentional at all but I turned him — we both went spinning off the back straightaway into the dirt, up a 10-degree banking. They black-flagged me for that and I lost points for the heat race. I thought that was kind of unfair because I'd just been racing hard, trying to get by him, but ended up going into him instead. I started at the back of the feature and came through the field to reach second. With a handful of laps to go, I got underneath Rod and managed to drive past him. Then he started shoving me all the way down the back straightaway. It was blatant. I decided that if he was going to mess with me, he was fixing to pay for it big time. I was going to teach this motherfucker a lesson. As we went into a turn, I backed off to give him the lead and then turned early so I could hook his right rear bumper. It turned him completely and instead of spinning out, he shot off the banking. It was about an 18-degree angle with no wall. It simply dropped off, and he disappeared over the bank. I thought for sure they'd black-flag me for that but they didn't. They must have seen him screwing with me earlier so they let it go, thinking turnabout was fair play. They sent a wrecker down to pick him up; he was done for the night. When he went off the track, his motor spun backwards. That messed his car up pretty bad. I won that race and got a lot of points on him.

He changed his approach after that — his team started protesting my car and saying I was cheating. It got ridiculous. One night, after I'd won the race, they protested the exhaust on my car because it was two inches too short. They disqualified me for that, so Rod won by default and got all the points. Another time, one of the guys took me aside and told me that he'd heard Rod was planning to protest the size of the number on my car after the race. I thought it was pathetic that his team was going to stoop to that level. I took some duct tape and outlined my number to give me an extra inch. Rod won the race that night but he couldn't protest my second place so I didn't lose too many points. His team was just going to try and find every way to fuck with me and win the championship.

He had a buddy who raced sometimes, a guy named Tommy Daniels. With four weeks left in the season, I was leading overall so all I had to do was make sure I finished in front of Rod. Places were important in the heat race too, because there were some points on the line. I was behind Tommy but in front of Rod, so I figured I would just stay put and not try anything fancy. That was until Tommy pushed up a bit, so I thought I'd get another position and pushed my nose up there to pass him. He suddenly turned a hard left into me. His job that day was evidently to take me out and he damn sure did that. He turned me completely around and I T-boned the guard rail. It ended up being a four-car wreck. I didn't manage to finish that heat race because there was so much damage, but Rod finished third and got a lot of points on me. Rod and Tommy got out of their cars after that race and were laughing and high-fiving . . . I was about ready to kill Tommy for what he did. Jimbo told me to calm down and to get new tires mounted. I was too mad to do anything so I just sat there, trying to keep calm and mind my own business. At that point, Tommy wandered over casually and stopped about 10 feet away. Sipping a cup of coffee, being all cocky, he said, "Tore up your car, huh? That's too bad."

That sent me over the edge — I went over there and fucking drilled him. It was like a cartoon; his coffee flew into the air, and he flew backwards, landing hard on his ass. One of his buddies picked him up and they hurried off. I thought that was the end of that, but a while later some officials came over to me and said Tommy had told them that I hit him. I tried to explain myself but they didn't care. They told me to load my car up and go home.

Jimbo was pissed off with me for losing my cool. I thought it was just sad that I got disqualified because Tommy went and tattled on me like a schoolboy instead of being a man and dealing with it. And that wasn't the end of it — Tommy pressed charges that night and they took me to jail. When I got out the next day, a letter from the racetrack was waiting for me, informing me that I was suspended for two weeks for fighting. That made no sense because, just the week before, one of the other drivers had started a fight and he got to come back and race the next week. They were doing everything they could to help Rod win the championship. In the two weeks I was out, Rod caught up and passed me overall and ended up 25 points in front of me. I was furious. There was no way I was going to make up 25 points in the last two weeks of the season.

I guess luck was on my side in my first race back though. Rod ended up wrecking in the heat race and I won, so I got some points back there. Then he wrecked again in the feature and couldn't come back because he tore up his car so badly. I had nothing to do with it, in case you were wondering. I came fifth in the feature because Tommy spun me out on the last lap, but I still got a heap of points back on him because he scored nothing that day. I ended up back ahead of him by seven points going into the final race of the season. It was tense to say the least.

In that final race, I wouldn't even have to beat Rod and I'd still come first overall. If he beat me, as long as it wasn't by much, I would still win the championship. I didn't care about winning that one race; I was riding to finish ahead of or near Rod. As it was getting down to the final couple of laps, I was in third with Rod two cars behind me. I figured I had this one in the bag and then, all of a sudden, I heard this horrific knock. My engine started making a noise and I began to lose oil pressure. All year long, I hadn't had a single mechanical failure and here we were, two laps to go in the whole season with the championship on the line, and my car was slowing down. I could not believe it. I had it floored and it wasn't going anywhere. Cars started passing me. I was trying to count them to see how many points I was losing. I couldn't see where Rod was anymore. One of my buddies tried to stay behind me to help me get as many points as I could, but I was going so slow he had to pass me. It was horrible. My heart was in my throat. Finally, I crossed the finish line. I knew I'd lost and that Rod was the champion.

When I got out of my car, Jimbo told me that Rod hadn't won the race and he actually finished quite far back, so it wasn't a sure thing that I'd lost. The officials calculated all the points and found out that he got seven points back on me that night, so we ended up tied for first on paper. They also found a discrepancy in the calculations for the season so they wanted to go back and do a recount for all the races. It was the final race of the season, and usually you would find out who won the championship and get to celebrate. But all they could tell us on that night was that they didn't know who had won overall. We loaded up and went home, and I started looking through my records, trying to figure out how many points I had for the season. They called me a few days later and asked me to come down to the track so they could go through all the points for each week, all the heats and features, with the officials and both me and Rod there.

I got there and met Rod. Everything was fine between us, the season was over and we both just wanted to know who won. They went through the whole year, recalculating it all, down to the last race, and found out they had made a one-point mistake. They checked it through to confirm it and finally said, "Bob, you won the championship by one point." I was glad that I'd won, but the fun had been taken away since we were sitting in an office a week after the final race. It felt kind of flat. I got a trophy and the winner's check — I won $2,500 for the year. For local track racing, that's decent. It was always a hobby for me, never a job. I figured I'd take that money, invest it back in the car, work on it over the winter, and come back for the '94 season to win by more than one point. Meanwhile, I kept on working at Cowin Equipment. I had no reason to want to go anywhere else; management was so nice that it made you want to work hard for them. They believed the better they took care of their employees, the better their employees would take care of them. They were right — I loved working there.

My life was going well and I was pretty damn happy. Then, one day in November 1993, I came home from work and found a message on my answering machine from J.J. Dillon.

CHAPTER 10
WHO THE F*CK IS THURMAN PLUGG?

It was Paul Bearer who got my foot in the door. Lenny had grown up with Paul in Mobile and the two were so close that they originally shared the same surname for their wrestling personas — they were Marcel and Percy Pringle. Percy had gone on to join the WWF as Paul Bearer, the manager of the Undertaker. 'Taker had become one of the group's top stars and Paul was right there by his side, doing the talking for him.

Lenny, as I said before, didn't want to get into the WWF because he didn't feel he could handle the travel. But, for me, getting into the WWF was my main wrestling goal. I honestly hadn't been thinking about wrestling since stepping away from it in 1992; I had become wrapped up in my car racing. Lenny had gone ahead and given the tape of my matches to Paul, asking if he could pass it on to the powers that be up in Stamford at the WWF headquarters. It had taken a long while to get looked at, but evidently they got around to it and liked what they saw. Paul didn't have to do it but he had seen something in me and kept pushing for them to check me out. Paul's a great guy and I've always been grateful to him for helping get me started with the WWF.

J.J. Dillon was in charge of hiring and firing at that point and he was looking to add some workers to the roster. He said he'd arrange for the WWF to fly me up to Stamford so that he could interview me. Of course, I was happy to do that. Even if I wasn't as into wrestling as I'd once been, I figured there was no harm in hearing what they had to say. I didn't know what was going on in the wrestling scene at that point. I didn't even know who the main stars were. When I stopped watching, Ric Flair had just gone to the WWF, the Ultimate Warrior and Randy Savage were working on top, and the Undertaker was starting to become a big deal.

When I got to Stamford, I sat down with J.J. and Vince McMahon for my interview. Everyone in the WWF HQ was very polite to me, including Vince. My first impression of him was that he was a nice guy. The interview didn't last long — we talked a bit about what I'd been doing for the last few years and I told them about my job and the car racing. They told me that they'd seen my tape and thought I was a solid worker. They were refreshing the roster and had dropped a lot of the guys who had been around a while and never got over, so they were looking to add some solid workers to the company. They didn't explain anything about what I would do, who I would work with, how they would use me, or even what my name or gimmick would be. They just said that they'd send me a contract and give me a job as a wrestler. That was good enough for me. Going up there for the meeting made me remember how much I'd wanted to get into the WWF, how hard I'd worked to make it. Sleeping in my car in rest areas, eating nothing but crackers and sausage, getting cut open for $25, traveling ungodly distances after a full day of work to do a house show in the middle of nowhere, being tortured to the point of exhaustion by Bob Sweetan . . . it had all paid off and I was going to get a WWF contract. I had finally made it to the big time and was going to make lots of money.

After the meeting with J.J. and Vince, I did some research on the company and found that some things had changed. The biggest surprise was that they had TV on a bigger scale now — they had started a show called *Monday Night RAW* in '93 and were taping in front of arena crowds. They were doing a lot of the shows live too. It was pretty impressive.

Another surprise was that a lot of the top wrestlers weren't as big physically anymore. Where they'd had muscle guys like the Warrior and Hogan before, they now had my old favorite Bret Hart as their top babyface. The Undertaker was a close number two. Shawn Michaels, a guy I had known mainly as a tag team wrestler, was now a heel and one of their best workers.

They still had some big guys, like Lex Luger, but the crowd wasn't into him as much as they were into Bret and Shawn. It was weird because they had these straightforward, good wrestlers working at the top, but underneath they had a lot of cartoon character gimmicks, like Adam Bomb (a radioactive wrestler), Bastion Booger (a smelly hunchback), Ludvig Borga (a Finnish strongman who was pissed off about the environment), and Doink the Clown (a wrestling clown — obviously). Wrestling had always had cartoon gimmicks, but these gimmicks seemed a little too silly to me. It made me wonder what sort of gimmick they were going to give me.

When the contract arrived shortly afterwards, the first thing I noticed was the name of my character. Thurman "Sparky" Plugg. "Who the fuck is Thurman "Sparky" Plugg?!" I thought at first. But you know what? It was the WWF, I didn't give a damn what they called me because it was worldwide TV and everybody in wrestling wanted to get in the WWF. If other wrestlers were going to make fun of me for being called Thurman Plugg, I didn't care because I was there and they weren't. If the WWF came knocking on their door and offered them a job, they would accept any damn name they were given. I couldn't tell them, "No, that's not the name we're going to go with." I was the one who wanted a job. They wanted me to be Thurman Plugg so, okay, I was going to be Thurman Plugg.

I recently found out that it was actually J.J. Dillon who came up with the name and character. They had gone off my racing background and wanted me to be a "two-sport superstar," a guy who went full speed both on the racetrack and in the ring. It wasn't what I would have chosen, but I figured it could have been worse. Over the next couple of years, they would bring in some truly ridiculous gimmicks like Duke Droese (a wrestling garbageman), Henry Godwinn (a wrestling hog-farmer), and Mantaur (half-wrestler, half-bull, total bullshit — and, yes, I'm serious; he even had a cow costume to wear to the ring). So I figured I got off lightly, all things considered. It didn't matter what they wanted me to do; I was going to be laughing all the way to the bank.

They didn't negotiate their contracts. You either accepted the deal or you didn't. There wasn't a downside yearly guarantee at that point; all they said was that they would guarantee you $50 per match and pay for your airfare. If the show you were wrestling on did well on pay-per-view (PPV) or on TV or at the box office, you'd get paid a lot more than that 50 bucks though. If your character got over and you had merchandise on sale, you'd get a cut of that too. Thurman Plugg T-shirts, baseball caps, bobblehead dolls for cars . . . well, I wasn't sure about any of that but the perception was that the guys working for the WWF made hundreds of thousands or millions, so I figured I'd make at least a couple hundred grand after a year or so. Boy, was I wrong . . .

I signed the contract and sent it back in November '93. It had been about 18 months since I last wrestled, so I hit the gym hard to get back into ring-shape. The problem is that you can't really do that without actually wrestling. I did as much cardio as I could but doing a wrestling match was a whole different game.

They sent a camera crew down to meet me at the racetrack in Pensacola, Florida, and we filmed some vignettes to air on WWF TV shows before my debut. The idea was that they'd introduce my character to the viewers and make me seem like a star before I got there. I thought the vignettes were silly. They had me getting into my car at the track, acting like the happy-go-lucky race-car driver who smiles 24 hours a day: "Hey there, guys, my name is Thurman Plugg but my friends call me Sparky . . . you can call me Sparky too!" It was one step away from "gee whiz" and "golly, hey, guys!" and that's totally not me. But hey, what was I going to do, tell them no? They gave you something, told you what to say, and you said it. The end.

PART 2: LIFE ON THE ROAD

If you want to make a living in the wrestling business, you'd better get ready to work your ass off. People think it's all glitz and glamor, but it's not easy. The part that people see, the 10 to 15 minutes in the ring, is the best part of our day. The other 23 hours and 45 minutes on the road is the work. Most people work an 8 to 10 hour day and then go home. You can kiss that goodbye if you're going to be a wrestler.

When I started with the WWF, we were on the road all the time. You got back to the hotel at 1 a.m. and if you had an early flight, you would grab three or four hours' sleep and head to the airport. On TV days, we would tape four or five shows in a night, so we'd be there from noon to 2 a.m. We'd do double shots on the weekends — do a show at midday on Saturday, stay in our gear, travel to the next town, and do another show at 8 p.m. Same on Sunday. We were doing nine shows a week. After four or five weeks, we'd get two or three days off, and we'd either sleep through those or get caught up on stuff at home. Then it was back on the road. It's a rough way to live. The newer guys have no idea how easy they've got it in comparison because they get at least a few days off each week. They get proper breaks at New Year's, Christmas, and Thanksgiving now — we didn't get that back in the '90s. I used to fly home on Christmas Eve, arrive at 11 a.m., have Christmas Day off, and fly out first thing the next morning. Vince hates holidays; he thinks everybody needs to work, but not everybody is built the same way as him. Sometimes you've got to take a break.

CHAPTER 11
STARTING THE ENGINE

My first match in a WWF ring was on January 11, 1994. It was at a TV taping but the match didn't air until much later in the month. I wrestled Barry Horowitz, a guy who had been a long-time jobber for the company. He was very gracious to me that first day. I felt kind of guilty when they had me beat him because here was this guy who had been in the locker room for years, losing to everybody and never catching a break, and I had just got there and was going to beat him the first time out. I actually apologized to him for beating him and he said, "Hey, man, it's what I'm here for." He knew what his job was in the big picture — they paid him to go out there and get other people over. He did his job and he got paid. He didn't have an ego about being on TV, and he knew that being a wrestler was, fundamentally, just a job. He ended up finally getting a push in '95 and the fans loved it, but management seemed to lose interest pretty quickly. He ended up getting lost in the shuffle by the end of the year and was gone shortly afterwards. I felt bad for him, patiently waiting years for a break and then, when it finally came, it was over before it started. The match he and I had was nothing special. We did about three minutes and kept it simple — I spent most of the match working his arm and then got the win after a splash off the top rope. I was sucking air pretty badly in that match because I was so out of shape. Running to the ring then a couple of minutes of wrestling and I blew up! I knew I had to get in better shape — and I did, eventually.

I was nervous as hell the first time I walked into that locker room. I introduced myself to everybody, found a spot where nobody was, sat down, shut up, and listened. I didn't say anything or try to fit in; I just did my thing, spoke when I was spoken to, and hoped they accepted me. I knew a few of the guys there — I'd met Paul Bearer on a few occasions through Lenny, and I'd also worked with Scott Steiner. My old "friend" from Mid-South, Jeff Jarrett, had just started there too, and they were going to push him big time. He'd been given a country-music gimmick and a lot of vignettes to make him look like a superstar coming in — and the only reason they were running with him was that his daddy was now working in the WWF office. Interestingly enough, that was when everybody's pay in the WWF got cut. I can just imagine the conversation: "Hey Vince, you ain't got to pay these guys what you're paying 'em; they'll work for nothing!" Working for Jarrett was one step up from slave labor and the only guy who ever benefited from it was his son. I honestly don't think Jeff would have gone anywhere in the wrestling business if he hadn't have been Jerry Jarrett's kid.

The first time the WWF fans saw me onscreen was at the Royal Rumble in '94, which was one of the big pay-per-view events and probably the third most important show of the year at that point. I wasn't meant to be in the match but was backstage because, even then, they flew all their talent in for PPVs, just in case they needed them. Sean Waltman, who wrestled as the 1-2-3 Kid, was injured, so they decided to put me in the Royal Rumble match in his place. I was on cloud nine when I found out. It felt like I'd finally made it and now I just had to stay there. I couldn't believe I was going to get to make my TV debut in the Rumble match, where the winner gets a title match at the biggest wrestling event of the year, *WrestleMania*. The Rumble is an "every man for himself" match with 30 guys coming in at intervals. You get eliminated by being thrown over the top rope to the floor. I figured I'd probably be in there for about a minute before they threw me out. I was pleasantly surprised that they ended up putting me in there at number 17 and letting me stay for over 21 minutes. I was quietly amused that my buddy Jeff Jarrett was in for less than two minutes — not a great start for him, but a promising start for me. I was one of the guys who was out there the longest that night and, on commentary, they put me over as a new guy with a lot of potential. I was eliminated by my old idol Bret Hart, who went on to win the match (along with Lex Luger in a screwy finish in which they were co-winners).

Being in the same locker room as Bret was pretty neat, given that before I joined the WWF, I thought he was the man. He was always pleasant to me in the locker room, but I never did feel like I had a connection with him. He seemed to alienate himself from everybody and was very quiet. He would talk to you if you talked to him and he was never unpleasant to anybody, but it was one of those deals where you had to go up and talk to him because he wasn't going to come to you. If I asked for advice, he'd be helpful, but even after I'd been there a while and he knew who I was, we never connected.

Connection or not, I always wanted to work with him because he was such a good wrestler. He could go out there, take someone who couldn't work, and make him look like he was a decent wrestler. A match between him and me when I was at my peak would have been off the hook, especially because of the way his mind works and how he goes about telling a story. I never got to wrestle him because I never got to a level where it would have worked. I could have pitched a story to management but they would have looked at me like, "Really? *You* want to work with Bret? Like *that's* going to happen!" Thurman Plugg vs Bret Hart wouldn't have gone over well. I *was* in a six-man tag with him, on his team, where Bret, 1-2-3 Kid, and I beat Yokozuna, Owen Hart, and Hakushi — and I was the guy who got the win too, pinning Owen after about six minutes. It wasn't a big deal though; it was one of those things where I was in the ring with bigger stars and just making up the numbers. I'll tell you how momentous it was — when I recently saw the match again, I couldn't remember how it finished but I was sure it would end with one of the heels pinning me. I totally forgot that I pinned Owen.

Bret was never a dick to me but we didn't bond. Two guys who I *did* bond with quickly were "Macho Man" Randy Savage and "The Model" Rick Martel. For the first couple of weeks, they hung back, probably thinking, "Let's get to know this guy and see how he is." Once they realized I wasn't a big-mouth and didn't try to force people to like me, they did everything they could to help me. They helped me understand the dos and don'ts of the locker room and were forever offering me advice. If I had a question, they were always there to help me out. I can't thank those two guys enough for helping me as much as they did.

Martel helped me out in the ring too. When I first got to the WWF, I was working with him at house shows every night for what felt like forever. I learned so much from him — he was a great wrestler, very smooth in the ring and a good storyteller. Some people thought he was boring but those people don't understand wrestling. Like Bret, everything Rick did was for a reason. He kept it technical and he wouldn't do the fancy high-flying stuff, and there was always a reason he went back to a headlock or to working on the arm. It was all part of telling the story of a match. Once you understand wrestling, you understand that Rick was anything but a boring wrestler. I enjoyed our matches and they helped get me back into ring-shape. When I found out that I was going to be working against him at *WrestleMania X*, I was over the moon. I'd only just got to the WWF and I was going to be in a 10-man tag team match on the biggest show of the year. It was going to be me, the 1-2-3 Kid, Tatanka, and the Smoking Gunns against Rick, IRS, Jeff Jarrett, and the Headshrinkers. I knew it was only going to be a filler match but I didn't care — I was going to be on the *WrestleMania* card! It's what every single wrestler in the business works towards.

The big day came. The match was at Madison Square Garden in New York. We were told that we were on right before the main event. Everything was going great; Bret and Owen had gone out and had one of the all-time great matches, the crowd was into the show, and about the only person who wasn't happy was Adam Bomb, who was whining and bitching backstage because he had to put Earthquake over in about 30 seconds. Shawn Michaels and Razor Ramon (Scott Hall) were out there doing a ladder match when I got to Gorilla (the area right behind the entranceway, named after legendary wrestler and announcer Gorilla Monsoon). They were having a great match and bringing the house down. I overheard the guy who was timing the show tell the referee over his ear-piece that it was time to go to the end of the match. I kept on warming up, adrenaline pumping . . . I was about to wrestle at *WrestleMania* in

Madison Square Garden. It doesn't get any better than that. Shawn and Scott were still going. And going. And going . . . The timekeeper was screaming at the referee over and over, telling him to get them to go to the finish but Shawn and Scott ignored him. All the guys in Gorilla were trying to figure out what to do and then I heard the sentence that made my heart sink: "We're going to have to pull the 10-man." They canceled my match and went straight to the main event. I was so disappointed. I wasn't mad at Shawn and Scott because they had a hell of a match, one of the best in wrestling history, and I was just this new guy. Who was I to say anything?

Randy Savage was mad though. He was *pissed*. When Shawn and Scott came back through Gorilla, I thought he was going to jump on them. He was screaming and cussing at them, calling them every name in the book. He ripped them a new asshole and called them selfish motherfuckers. He told them that they had disrespected the other boys by taking their TV time and their spot on *WrestleMania* in order to go over their time allowance. Randy felt it was a "screw you" to everyone else, that Shawn and Scott thought that their match was going to be so good that they could screw 10 guys out of a *WrestleMania* appearance and a payday. Management always said in meetings that the golden rule was to always hit your time cues because if you went long, you were taking away from somebody else. Shawn and Scott only cared about themselves. Nobody had doubted that they would have a great match because they'd worked to perfect it for two months straight on the house show circuit. Randy was furious because he felt they were going into business for themselves and were disrespecting everyone else in the locker room. Randy fucking hated Shawn and his buddies because he thought they were taking over the locker room and starting to run the show.

I loved Randy as a friend and as a wrestler — he was very charismatic, very flamboyant. He wasn't a *great* worker but he was definitely good enough to be on top. He did great promos, had a great gimmick and character, and absolutely had what it took to be one of the top wrestlers in the world. By the end of 1994, Randy left the WWF. I hated to see him go. He didn't tell anybody, he just upped and went. He told Vince that he was quitting wrestling and then, all of a sudden, he turned up in wcw. Vince felt Randy had betrayed him, so Vince blacklisted him. Now Vince is a businessman first and foremost, so even when someone screws him over, if he feels he can make money with them, he'll put his differences aside and work with them — but he never worked with Randy again. There have been rumors going around for years involving Vince's daughter, Stephanie, and Randy. I won't say anything other than Randy was always pretty friendly with her.

But Randy was right: Shawn's little group of buddies, the Clique, as they called themselves, were taking over. It was Shawn, Scott, Kevin Nash, and the 1-2-3 Kid. Triple H would ass-kiss his way into the group when he turned up in 1995 and kept ass-kissing his way to the top of the industry. Before Triple H, Shawn was the biggest asshole in the company. He was a complete dick. When I started, he had been decent to me, but as time went on, he turned into an arrogant smartass. We were in Europe when I first butted heads with the Clique.

When we were overseas, we were given cards to fill out to order food for the bus after the show. I had been with the company about four months at this point and I was working mainly with Rick or with Savio Vega (when he was wrestling as Kwang — a good worker who knew what he was doing). After my match on our first night in Germany, I got showered and dressed, then went to the kitchen to get my food. It wasn't there. I thought that was a little strange. Same thing the next night . . . and the night after that. I went with Rick into the kitchen the next day and, again, my food wasn't there. Rick asked what was going on and I told him my food had been missing for the past three nights. I said I'd been filling my card out but there was never any food. Rick looked around with me — he didn't find my food but he found my card. It was torn into pieces on the floor. I figured this was somebody's way of ribbing me, but to me that's a dirty rib. You don't mess with somebody's food or clothing.

The next night, I was in catering, eating with Randy. Rick came over, sat down, and said, "Hey Randy, Bob's food has been missing after the shows and we found his card torn up." Randy, in his growly Macho Man voice, said, "Well, I saw someone tearing up a food card so I know who's doing it, brother . . . it was Shawn. And you've got to stop it now before it gets any worse." So after my match, I took my shower and changed. Sure enough, in the kitchen, my food wasn't there. Rick was with me and asked what I was going to do. I said, "Just watch." I stormed off down the hall. Randy spotted me, saw that I was pissed, and asked what I was doing. I said I was looking for someone. He replied, "He's in the shower."

Randy and Rick followed me and stood outside the door of the room where the Clique were changing. They had set up their own little area away from the other boys. Before I went in, I said to Randy and Rick, "Don't worry, I've got this," and I shut the door behind me. Scott Hall was milling around and Shawn had just got done in the shower. I said, "Shawn, what's your fucking problem with me?" He looked at me and said, "I don't know what you're talking about." I said, "The fuck you don't know . . . I don't think I need to remind you. If you've got a problem with me, you come up to me and you discuss it with me, but the next time you touch my fucking food, I swear to God, I will cut all your fingers off with bolt cutters. Do not fuck with me." Scott jumped in and tried to be a tough guy, so I turned to him and said, "Motherfucker, don't come any closer or I will fucking drop you." He backed up, playing all cool and everything, and said, "Hey, come on, there's no need for this. . . ." I responded, "I'm nobody to fuck with, Scott. Don't try me." Shawn didn't say one word. I turned around and walked out of there. Randy and Rick were standing outside the door, laughing and carrying on. Randy looked at me and said, "That's the way you fucking handle things, right there. . . ."

I wasn't done with the Clique though. The next day, as I was heading into catering, I saw Scott and Kevin Nash sitting on one of the stage equipment boxes, being dicks to everybody who went by. Kevin smarted off at me so I stopped, looked him straight in the eye, and, in front of everybody, said, "You say one more word to me and I will knock your ass out." Then I drew an X on his chin with my finger and said, "This is where I'm gonna hit you." Nash couldn't believe it. That sumbitch just sat there and looked at me as if to say "What do I do now?" They never fucked with me again.

The international tours were tough and it didn't help that the money was nothing close to what I had expected. After I'd been with the company for about a month, I still hadn't seen a paycheck. I enjoyed the work and being with the WWF, but we'd been on the road for seven days a week most weeks. The office would give us a $200 advance each night to use for paying road expenses — they might have picked up our flights but we had to pay for car rental, gas, food on the road, and hotel rooms. When they worked out what you made from the shows you were on, they would deduct the advance they paid you and your paycheck would be the difference. About six weeks after I started with the WWF, I finally got the check for my first two weeks with the company. It was for a couple hundred dollars. What the hell? $200 for two weeks' work? Were they kidding me?!

It didn't get any better after that. One time, I was on the road for five weeks without a break and I got a check for $50. Fifty fucking dollars. All the boys told me, "Always get your advance every night because you don't know when you're going to get paid." There would be four of us piled up in a rental car, four of us sharing a hotel room; we spent 24 hours a day together, 7 days a week. You did what you had to do to cut expenses since it was the only way you could actually make any money if you weren't one of the very top guys. Nobody in the mid-card or below was making any money. You earned enough to pay your road expenses, your taxes, and your bills at home and that was basically it. We were working for this mega-million dollar company, yet pretty much nobody was making any money. And I was right at the bottom of the earnings barrel. If you didn't watch what you spent on the road, you'd come home with nothing and not even be able to pay your bills. It was a lot of work for not a lot of return. I started to second-guess myself. Was this what I really wanted to do? I figured that the only way it was ever going to work was if I was able to stand out and start moving up the ranks.

I kept working hard, learning, and making sure I had good matches, but I also tried other things to get noticed. I got new wrestling gear made, with bold colors that would help me stand out. This was a trick I always did with my race cars, so I got my gear made the same way. One of my outfits was a lime green singlet and pair of tights. Looking back, I realize that everyone probably laughed at it and thought I looked like The Great Gazoo, but I just wanted somebody to notice and give me a shot.

After I'd been with the company about six months, I decided to go for broke and talk to Vince about my name. I was nervous as hell to bring it up, because I didn't want him to think I was ungrateful that he'd given me a job. But I knew that nobody would ever take me seriously with the name

"Thurman Plugg." I made sure to thank Vince for the opportunity before explaining my thoughts about the name. He understood and asked what I suggested changing it to. I told him and he was okay with it — I think he respected me for actually bringing it up to him — so after that, I became Bob "Sparkplug" Holly. I was happier with that name. I didn't like the Sparkplug bit but I figured we'd take one step at a time. I still had the race-car driver gimmick and that gave me an identity, so that was fine with me.

That first year with the WWF didn't really have any highlights for me because I didn't do anything. I was in the Royal Rumble, sure. I was nearly in *WrestleMania* but didn't get on the show thanks to Shawn and Scott. I didn't have any storyline or anything. I won some matches, I lost some matches. Nothing important. I was an enhancement guy. I got to beat other enhancement guys and jobbers in order to give a win over me some meaning, but then I'd lose to the guys who were actually going somewhere. I wanted to be more than just enhancement, so I told myself that my time would come and I had to be patient, do as I was told, and wait my turn. Everybody has to start somewhere and I always thought I would put my time in, keep my nose clean, pay my dues, and wait for a better spot in the company to open up. 1994 had seen me get into the company. I was hoping that 1995 would see me start to move up the ladder, but I couldn't see where the opportunity was going to come from.

As it happened, a spot opened up when Shawn and Kevin got moved up into the main event and vacated the tag-team championship. The WWF wanted to mix things up in the undercard, so they arranged an eight-team tournament to crown new champions. I was put in a team with Sean Waltman, the 1-2-3 Kid, who was part of Shawn's Clique but less of a dick than his buddies. I didn't think anything of it and figured that, as a makeshift team, we'd just lose in the first round and I'd go back to putting people over. We ended up winning the first match and the next one too — and, just like that, I was in the final and the tag team title match at the Royal Rumble in January. It didn't matter to me that we were basically just being set up for Bam Bam Bigelow and Tatanka — two guys much higher up the card than me or Sean — I was finally getting a title match on pay-per-view. That was a definite step up as far as I was concerned. Maybe 1995 would end up being a decent year after all . . .

PART 3: FLYING HIGH

As a wrestler, it feels like you either spend your life in a car or in an airplane. You fly so much that you get automatically upgraded a lot of the time. That's something you've got to be careful about politically. There's an unwritten rule in the locker room that if you're given an upgrade and you haven't been with the company long, you offer your seat to a veteran who is sitting in coach. Some guys who came in and somehow got upgraded would get heat, even if they paid for it themselves. It just wasn't the done thing.

When I started out, I got upgraded a few times. I stuck with the rule: always offer the seat to the vets. If they didn't take it, you wouldn't get any heat for sitting up front as long as you had offered and they vouched for it. Later in my career, when some of the new guys offered me their seat, I wouldn't take it. I got to sit in first a lot during my career, so it was nice for the young guys to get a chance to do that. I was thankful for the offer but I wasn't that uncomfortable in coach, to be honest.

I would offer my upgrade to the big guys if I had the chance. Bam Bam Bigelow, for example. When I first came in, I made sure to offer him my seat if I got an upgrade. He was a large guy and he wasn't going to be comfortable in coach. It's kind of ironic that I got him out of coach — because he ended up throwing me under the bus.

CHAPTER 12

THE MAN WITH THE FLAME TATTOO

Heading into the 1995 Royal Rumble, I was feeling positive. Although I didn't think that this match would be the turning point for me in my WWF career since I was sure we were just there to make Bam Bam and Tatanka look good, getting a match on pay-per-view was always good. That's where you made your money — or so I had been told.

This is how it works: management looks at the match you are in and considers how important it is to the show, then looks at what the live gate is and how many people buy the show on pay-per-view. After however long it takes them to make the calculations — and usually it takes several months — they send you a check with whatever figure they worked out for you. There is no formula; they could just pull a number out of a hat for all I know. But you could end up with a nice chunk of change, so getting a pay-per-view match is good news.

The Royal Rumble was at the USF Sun Dome in Florida that year. When I got to the building, Pat Patterson, who was the agent for our match, came over and told me and Sean that Bam Bam was going to do something with football legend Lawrence Taylor after the match, which would lead to a match with him at *WrestleMania*, so we were going over and winning the tag titles. I was tickled to death about that — I thought it was fucking cool. Everyone in the wrestling world aspires to be a champion in the WWF and here I was about to become one of the world tag team champions. It was awesome; I figured I was on my way to making some good money . . .

I was looking forward to being in the match with Bam Bam and Tatanka, because they were both guys who had worked near the top of the card. Bam Bam, in particular, was gracious as hell to me. When we went through the match beforehand, he said he wanted to make me look good. So did Sean. When we were laying out the match with Pat, he said he wanted Sean to get the pin on Bam Bam. Sean said, "I get to win a lot so why don't we give Bob the win on this one?" He figured it would help elevate me. I thought that was very decent of him. For whatever reason, Pat didn't go for it and insisted that Sean get the win, but I didn't really mind. Whether he got the pin or I did, we were still going to win the tag team title.

We went on right before the Rumble match itself and I enjoyed it — I thought it was a pretty good match and I put in a good performance. It was a nice feeling to hold that tag title belt in the air. I thought to myself, "I could get used to this."

They had us lose the title the very next night.

We were working with the Smoking Gunns, Billy and Bart, two guys who'd been traveling with us a lot, and we were told that Kid and I were going to drop the belts. They had always wanted the titles to end up on the Gunns, so I don't know why they didn't just put them over in the tournament in the first place. I wasn't about to complain though. I thought it was a waste because me and Kid had got over as a good underdog team and could have run with the belts for a while, but that wasn't my call. I was going to do what I was told.

The night after the Rumble, we taped three episodes of *RAW*; one went out live and the others were for the next two weeks. On the live show, at the end of the match, I took a move called the Sidewinder, where Bart lifted me up on his shoulder and Billy jumped towards me and hit me with an elbow as Bart dropped me. I don't know how it happened but I smashed my head on the canvas and knocked myself out. It was the finish of the match anyway and Billy pinned me to win the title. When I came to, I had no idea where I was. It turns out I'd got my first wrestling concussion. I was able to walk to the back by myself but I was real confused. Once I got backstage, I couldn't remember where I put my stuff. I didn't know whether to go right or left so I just stood there. Somebody came over and asked if I was okay. I said I didn't know where the locker room was. He said, "You're kidding me, right?" I honestly had no idea. We didn't have doctors or trainers backstage back then, so I could either go to the hospital or get on with it. Pat came over and checked to see if I was all right. He said that we were supposed to do a rematch with the Gunns in about half an hour and asked if I could do it. I wasn't going to tell him no. You just didn't say no. After that, it's all a blur. I can't even remember sitting with Billy and Bart to go over the match. I do remember going out there later, and the rest is hazy. Billy told me that he could see I had no idea what was going on, because I was doing things in the ring for no reason at all. I got really sick the next few days on the road, but that was how it was back then. You didn't complain; you just got on with it.

When the check came in for the match I had at the Rumble, I was happy. I made $2,500. Back then, I thought that was great. In hindsight, knowing what I do now, it wasn't that good. In the grand scheme of things, given how much money the pay-per-views generate and how much the company takes from that, $2,500 is nothing and I probably should have seen more for being in one of the featured matches. Back then though, the way I looked at it was that I hadn't been there very long and I still had to prove myself. I hoped that later on, I'd make more money. Some of the other guys would sit in the back and complain because they weren't making money or being pushed, but I hadn't been there long enough to buy a watch, so who was I to say anything? I just listened and basically learned from others what not to do. I think one of the reasons I had such a long career with Vince is that I didn't complain or get pissed when I had to put somebody over. I just did my job.

My job continued to be making other people look good, and one of the people who needed to look very good in the lead up to *WrestleMania* was Bam Bam. He was going to be in the main event with Lawrence Taylor, so he needed to get as much momentum as possible. I worked with him several times, putting him over. Everything seemed fine and he was pleasant and easy to work with. But one day, without warning, he

threw me under the bus. I was really shocked. Somebody came up to me backstage and said, "Hey Bob, I heard you didn't want to put Bam Bam over last night?" Everyone was apparently saying that I hadn't wanted to do the job for Bam Bam. That was bullshit and I said so — I never refused to do a job in my career. I *had* suggested that we used a different finish to our match the previous night. We had been doing the exact same finish in all of our matches, so I thought it would be good to switch it up (but still have Bam Bam win). He agreed to go with the different finish. I was trying to make him look versatile and I guess I shouldn't have bothered.

Anyway, I asked around and found out that Bam Bam had told one of the agents that I didn't want to lose to him. I confronted Bam Bam in the locker room in front of everybody and asked why he had said that I didn't want to put him over. He said, "I didn't say that . . ." I demanded, "So what *did* you say?" and he responded, "All I said is that you wanted to change the finish. . . ." He didn't tell them that I'd only suggested altering the finish but not the result, and he didn't explain that it was only because we were using the same finish all the time. He just didn't say anything. I told him that it was a chickenshit thing to do. He apologized and said that he was having a bad day, he took it wrong, he didn't mean to make me look bad and everything. I couldn't believe it. Hell, that "misunderstanding" could have cost me my job! That was my first lesson in not trusting anybody. I didn't want to get a reputation as a troublemaker. You don't want that reputation in wrestling.

I made sure to talk to Pat Patterson about it and explain what really happened. Pat was understanding and said it was fine. I wanted to make sure I didn't have any heat with the office. I learned from the situation and I didn't let any more trouble happen with Bam Bam after that. Whenever I worked with him, I kept it simple. I said he should just tell me what he wanted to do and I would do it. That way, he couldn't go back and say that I wasn't cooperating.

Bam Bam wasn't happy about a lot of things at that point, so I guess that's why he was acting out. He knew he was going to be losing to the football player at *WrestleMania* in front of a huge audience and he didn't like it one bit. I agreed with him — I thought he had every right to complain. They were bringing in a guy from outside our world and having him beat a professional wrestler. If somebody from the outside comes in, they shouldn't be able to beat us at what we do. It would have been one thing if Lawrence Taylor had been fighting a nobody who lost to all the wrestlers. You wouldn't expect a wrestler to beat Tiger Woods in a game of golf, for example, so why should a wrestler be expected to potentially sacrifice all the credibility he's built up over the years in order to put over somebody who isn't even in the industry? Bam Bam was your consummate tough-guy wrestler, well over 300 pounds and feared in the wrestling world, and now he was going to lose to a retired football player? That didn't seem right to me. I didn't like the match either — Bam Bam just about killed himself to get L.T. over and had to lead him through everything. L.T. had no idea what he was doing and Bam Bam was pretty much holding his hand through the whole thing and sacrificing himself. He main-evented *WrestleMania*, something everyone in wrestling aspires to do, but he wasn't happy about how it went down.

They tried to keep Bam Bam happy afterwards and gave him a huge payout for the match. I heard it was something like a quarter of a million dollars. They promised that they'd turn him babyface after 'Mania and give him a big push to get him to the top of the card in order to rebuild his credibility. That didn't work out. Shawn and Kevin were deep in Vince's ear by this point and made sure that most of the attention was on them, so Bam Bam didn't really have a chance to get over as a babyface. Not happy with the way things were going, he left the company later that year. He main-evented *WrestleMania* in April, received the most mainstream publicity of any wrestler in the world at that point, and was gone by November. That's fucked up. But that's how things were once the Clique took over.

CHAPTER 13
TREADING WATER

By this point, Kevin Nash (as Diesel) was the WWF champion, and Shawn and Razor (Scott Hall) were working on top too. Even though Nash was drawing nothing as champion and business was down, they had a lot of stroke and they were damn sure using it. The only other guys who were getting anything were Bret and 'Taker because they were already at the top when the Clique got there. I was convinced that Shawn had something over Vince. I had no idea what, but there was something there. How else could Shawn have had so much power? Vince allowed the Clique to manipulate everything, the way every storyline went, the way every talent was used. They dictated everything. I didn't like it but hey, if I didn't like working there, I could have quit. I kept my mouth shut and did my job. My opinion didn't matter.

'Taker and Bret were both respected in the locker room, great workers who had Vince's ear but didn't abuse their power. Bret made sure to look after his brother Owen and his brother-in-law Davey Boy Smith as much as he could, but at least he never fucked with anybody else's career. It was a shame to see Shawn acting up, because he was such a talented worker that he didn't need to resort to politics and being a jerk. He was messed up all the time too — always drinking, always doing something. A lot of the boys were frustrated with his behavior but they didn't say anything.

Everybody knew how much the Clique had Vince's ear and that, if they didn't like you, they'd bury you in a heartbeat. Take Shane Douglas, for example — Shane was getting over. He had great promos, he was a good worker, and he knew how to get heat. I thought he was going to be one of the top guys because he was damn good. Shane didn't act like he thought he was a big star or anything but Shawn and his buddies didn't like him, so they shoved him right out the door. They did the same with "Sycho" Sid Eudy. It seemed to me like they were just afraid somebody was going to get over more than them, so they held everyone else down. They were making a ton of money and I didn't get why they had a problem with someone else making money too. After all, the more people we have making money for the company, the more we all get paid. But all Shawn wanted to do was work with his buddies. It was clear that Bret didn't like the way things were going either — Vince was the owner of the company but you had these two guys, Shawn and Kevin, who were dictating how everything went and who was going to do what.

Bret stuck it out and kept trying to balance things but other guys didn't stick around. wcw had Hulk Hogan, Randy Savage, Sting, and Ric Flair, and they were just about to launch a live TV show to go head to head with *RAW*. They were genuine competition for the first time and they had an aggressive boss in Eric Bischoff, who wanted to prove he could beat Vince. They also had the unlimited financial resources of Ted Turner, who owned the company. Jumping to wcw became a very realistic possibility for the boys who weren't happy. I remember flying back home the week after *SummerSlam '95*. I was in first class, sitting next to Lex Luger, and we were talking about working out. Lex had been traveling by himself but it sounded like we had a pretty similar schedule, so I said I'd like to work out with him in the future. He gave me his number so that when we started back on the road we could travel together and work out together. The next thing I knew, he showed up live on *WCW Nitro*. I called him but his cell phone number had changed already. We'd talked for hours on the plane and he hadn't said a word about jumping ship. I guess he'd had enough of being ignored in favor of Shawn and his gang. Still, no matter how I felt about the Clique, I felt like Luger was a traitor. None of the boys could believe it. Vince had invested huge money in Luger, paid him well, and given him every chance to be the biggest star in wrestling, including a highly publicized bus tour around the country to build a fan base. Yet Lex just upped and left. Where's the loyalty? I've always felt that when someone is good to you, you have to be loyal. And Vince was very good to Luger. I thought that he just never clicked with the WWF audience. He fit in better with WCW because that's where he started — he seemed like a fish out of water in the WWF. That's no excuse though. You don't just up and leave without a word of explanation.

Luger wasn't the only one who acted like a jerk that year — Jeff Jarrett took his ball and went home too. He was about to work a program with Road Dogg and he didn't like what they were planning to do, so he decided to walk out on the big company that had made him a star so he could jump to WCW. And he and Road Dogg were good friends — or so Road Dogg thought. When Jeff wanted to leave the WWF, Road Dogg stuck with him and left too, but when they got to Atlanta, WCW only wanted Jarrett. Jeff didn't go to bat for Road Dogg; he just took the offer WCW gave him and left his so-called friend behind without a job. Jeff's a charming guy to your face but I wouldn't trust him as far as I could throw him.

He might not have been trustworthy but he was good enough in the ring. I had a number of matches with him earlier in the year and it looked like they might actually go somewhere. The company had put a lot of effort into Jeff and he'd been the Intercontinental Champion a couple of times. He and I had a match for TV that was going to be for the IC title, and they told me before the match that I was going to win and become the champion. I was glad to hear that, because the IC title was second only to the WWF Championship at that point. We did the match and it went well, and the finish came off fine, with me hitting him with a clothesline off the top. I went for the cover and Jeff got his foot on the rope to break the pin, but the ref didn't see it and counted three. I'd been told to get out of the ring quickly, grab the belt, and come straight to the back, so I did. My music was playing, I was high-fiving the fans, and Jeff was kicking up a stink in the ring with a bunch of referees because his foot had been on the ropes. The idea had been to use the controversy to build up to a rematch for the title at the next pay-per-view. When I got backstage with the belt, they told me that I was going to go back out there, they were going to announce the title was vacant and I'd never actually won it, and we were going to do the rematch right away — and Jeff was going to win. It was incredibly frustrating; they kept nearly going with me and then pulling back at the last second.

We didn't get to do the match on pay-per-view after that. Instead, Jeff and Road Dogg found themselves in a match with Razor Ramon and the 1-2-3 Kid. I wasn't surprised to see Shawn's buddies in that match instead of me. Heading into that event, Kid got injured, so Razor needed a partner. You'd think I would have been the logical choice, given what had gone down between me and Jarrett, but they just had Razor fight two guys by himself. God forbid anyone else got a chance to get over or collect a payday. So, in the end, I never won the IC title. Interestingly enough, the guy who won it from Jarrett a couple of months later? Shawn Michaels. He was meant to go on to *SummerSlam* to defend the title against Sid. At the last minute, plans changed and Sid was taken out of the match for no reason. Guess who replaced him? Razor Ramon. They controlled everything.

I did, at least, get a pay-per-view appearance on that *SummerSlam* show. My job was to help kick-start the push of a new guy named Hunter Hearst Helmsley. He had just come in from wcw and had kept to himself in the locker room — he was quiet, spoke when he was spoken to, and took everything in. I liked him back then and we worked a lot of house shows leading up to *SummerSlam*, so we were able to perfect our match. Hunter is probably one of the easiest people to work with. No matter what else I might say about him — and we'll get to that later — he is really fucking good and there's no other way to put it. He knows what he is doing; he knows where to be and when it's time to do certain things. He's not selfish, he doesn't do things off the cuff, and everything he does makes sense. He's a great storyteller in the ring.

I liked our *SummerSlam* match — he looked strong and I looked competitive. He got the win and started to move up the ladder. I didn't mind — I figured one of these days, it'll come back to me. I'd started proving that I could hang with these guys and wrestle just as well as them. Even though I was putting people over, every time I went out there I proved I could work. That was almost the problem — the office ended up thinking,

"Bob's a good hand — he can make people look good so let's keep him in that role."

They had me do the same at some of the other pay-per-view events. I put over Jean-Pierre Lafitte at *In Your House 1* and Goldust at *In Your House 3*, and actually got to beat Rad Radford at *In Your House 4*. All three matches were dark matches — untelevised bouts to get the crowd warmed up before the main show. It felt like management thought I was good enough to wrestle in front of an audience but not worth paying to see. That was demoralizing.

The money hadn't got better, either. The most I'd got paid all year was still the $2,500 from the *Rumble.* I got something like $1,200 for my *SummerSlam* match with Hunter. The other pay-per-view matches were about a grand each. Nothing special. Don't get me wrong, I appreciated any money they paid me and I appreciated any time I got on the big events. I just wanted to be more than the person they turned to when it was time to put a new guy over or they needed a last-minute fill-in. At *King of the Ring* in 1995, I wrestled Road Dogg and lost to him. Up until that point, he had only been acknowledged as Jeff Jarrett's roadie (hence the name) and not a wrestler, so like Bam Bam and the football player at 'Mania, it looked like a non-wrestler was beating a wrestler. I didn't appreciate that. How the hell was I supposed to have any credibility if I couldn't beat a roadie?! That was the night I really started to question company politics and began to think that it didn't matter how good somebody was. Road Dogg had the connection to Jeff. The other guys they were pushing on that show weren't good workers. Kama, Mabel . . . neither were good wrestlers but they were buddies with the Undertaker. Since they wanted to get those guys over, they needed a good wrestler to help people believe in them. It felt like I was doing all the work and they were getting all the rewards. Jerry Brisco even said to me, "We need guys like you who can wrestle to get over the guys who can't." That seemed fucked up to me. Why not just push the guys who *could* actually wrestle? I knew what I was doing and I didn't screw up spots, but I felt like I was getting penalized for being good at my job. They kept beating me with guys who were not good at their job until the fans were programmed to say, "Okay, he's going to get beat because he's lost every night for the past year." Everybody was conditioned to see me as a loser, so how the heck was I meant to get over or make any money?

By the end of the year, I was only on pay-per-view as a last-minute fill-in. At *Survivor Series* in November, they pulled Al Snow from an elimination match because they'd tried to get him over with a new gimmick and he'd fucked up his finish move on *RAW.* They lost interest in him right away and put me in his spot in the match. I even got to beat Tom Prichard before they eliminated me. I was sure they wouldn't have made me look strong by beating someone else unless they were going to do something with me but, as usual, that was just wishful thinking. 1995 had started with promise and ended with disappointment. I had moved down the card over the course of the year rather than up, and, believe it or not, the next few years were going to get even worse.

At this point in my wrestling career, the most notable thing I had done was back on the racetrack. In the first year or so after I joined the WWF, trying to get myself a push, I went to Vince with an idea to expand our fan base. I said that the car-racing demographic was similar to ours; racing fans were like wrestling fans. If we reached out to that community, we might draw more interest. Since I was a race-car driver for real, I suggested the WWF sponsor me in all the pro-circuit races, using a WWF car to get us some attention. I was upfront with Vince and told him that it would cost a lot of money to get started, but he liked the idea so much that he asked me how I would act if Frito Lay was sponsoring me? I told him that, if it was a big corporation like Frito Lay, I'd get whatever I needed. He said, "Run the race car just like that then — get whatever you need." He left me in charge of an unlimited spending budget. The company bought three motors, at about $25,000 each, and two Super Late Model cars. I had one of the cars out with me on the tracks and the other one, brand new, sitting in my workshop. Vince was fucking great to me — whatever I needed for the cars, I got. I always told Vince that I would treat his money like my own and try to shop around to get the best deals possible. I kept track of every dime we spent. Vince appreciated that.

A friend of mine named Ricky Crawford hooked me up with Randy Dorton, who worked for Dale Earnhardt — they built our motors at Automotive Specialist and they were top of the line. Vince wanted the best of everything and it was all high-dollar stuff. Ricky did everything he could to help me, pointing me in the right direction and guiding me along the way. He was running the All Pro Series against me, but even at the racetracks he'd come over and help me as much as he could to make sure my car was running well — a really good guy who went on to bigger and better things and ended up in NASCAR. To this day, I'm grateful to Ricky for all his help back then. He's the promoter for the Mobile International Speedway now and doing a great job.

It was great to be racing again, and getting into the All Pro Series was a big deal — some of the races were even on TV. It was the Late Model series that everybody in racing wanted to be in. I found it hard doing the traveling involved. I was used to racing at only one track. Since the All Pro Series was a traveling event, I was going around to different tracks in the southeast. That by itself would have been fine, but I was still doing the wrestling shows at the same time. When there was a race every couple of weeks, I'd fly home from a show, drive out to whichever track we were at, do the race, drive home, fly back out, and wrestle somewhere else. At first, I was okay because I was still young and my body wasn't beaten up yet, but after a while it wore me down. I couldn't fit everything in, either — when you're racing, you've got to work on the car every single day — so I told the WWF I needed to hire somebody to work on the cars when I was out working the wrestling shows. They told me to choose someone and they would put him on payroll, so I gave the job to Jimbo Walker. It was pretty cool that I was able to get my buddy that job. He was so good to me in helping me win my championship back in 1993, so my loyalty lay with him. It was an eight-hour-a-day job, just like any other. Nine to five. Jimbo started out doing that, but as we got more into the racing he got a little bit lazy. Sometimes, I'd be on the road with the WWF and I'd get a phone call from the workshop to tell me it was midday and Jimbo hadn't arrived yet. I tried to get him back on track but it turned out he was doing a lot of cocaine, so I had to let him go. Emotionally, that killed me but I couldn't have someone who was doing drugs working on my race car, no matter how much I liked him. That could have *literally* killed me.

Without Jimbo, I had to cover the work on the cars by myself and it got to be so much that I ended up missing races. I was working every

hour of every day. I'd get to the track with the car and start working on it right there, trying to get it ready. When you show up to a track, that car needs to be ready as soon as you unload it from the trailer. Maybe you'll have little things to do when you get there but you'd better be ready to race. I was pulling the truck and trailer ten hours to a racetrack, trying to get ready at the last minute, failing to qualify because the car wasn't ready, missing the race, driving back home, and then flying out to wrestle. I kept interviewing people to help out but I couldn't find the right person. I wasn't about to hire any person off the street. Doing everything by myself was exhausting but I still enjoyed getting the chance to race at some great tracks. We were coming up to a race in Bristol, Tennessee, and I was so excited about that. Some of the best racing in the world goes on there. It's a super-fast track — a half-mile oval with 36-degree banking in the corners. You can flat-foot it around that track in a Super Late Model and not even lift.

About a week before the race, I got a call from Vince telling me that he was going to have to cut the racing program. I felt like somebody had popped my balloon — why couldn't they have just waited another week until I'd been able to do Bristol? Vince explained that the company had lost a lot of money through the steroid trials in 1994 and business hadn't been great for a few years, so he had to cut a lot of stuff. I understood, but I was disappointed that I didn't get to race Bristol. I told Vince that I would sell all of the equipment and get him his money back. He said that since I'd been behind everything and loved racing, he wanted to sell it all to me. There was about $300,000 of equipment and I couldn't afford that. He told me, "Don't worry, you can afford to buy it, I want to sell it to you . . ." He had his attorney on the phone too. "I'll just take the money out of your check." If he'd done that, he wouldn't have paid me another dime for years! I protested, telling Vince that I was glad he'd let me race, but there was no way I would ever be able to afford all the equipment. He said, "I'm going to sell it to you . . . for $100."

I didn't know what to say to that. I told him again not to worry, that I would sell everything and get him his money back and he just said, "No, I want you to have everything. I'll write it off." No matter how much I protested, he wouldn't have it any other way. He said it was a done deal, his attorney would FedEx me the paperwork to confirm it was all being transferred to me and that they'd take the $100 out of my paycheck.

I ended up racing on my days off — just local tracks at Mobile and Pensacola. I did that for another year but I was on the road with the WWF so much that I'd be gone for weeks and home for only a couple of days. I just didn't have time for racing any more. I sold everything and got a good chunk of money for it. I made sure to offer the money to Vince, but he didn't want it — he just said, "Bob, that was your stuff, you keep the money." That's one of the main reasons I was always loyal to Vince — he took care of me. Whether it was letting me keep all the car equipment or making sure I was fully paid whenever I got injured, he always took care of me. The only thing I question about him is why he lets other people dictate how he runs *his* show. Apart from that, I have nothing bad to say about him.

And, in the end, he never even took that $100 out of my paycheck.

CHAPTER 14

THE CLIQUE TAKES OVER

Heading into '96, management seemed to have given up on Kevin Nash being the top guy since we were getting godawful ratings with him as champion. Instead, they were going to go with Shawn. People voiced their opinions pretty gingerly but it was obvious that Shawn and Kevin were running the show, and almost nobody liked it. Everyone tiptoed around backstage because they knew the members of the Clique had a lot of influence over Vince and were more than happy to use it. Everyone was job-scared.

Drugs and alcohol were everywhere. It wasn't something anybody talked about; you could just see who was in and who was out. I was out. I was never a drink or drugs guy, so I'd just go to my room after the shows and go to sleep. As I said earlier, I've never felt comfortable in a bar environment. The problem was that the attitude seemed to be "if you don't go out with the guys, you're not going to fit in." I'm not a follower and I don't care what other people think, so I wasn't about to give in to peer pressure. I felt like I shouldn't have had to go out with the guys to fit in. If they were going to like me, they were going to like me whether I went to the bar or not. If they didn't like me because I didn't go drinking, fuck 'em. I was going to stay true to myself. I'd gone out a couple of times when I first got to the WWF but it wasn't for me — just one of those things. Even though

I didn't go out, I still heard from the boys in the locker room about the events from the night before.

Right in the middle of it all was Shawn — he was the ringleader. He dictated everything that was going on. He'd go out partying every night, drinking, taking drugs, getting in fights . . . he'd show up the next day hungover as hell but still work like crazy. He never screwed anything up — whatever mind-set he was in, he still went out there and put on the best match of the night. He was a machine. Not a great ambassador for the company though — and not a great influence backstage. The Clique just kept on fucking with people and wanting to work only with each other, hogging all the money. Anybody who looked like he could get over and make some money was put in his place. The prime example of that was Sid Eudy — Kevin and Shawn didn't like him. Sid is misunderstood; he's very humorous, in a sarcastic way, and people take it wrong. He was always good to me. When we traveled together, he knew I wasn't making a lot so he paid for our rental car, the hotel, a lot of my meals. I wouldn't have made it without him — I owe him a lot. I think I helped him out a lot too, by keeping him sane!

Sid wasn't a good worker but he cut a great promo and he had a great look. He was over huge, so of course Vince was going to use him to draw. I guess Kevin and Shawn didn't like the thought of someone else getting a piece of the action so they stepped in. Nash, especially, felt threatened by him because they were both big men, but Sid was over and Nash just hadn't worked out as champion. They butted heads a lot when they were going over matches. Sid was set in his ways and wasn't about to back down to anybody. He wouldn't let upper management or the other boys push him around or abuse his character.

After the Clique pushed Sid out of the main event picture, they kept sticking it to him — I guess to prove a point or something. In January 1996, they pushed it too far. He and I traveled to the arena together. Sid came up to me a while after we'd arrived and said, "How do you want to beat me?"

"You're fucking with me, right?" I replied.

"No," he said, "we're wrestling tonight and they want you over." I asked him if he was mad at me. "Fuck no," he said, "It's them . . . they're fucking with me. Fuck this place. I'm done after tonight." I wasn't offended that he was mad at having to lose to me — it was an insult to him. Here you have me, who loses to everyone all the time, and there you have Sid, this big monster, and he had to put me over clean? I was very uncomfortable. He was pitching an absolute fit backstage and I was caught in the middle of it. We did the match and it was fine — I won with a cross-body off the top or something like that. The whole time we were out there, though, I felt so bad for him. It wasn't right, what Kevin and Shawn were doing to him. But what could I do? I did what I was told or I found another job; it was as simple as that.

Afterwards, Sid came backstage and was selling that he got injured. He said he hurt his neck. He was lying about that — since we had been traveling together, I knew the truth. He just didn't want to deal with all the politics anymore so he left. Long before *WrestleMania* that year, Sid was gone. After *'Mania*, Bret Hart took some time off. 'Taker was still around but the Clique's influence was everywhere. Shawn was the champion now and Kevin was still on top. Shawn's first challenger as champion was going to be Kevin. Scott Hall and Kid were still hanging around with them. The Clique had managed to push all of the other top guys out of the picture (except for 'Taker, and ain't nobody pushing *him* anywhere . . .) so now they were free to work with each other and dominate the company. They'd even added a fifth member . . .

How Hunter got hooked up with the Clique, I don't know. He'd been in wcw for a while before he came to the wwf, so he'd seen how the game was played. He figured out pretty quickly that if you wanted to get somewhere, you had to be in Shawn and Kevin's circle, so he went right for the kill. If you ever meet Hunter, he'll suck you right in — he's a likeable guy. He comes across well, he's very intelligent, very charming, and he has a great mind for the business. Shawn and Kevin let him in, although they sort of used him as a bag boy for a while to carry their luggage. He didn't care about sucking up to get ahead.

Maybe that's where I went wrong. All my life, I was never into sucking up to anybody. When I went to the wwf, I didn't know how the game was played and I thought I would just sit back, mind my P's and Q's, not step on any toes, and let my work speak for itself. If I'd gone up to

Shawn and kissed his ass, maybe I would have had a bigger push. Instead, I traveled with guys who they didn't like so I ended up "guilty by association." Politically, I went in the wrong direction — but number one, I didn't know what was going on when I first got there and number two, I didn't care about locker-room politics. I wasn't going to kiss ass to get ahead. I thought I could make my own path without anybody's help, but in WWE you need *everybody's* help. It's often not what you know, it's who you know. It's funny that after I broke in, my first road trip was with Paul Bearer and the Undertaker. Politically, that was a hell of a connection to have for a new guy, but I wasn't interested in playing that game. I was a guy who wanted to go work out and 'Taker wasn't. Paul definitely wasn't! But 'Taker is as cool as hell. He's kind of quiet but very accommodating and fun to be around.

As much as they claimed to be tight, the Clique's members were a bunch of cowards who wouldn't go to bat for each other when things got rough. At one point, when we were overseas on a tour, we heard about an incident that happened back in the States. The agent report was phoned through to us the day after the other crew had done a show in Madison Square Garden. Shawn had been smarting off — as usual — to the boys earlier in the day. He'd made the mistake of smarting off one too many times to Ronnie Harris. You don't fuck with either of the Harris Twins. By now, Shawn and Kid didn't change with the rest of the boys; they'd got themselves their own private dressing room. The Harris boys paid them a visit. Donnie stood outside the door to make sure nobody got in. Ronnie went inside, propped a chair up against the door, and put a table in the way to make sure nobody got out. He grabbed Shawn by the throat and slammed him up against the wall, then slammed him on the table and started choking him out. He was practically killing him and Kid just stood there and watched. Didn't say a thing, didn't do a thing. Now, if I were to see my friend getting choked out, regardless of whether he had it coming or not, I would intervene. I never understood why Sean didn't.

When the agent explained what had happened, I was sitting at the back of the bus playing trump with Kevin Nash, Scott Hall, and Yokozuna. Nash was furious. Being the tough guy he is, he said, "If I was there, that wouldn't have happened. I ought to go to Ronnie Harris's house, knock on his door, and beat his ass." Nobody else said anything until I said, "That's exactly what you need to do, Kevin. You need to go beat his ass." Nash just looked at me and didn't say a word. He didn't say a word to Ronnie Harris either when he saw him next. That was Kevin — he was always talking tough. Whenever stuff went down between Shawn and Bret, Kevin said he would kick Bret's ass. Nash is the biggest seven-foot-tall pussy I've ever seen in my life and Bret Hart would have eaten him for lunch. I'd tell Nash that to his face too — because he wouldn't do jackshit to me.

CHAPTER 15
THE BEGINNING OF THE WAR

Everything changed in the middle of '96 when it came out that Nash and Hall had signed with the opposition. wcw had been gaining ground and were trying to sign a lot of our guys, but everybody in the locker room was shocked when Hall and Nash quit. I couldn't believe it — after all Vince had done for them, they showed absolutely no loyalty. Before they got to the wwf, they were nobodies. Vince took care of them, paid them well, made them who they were, and they shit on him. Loyalty didn't mean a damn thing to those guys. They had been pushed to the moon, they beat everybody else on the roster, and then, boom, they were gone. All of the other boys on the roster worked hard, put Hall and Nash over, and then they just upped and left? They were making tons of money while none of us were making any. They deserved to have their asses kicked.

Being a bunch of jackasses, they couldn't just leave the company without doing something stupid too. I got back from (another) tour in Europe and Jerry Brisco told me what had happened at Madison Square Garden on Kevin and Scott's last night with the company. Shawn and Kevin worked together, Shawn as the babyface, Kevin as the heel. After the match was over, Kevin got up and they started hugging and saying goodbye in front of the fans, despite the fact that they'd been fighting in a cage match just minutes before. Then Scott — another babyface — went out and joined in. Hunter was standing in Gorilla with Vince and Jerry and said, "Should I go out there and join them?" He knew that Jerry would have wanted to stop him, so he was looking to Vince for approval. Maybe it was because Shawn was his golden boy and he didn't want to piss him off, but apparently Vince looked at Hunter and didn't say a thing. Hunter went off and joined his buddies in the ring. Hunter was a heel and had fought Scott earlier in the night. Suddenly all of these guys were in front of the audience shaking hands and hugging and doing their little Clique hand sign like a bunch of fucking idiots. Jerry wanted to rip Hunter apart. He and Vince were both pissed.

Management couldn't do anything to Hall and Nash because they were leaving. They wouldn't do anything to Shawn because he was over, making the company a lot of money, and I'm sure there was something going on behind closed doors with Vince too. Hunter took the fall. He was scheduled to win the *King of the Ring* tournament so they took that away from him and made him do jobs for a couple of months. Steve Austin ended up winning the *King of the Ring* that year and took off.

I don't think the punishment fit the crime for Hunter. Sure, he lost a bunch of matches for a while but he didn't do a job to me or any of the other guys who could have gained from it. If he'd been made to do a job to me, *that* would have made a statement — especially since I'd busted my ass putting him over so much the summer before. After a couple of months, they figured he'd paid his dues and they gave him the Intercontinental title. That sure showed him.

As for Nash and Hall, as soon as they got to wcw, they ran an angle where it looked like they were outsiders invading the promotion. It got hot real quick. wcw took off and suddenly started beating us in the ratings. They signed anybody they could take from us to build up their roster. Kid showed his loyalty to the wwf by jumping ship to join Nash and Hall pretty quickly. Other people stabbed Vince in the back too. It seemed like people would do anything for a bit of money. For example, Madusa, the wwf women's champion, turned up on wcw tv and threw the title belt in the trash. They were definitely turning the volume up.

I thought it was great that we had real competition at last. When you've got good competition, you strive to do everything you can do to be the best company on the planet. The locker room bonded together, tightened their bootlaces, dug deep, and worked harder. We were determined to put on a better show and prove to Hall and Nash that they had fucked up by leaving. It was like everybody wanted to say, "Just because you guys had a hit with the nWo, you just made us all work harder to become number one again." We had monitors in the locker room when we were taping *RAW*, and sometimes we'd watch some of *Nitro* to see what the competition was up to. I didn't think their show was that good. I was biased, obviously, but I thought our show was a lot better. The competition between the companies got pretty intense. We weren't allowed friends in WCW. WWF management didn't want us talking to *anyone* associated with WCW at all. They even sent out a memo with our travel itineraries, telling us that if they found out we were talking to anyone at all in WCW, we would be fired. Nobody backstage could believe it. Who were they to say who we could and couldn't talk to?! There were guys we'd been friends with for years and suddenly we weren't allowed to talk to them? As usual, I kept my head down, did my job, and didn't complain. If I didn't like their rules, I could leave. Nobody was forcing me to stay. But I bet Hunter and Shawn didn't stop speaking to Scott and Kevin. The rules didn't seem to apply to them back then.

Mind you, with more than half of their members gone, the Clique couldn't hold a gun to Vince's head anymore. Shawn was the lonely man on the island backstage at that point. His behavior got even worse after Hall and Nash left; he was drinking more, doing more drugs. He was in a whole other world. The office sent one of the referees, Timmy White, to travel with Shawn and try to keep him on the straight and narrow. They were worried Shawn was going to do something stupid or just disappear. He was always getting into trouble. Timmy almost quit the company over that because he couldn't take riding with Shawn. I don't know the details but from what Timmy told me, it wasn't fun — he described his time babysitting Shawn as one of the worst periods in his career. I don't believe there's a place for people like that in the industry. Why should somebody else have to take responsibility to get you to the show on time? If you're a grown man in the wrestling business and you can't get yourself to the arena or take responsibility for what you've got to do to get there, you have no place in the industry, no matter how talented or how much of a draw you are. Shawn kept abusing his power and getting away with it because Vince was feeling the pressure from wcw. He was doing whatever it took to make sure his top guys were happy and the wwf stayed in the game, but he started making decisions that Shawn couldn't have liked, including bringing back some top guys that Shawn definitely didn't like.

Despite a huge offer from wcw, Bret came back at the end of the year. Sid was brought back halfway through the year, on some conditions: Shawn couldn't fuck with him anymore, and guys like me wouldn't go over on him to make him look bad. I don't blame Sid for trying to protect himself. Another of these conditions was that Sid would get the World title, which he actually ended up winning from Shawn himself. I thought that was quite fitting and pretty funny.

As for me, I wanted to do my bit and make a difference. All of these guys had been defecting to wcw and I was still with the wwf and working hard. I figured I'd finally get my shot. After all, I was loyal and talented, and, through the ups and downs, I had always figured my talent would eventually dictate how far I went. It turned out that my talent actually held me back because I was a good enough, reliable enough worker that I was used to make other people look good, even when they were absolutely terrible. And so I carried on in the role of the guy who went out there and lost to everybody to make them all look good, and it didn't do a damn thing for me. I wasn't even making decent money and they were using me less and less. In 1994, I had over 200 matches. In 1995, I had somewhere around 150. By 1996, they had me working less than 100 matches, and in 1997, I only had 50 matches. I'm sure that traveling with Sid was one of the reasons I got fewer matches in '96. But, in '97, Sid was the only reason I got *any* matches — he went to Pat Patterson and said, "If you don't get Bob back on the road, I'll be quitting." He said that I kept him sane, helped him drive when he was hurt, that sort of thing. That was why they got me back on the road and working the shows. Sid had a lot of stroke but they never used him properly — they could have made a lot of money with him if they'd figured out how.

Even though they brought me back, Sid still couldn't deal with Shawn being a prick, so he dropped the wwf Championship to 'Taker and left shortly afterwards. I got used less and less again, and I ended up sitting at home for a long time as the war between WCW and the WWF went on. They were cycling their enhancement guys in and out, seeing if any of us would catch on with the audience. They were just throwing shit at a wall and hoping something stuck. None of us were making any money. I was still paid by the WWF and got calls to go to the TV tapings and the pay-per-views, but it wasn't enough and I had no idea when they would bring me back full time. Then a friend of mine, who was a foreman with Harmony Construction, called and said that he needed a TIG welder. I didn't want to do that, I just wanted to get back to the WWF and get on with my job there. I told him this but next thing I know, he turns up at my door on a Monday morning and says, "Jump in the truck, let's get you a welding test. . . ." I figured, "Why not?" so I went ahead and did it and ended up getting a job with him. I was making good money as a welder during the week and started racing on the weekends again, so I was actually pretty content.

After several months, Bruce Prichard from the WWF called me and said he needed me to come back to work full time. I told him I didn't think I wanted to come back, that I had a good job, was enjoying racing again, and was home every night. He kept at me until I said that if they wanted me back, they were going to have to make sure I made at least what I was making at my welding job. I left it with him but I wasn't concerned either way. Like I said, I was content with what I was doing at that point.

I know a lot of people think that we were on TV and so we must have made huge money but it's just not true. I was making $1,000 a week welding. After road expenses, I was making nowhere near that with the WWF. Only the top guys were.

Bruce called me back later and said that they would match my salary and they wanted to bring me up to Connecticut to do some training, knock off the rust, and get me back into ring-shape. They started paying me right away but didn't get me up to Connecticut for another four weeks, so I ended up making two grand a week for a while. That was pretty nice but it's definitely not the sort of money that most people think a wrestler with the WWF makes.

PART 4: MAKING MONEY

One of the things you hear the most in WWE meetings is that "you've got to make your own push." That is such a load of crap. I always used to give them ideas for me and those ideas would get thrown back at me every time. It gets to the point where it's useless to try and it doesn't do any good to complain, so you just go out there and do your job. You will go as far as they want you to go. If they get behind you and stay behind you, they will push and push until you get over. If they lose interest, you're done.

It all comes back to what they want to do with you. They decided I was going to put people over and I was stuck in that role. It didn't matter how great my ideas were. You can get over by jobbing but only so much. If you get beat week in and week out, people are programmed to expect you to lose, and who is going to support a loser or buy his merchandise? You can't get over and stay over with three to five minutes of TV time per week when you lose all the time.

Look at Mark Henry — he was basically a nothing guy for 14 years. Then the company figured out how to use him, got behind him, pushed the hell out of him, and he was suddenly World Champion. Good for Mark, but why did it take the company so long to figure it out? Without the machine behind you, you're going nowhere.

Take the recent example of Zack Ryder. He was sitting at home, not going anywhere, so he came up with an internet show that got him a cult following and forced management's hand. They put him on the main shows but they still treat him as a joke. Even if you "make your own push," you're only going to get as far as management wants to let you get. He's a good worker too. I remember him from when I spent some time in Deep South Wrestling. He caught lightning in a bottle with that internet show. Back in my day, the internet wasn't as mainstream; plus, we were on the road so much that we didn't have time to do stuff like that! There are only so many different ways of trying to get over, and most of the time, WWE doesn't like it if you think outside the box.

I did ask Vince what I needed to do but the thing you have to understand about him is that you have to come at him with ideas. I asked what I could do better and he told me, "You have all the skills, you just have to come up with ideas." So I went away, came up with ideas for angles, programs, and catchphrases and they would either throw them away or use those ideas for other people.

I took an idea for a shirt to the merchandising team once, something that Shelton Benjamin came up with for me. He couldn't use it for himself but he thought it fit my character perfectly. Undeniably, it would have sold. The merchandise guys agreed it was great, put together three different versions, and ran them past Vince. He shot the idea down, saying I wasn't one of the guys they were pushing and they only had so much space in the merchandise catalog. When that next catalog came out, there were three new Chris Jericho shirts. There's a lot of money to be made with merchandising but if they won't give you anything, you can't make any money.

It gets to the point where you just resign yourself to the fact that they'll only push you if they want to, no matter what you do. Meanwhile, you do your job, you cash your check, and you go about your business.

CHAPTER 16
MONTREAL

Even though I was under contract, the WWF didn't use me in a single match from the middle of August 1997 through to March 1998. They would call me up at the last minute on a Saturday or Sunday and tell me they needed me at the next day's pay-per-view or at *RAW,* so I'd get on a plane, get to the arena, and then sit backstage and watch the show. I still got paid for it but I never got to work. They just wanted me backstage in case someone else didn't turn up or I was needed for a dark match or something. I hated just sitting around and not working, but it did mean I was around backstage to see some really interesting stuff . . .

Everything came to a head between Bret and Shawn in '97. In the last six months that Bret was with the WWF, I was sure he was having a meltdown because he thought Shawn was being put before him and he couldn't stand it. I still had a lot of respect for Bret as a person and absolutely none for Shawn but even then, I still thought Shawn was hands-down the greatest worker to ever step foot in the ring. Honestly, I think the issue started because Bret couldn't stand that Shawn was better than him. In his own mind, Bret was the greatest wrestler who ever put on a pair of boots. He really believed he was a real world champion. No, Bret, you were a world champion because you were told to be a world champion. It's good to take it seriously to an extent but you've got issues if you truly believe that you're a real world champion once you go back behind that curtain. When I got backstage, I stopped being "Thurman Plugg" or "Sparky" or "Hardcore" and went back to being Bob Howard. I separated myself from my character, and that's why I have never felt that I absolutely had to be in the limelight. It was a job to me and if it weren't for the people I worked with who helped me, I would have been nothing. You don't get anywhere by yourself and you can't be selfish. Bret Hart was always a little wrapped up in Bret Hart. That told me a lot about his character. As '97 went on and his dispute with Shawn got worse, more cracks appeared.

Shawn was acting like a jerk, plain and simple. He went out on national TV and made a comment that implied Bret was having an affair with Sunny, one of the women on the roster. I thought that was a chickenshit thing to do, given that Shawn knew Bret was married with kids. Everyone backstage knew it was wrong but nobody was going to stand up to Shawn because even without his buddies he was still tight with Vince. Everyone was still job-scared. I just knew that when Shawn messed with me at the beginning of my time there, I called him out because I wasn't going to let that motherfucker humiliate me. If they fired me, they fired me but it was nobody else's business so I dealt with it. And that "Sunny days" comment by Shawn was Bret's battle to fight.

Now, I would have marched right over to Shawn and knocked all his teeth out but Bret got into a hair-pulling contest with him instead. Shawn was doing a pre-taped promo backstage and Bret snapped when he saw Shawn — he went running over to him and pulled his hair like a little girl. He pulled a big chunk of hair out of his head. Are you kidding me? He's supposed to be a man!

Was Bret having an affair with Sunny? I have no idea. You'd see people talking backstage and if one of the boys was talking to a woman, some of the others would think, "He must be fucking her." Same thing if one of the boys was eating in catering with one of the women or if they were watching the show together: "They must be fucking." That's the mind-set, and it's bullshit. I didn't see Bret and Sunny hanging out all the time so I don't know what to believe.

Shawn *definitely* saw some Sunny days though. Several of us walked in on him in the shower in Binghampton, New York, when he was having one of those Sunny days. I remember it clearly because Sunny's boyfriend, Chris Candido, was out in the ring at the time. Of course Candido found out, but he didn't do anything about it because he didn't like confrontation. Everyone lost respect for him after that. If somebody fools around with your woman, you stand up to them. It doesn't matter who it is — it doesn't matter if they can whip your ass or not, you stand up to them. Even if you take an ass-whipping, you'll earn more respect because you didn't let yourself be walked all over. You go down swinging.

All of this tension between Bret and Shawn backstage led up to their match in Montreal at *Survivor Series '97*. A lot of wrestlers who *weren't* around have given their opinion on the matter. I was backstage to see it go down, so here's my take.

Back then, it wasn't like it is today, with the internet everywhere and every piece of news (and thousands of rumors) reported all the time. You would hear bits and pieces now and then, but I really didn't know much heading in to Montreal. Nobody backstage knew what was going on. If they did, they were keeping their mouths shut. We knew that Bret was leaving for wcw at some point and, since he was the wwf champion, he'd have to lose the title before he left, but nobody knew how it was going to go down. Steve Austin had taken off by this point, so it was clear they were going to go with him winning the belt at *WrestleMania* the next spring. But nobody knew what was going to happen before that.

Management doesn't tell everyone who will be going over in a match, especially in the main events. They're very hush-hush about that. I didn't know who was going to go over but a lot of the boys had heard that Bret would win. We were watching the monitor backstage when it happened. Bret and Shawn were out there having a fucking great match — it was probably going to be the best they ever had — and then Shawn got Bret in the Sharpshooter. Within maybe four seconds, the referee, Earl Hebner, rang the bell and everybody scrambled. Earl jumped out of the ring and ran to the back. Shawn looked pissed. Vince was ringside with a bunch of officials. Bret spat right in his face. All of the boys were sitting there in the back going, "Holy fuck . . . what just happened? That wasn't the finish. . . ." It was obvious somebody just got fucked over.

Shawn came backstage first. As usual, he had Hunter and their female bodyguard, Chyna, with him. Shawn was cussing like crazy, yelling at the officials, asking what the fuck just happened. It was a great performance, very convincing. Shawn's a great actor. Bret was still at ringside, pitching a fit, breaking TV monitors and wrecking the equipment. Nobody backstage said a word. Everybody was in shock. When Bret got to the back, it like the parting of the Red Sea. Everyone got out of his way. Later, Vince went into the locker room to talk to him and when he came out, it looked like he'd had his ass whipped. Evidently Bret didn't hit him hard enough because he still walked out. If somebody is going to screw you over like that, you're going to want to make them pay, but all Bret did was punch him in the eye? Come on! Bret should have knocked him out. I didn't know why everything had happened and I wasn't in the position to give an opinion. I was in shock, and I wasn't ready to make a judgment until I got the facts.

When I arrived at *RAW* the next night, I still didn't know what had happened. I'd heard stuff but took it all with a grain of salt. At that point, it was all hearsay. At *RAW*, Vince had a meeting where he told us all basically that he did what he had to do and that "if you don't do things the way I want, you can leave." Then he just got on with putting on a wrestling show. There was no general feeling backstage about who was right. It was a point of discussion but something we talked about in private. Nobody wanted to get any heat for voicing an opinion too loudly.

To me, it looked like Bret was leaving the company and Vince couldn't let him take the belt with him. Vince had to protect the title and he had to protect the company. He couldn't risk his World Champion doing what Madusa had done and throwing it in the trash on *WCW Nitro*. I heard that some of the boys were worried: if Vince would screw Bret over like that after Bret had been with the company for 14 years, how the hell could everyone else trust him? I never thought like that. It never changed the way I saw Vince. I trusted Vince's judgment and figured that if he had screwed Bret, it was because he had been backed against a wall and had no other choice. All the years I worked for Vince, I never talked to him about Montreal. Who was I to say anything? It was his business to run as he saw fit.

Vince took the heat and became the most hated man in wrestling. It goes to show how smart he is as a businessman that he capitalized on it by putting himself on TV. As Mr. McMahon the heel, he let the fans spend their money watching him get his ass kicked. It was a business move and it paid off. To this day, any time Vince goes on TV, it pays off in ratings.

There was some worry backstage that he had alienated a huge portion of the audience who were Bret Hart fans, but, as I've said before, it was clear to everybody that Steve Austin was going to be the top guy in the business. We weren't worried. Sure, WCW would have the chance to get a lot more fans when Bret got there, but we had Steve. Whichever side had Steve was going to win; it was that simple. After Vince went on TV as a heel, business just got hotter. Then we ended up with The Rock coming through on top and we just left WCW dead in the water.

It was much later that I finally made a judgment on what had happened in Montreal. A conversation between Bret and Vince that was taped without Vince knowing ended up in the documentary *Wrestling with Shadows*. In it, Bret says he doesn't want to lose to Shawn and would rather hand over the belt on *RAW* the next night. That's when I lost every ounce of respect I had for Bret. It doesn't matter what else was going on, when he said he wanted to hand the belt over without doing a job, he pissed on the company and everybody who ever put him over. He didn't get to the top on his own. He couldn't have become the WWF Champion without everybody else putting him over, so for him to say he wanted to leave without losing to anybody was shitting on each and every person who ever helped put him on top. Imagine that a bunch of people at a regular job help you get promoted, then you decide to leave. Before you go, the guys who helped you get promoted, increasing your value so you can go elsewhere and make more money, ask for your help to cover the hole you're leaving. Do you just say, "No, I don't want to"? In wrestling, if you're leaving a company and you're a champion, you do the right thing and drop the belt to whoever the next person in line is and you do it 1, 2, 3 in the middle of the ring. Back before I started training as a wrestler, Bret was my favorite guy in the WWF, and it killed me to lose all my respect for him.

WWE recently released a DVD in which Shawn and Bret talk about the whole rivalry. Bret comes across as the guy who was wronged. Of course they're going to pacify Bret — they know the DVD wouldn't have happened without Bret's permission and it'll sell better with Bret in it. Shawn's going to play along too. It's about pacifying one person so they can all make a load of money. Shawn says that he always sought validation from Bret. Let me tell you this — the only person Shawn needs validation from is God. He does not need validation from Bret Hart.

Anyway, there were a few things said in that DVD that got me thinking. Bret said that he wanted Shawn to put him over at *Survivor Series* because Shawn had disrespected him backstage by saying that he wasn't prepared to put Bret over. Now, if somebody said that to me, I would think he was an asshole but I'd still do the right thing and job the belt on my way out of the company. It's a tough call and I think Bret's back was against the wall. Bret thought that no one had respect for him, including Shawn, Vince, and everyone in the locker room. The funny thing is that *everybody* had total respect for Bret — until Montreal.

Shawn hadn't helped by acting like a dick, but that was just Shawn back then. He had Vince in his back pocket and felt he could get away with anything. The thing is, if Vince and Shawn had agreed that Bret could beat Shawn in Montreal but drop the belt to Shawn the next night on *RAW*, Bret could have said, "I'm not going to do that." Hell, he could have just not turned up at all. Honestly, I think that even if they *had* put Bret over Shawn in Montreal, Bret would have just handed the belt over the next night and said, "Screw it, I'm not going to lose to Shawn." I've heard people say that because Bret had worked for Vince for 14 years, Vince should have trusted him, but it's the wrestling business. You don't trust anybody in the wrestling business. And you sure didn't trust anybody back when WCW and the WWF were at war. Vince just couldn't take that chance. If Bret *had* screwed Vince, I think Vince would have rebounded, but it would have left a black eye.

Later, Bret also claimed that he said he would drop the title to anybody anywhere except to Shawn in Montreal. I think Bret was just saying that and really had every intention of leaving without losing. Vince couldn't take him up on that offer and Bret knew it because they had built up the match for the pay-per-view in Montreal. If Bret had dropped the belt to someone else before *Survivor Series*, it would have killed the whole storyline for the main event, which was the bread and butter for that show. It had to be Bret vs Shawn and it had to be for the title. Vince should have tested Bret and said, "Okay, I want you to lose the title to this mid-card guy." I would bet that Bret would have said, "There's no storyline there and you haven't built this other guy up," and made excuses to keep himself from losing. Bret was just jealous and acting out because Shawn was better than him and he felt he was being pushed out of the promotion. Bret is one of the greatest storytellers ever in that ring but he's not the best. Shawn is hands down the best wrestler of all time and Bret needs to accept that.

If I had been in Vince's shoes back then, I would have done the same thing he did, no questions asked. I'm not excusing Shawn's behavior leading up to the match, but I would have waited for the pay-per-view and I would have beaten Bret the exact same way. I know why Vince told Bret he was going to win too — it was to get the best possible match out of him. If Bret hadn't thought he was getting his way going into that match, he wouldn't have put 100 percent into it.

I didn't like how long Bret held onto the whole deal, how he wouldn't let it go. He said that he forgave Earl Hebner for his part in the proceedings but that if he had been in Earl's shoes, he wouldn't have done it. That shows how selfish Bret is because Earl had to feed his family. What was Earl going to do? Tell Vince that he wasn't going to go along with the plan and then quit his job or get fired? Was Bret going to take care of Earl and feed his family for him? Of course not.

I thought it was a shame what happened to Bret down in wcw. He really was one of the greatest wrestlers ever but he looked out of place. Bret wasn't Bret after he left the wwf. He was never the same caliber of worker again after Montreal.

Some people still think the whole thing was a work, something agreed to behind closed doors by Vince, Bret, and Shawn. If it was a work, it was the best work in wrestling history. I don't think it was. It just boiled down to the fact that Bret didn't like Shawn, Shawn didn't like Bret, and somebody was always going to get screwed.

PART 5: SHAWN MICHAELS

I know Shawn much better now — he was off for several years because he broke his back, and in that time, he found religion and turned his life around. He's super humble now, a really good guy whom you'd love to hang out with. He helps everybody. I guarantee not too many people know this, but there was a couple in Shawn's church group who fell on hard times. The man lost his job and they were fixing to lose their house — Shawn stepped in and paid their house off for them. I thought that was such a commendable thing for him to do.

I talked to him a few months before I left WWE and told him, "You know, I didn't like you when I first got here." He laughed and said, "I don't remember half my life — I was so fucked up." I told him about the whole deal with him tearing up my food card in Germany and me confronting him in the locker room. He said he couldn't remember that at all, but he still apologized for being an asshole.

Shawn Michaels is the greatest wrestler of all time, hands down. If you want proof, go watch the hour-long match he did with John Cena on *RAW* in England back in 2007. Cena can't wrestle and he can't lead a match. Every single bit of that match was Shawn. He carried Cena for a full hour. That's absolutely incredible.

CHAPTER 17

PUNCHING THE CLOCK

After that whole deal in Montreal, the wwf took off. It wasn't about Bret, it wasn't about Shawn; everything was about "Stone Cold" Steve Austin. wcw was still doing well and wrestling was becoming mainstream, like it had been during the Hogan era. Now, Austin was going to be the man. The difference was that the Attitude era, as it came to be known, wasn't designed to appeal to little kids — it targeted the 18- to 30-year-old audience. The storylines were more realistic and the characters were reflections of the wrestlers' actual personalities. People started buying into the show because of the cool factor. Austin was cool, The Rock was cool, and people wanted to be like them. The fans could relate to our characters because we were like over-the-top versions of them.

The Hogan era had been much more like a cartoon, so nobody could really relate to those characters. It fit that era just fine and made a lot of money, but the cartoon thing spilled over into the '90s, when you had a wrestling garbage man, a wrestling plumber, a wrestling stock-car driver . . . none of them were going to catch on and strike a chord with anybody. Once Vince realized that he had to let people be themselves *as* wrestling characters, because it would give the fans stars they could relate to, wrestling became more popular and started winning people over.

Vince really had something special with Austin. Steve was always going to succeed because of his personality and the ideas he had. Sure, he won the *King of the Ring* in '96 and did his Austin 3:16 speech when they had originally planned to give the win to Hunter, but even if Steve hadn't won that night, he would have done his 3:16 speech at some point and got over just as much. Steve was going to be a huge deal regardless of when. *King of the Ring* just gave him an opportunity to make it happen a bit sooner.

I thought it was great that Steve was on top — he helped put wrestling back on the map, he appreciated becoming who he was in the business, and he gave back to everybody. If somebody takes off and becomes a superstar, I'm all for that because it makes money for everybody in the company. The funny thing is that Vince wasn't crazy about the idea, initially. The WWF brought Steve in as a borderline cartoon character, the Ringmaster, and Steve wasn't comfortable with it. He wanted to go out there and be a bigger version of himself; no-nonsense, middle-fingers for everyone, and cussing all the time. Vince wasn't too keen but there are far worse things done on TV than swearing and flipping the bird at your boss. Steve got to try out his ideas and do things his way. When his business went through the roof, I'm sure Vince's opinion changed.

Steve was always the same person. From when he was in WCW as Steve the movie projector guy to the Ringmaster to becoming "Stone Cold," he was the same person behind the scenes. Only the gimmick changed. I always thought that if somebody wasn't comfortable with something, they should change it. The talent should be comfortable because when they are, they will be able to give 100 percent of who they are in the ring. It worked with Steve for damn sure.

I hadn't caught on as a wide-eyed babyface, slapping hands and acting like I'd never had a bad day in my life, because that's not who I am. Because they were starting to make everything more realistic, I figured I'd stop being the wrestling stock-car driver and start being a proper wrestler with a realistic personality. I wanted to be a tough guy because that was me! It would have worked. The problem was that when they looked at me, they didn't see a tough guy. They saw a guy who was good in the ring and dependable outside of it. They'd just got me back on the team and had to find something to do with me, so rather than bothering to think of a new gimmick for me, they just gave me somebody else's.

The Midnight Express was one of the greatest tag teams in wrestling history. They sold tickets and had great matches in the Southern territories and the NWA. The WWF had something going with an internal NWA faction and were using the original Rock 'n' Roll Express against them. So I guess management figured they'd bring in the Midnight Express. While the Rock 'n' Roll Express was still running, the Midnight Express had stopped a long time ago, so they just took a couple of guys who weren't doing anything else — who turned out to be me and Bart Gunn — and called us the New Midnight Express. Their entire management of us consisted of them giving us some videotapes of the original Express and saying, "Be like Dennis and Bobby." Nobody can! Those two formed one of the greatest tag teams of all time. Throwing Bart and me together and hoping we'd immediately develop what took Dennis Condrey and Bobby Eaton years to get was plain stupid. We had new tights with "M.E." on them, Jim Cornette as our manager — just like the original Express — and new names to go with the gimmick. Bart became "Bodacious" Bart and I became "Bombastic" Bob. I knew it wasn't going to work.

At least I finally got to be in *WrestleMania* in some capacity. The night that Steve Austin won the WWF Championship for the first time, I was in the opening match, a tag team battle royal where they threw a whole bunch of guys in the ring, including some established teams and some guys just put together for that match, and said the winners would be the top contenders for the tag championships. The reality is that nobody cared about the match and it was just there to take up time. To show you how seriously management took the match, only two teams got entrances; the team that was going to win (the Legion of Doom) and a couple of guys who were buddies with the Undertaker (Ron Simmons and the Godfather). That tells the audience right there that one of those two teams is going to win and they shouldn't give a crap about anybody else. There were about 15 teams in that match, but the WWF totally buried everybody before the bell rang. You'd have thought it would come down to the two teams who'd had entrances but it didn't — Godfather and Ron got eliminated along the way and it came down to the Legion of Doom and the New Midnight Express. That went about as well as you'd expect — we put them over, made them look good, collected our paychecks, and went about our business. It definitely wasn't the *WrestleMania* moment I wanted.

Bart and I got along fine and tried hard to work well together as a unit but it was obvious to us and everybody else that we were just there to be an underneath tag team, take up some air time, and have some filler matches. As usual, time was passing, I wasn't making any real money, and I wasn't going anywhere. Austin was taking off and a few of the other guys at the top of the card were doing well, but there was a load of the mid-card guys floating around doing nothing. Then somebody had an idea about a shoot fighting competition, which ended up becoming the *Brawl for All*.

Our ratings were getting better and we had drawn level with WCW again, but Vince was always looking for ways to stay ahead in the ongoing Monday Night War. They decided to take 16 of the guys who weren't doing anything and put them in a tough-man tournament. They were going to have us go out there, on a live-TV wrestling show, and fight for real in an attempt to get some ratings. It was also an attempt to get a wrestler by the name of "Dr. Death" Steve Williams over. Jim Ross, who was in charge of talent, had been lobbying to bring his buddy Steve in for a long time but Creative didn't know how to do it. Steve had wrestled in Japan for the majority of his career and had a reputation as a genuine badass, so they figured they would introduce him in the *Brawl for All*, he'd walk through everybody, and boom, they'd have a credible guy they could leapfrog over everybody else to put up against Austin in the main events. Everybody backstage thought it was a bunch of bullshit. J.R. was shoving Steve down everybody's throats, saying he was going to destroy everybody. Nobody had a problem with Steve before, but J.R. was putting him over so often that the boys resented him and hoped he'd get knocked out.

They got together their group of 16 mid-card wrestlers who they figured were the tough guys. They put Bart in the tournament but I wasn't included. They didn't think that Sparky Plugg could fight. That pissed me off. Obviously, they didn't know that Ol' Sparky was a tough motherfucker!

Most of the people they had in there were pretty tough. Some of them talked a good fight but couldn't back it up. Tiger Ali Singh had been bragging that he was a shoot fighter and a bare-knuckle champion and could do this and that, but when it came to it, he chickened out and said he wouldn't do it. They needed a replacement and Bradshaw told Bruce Prichard, who was one of the guys in charge of organizing the whole thing, "Bob may not look like anything much but he'll surprise you. . . ." Bruce gave me a call to ask if I wanted in. I said, "Hell yeah, I don't know why you didn't ask me in the first place!" I was pretty excited because I figured I could make some decent money and I'd have a chance to show them how tough I actually was.

They explained the rules to us. Three rounds, one minute a round. We would get points for takedowns and knockdowns. A knockout would end it. We were told the winner would get $100,000 and that each time we fought, we would get five grand whether we won or lost. Sure, I thought — they're not going to pay us $5,000 each match for doing this! But they genuinely did.

As soon as Steve Blackman found out he was in the tournament, he started training for it. He was dead serious about hurting people, planning to take people's knees out to win that hundred grand. In the meeting when the rules were explained, they told us that it was anything goes. Steve said, "So that means that if I want to take somebody's knee out with a kick, I can do it, right?" Right about then they decided they needed to make *some* rules. I think they got worried that Steve might kill people and you know what? He probably could have. There is nobody more dangerous than Steve Blackman, period. He knows every element of the fighting game; he's strong, he's smart, he's lightning quick — he's a well-rounded fighter. Unfortunately for him but fortunately for the rest of us, Steve hurt himself training against a 300 pound guy who rolled on Steve's leg and blew out his knee. If that hadn't happened, Steve would have won the whole thing, hands down.

My first match turned out to be against my tag partner, Bart Gunn. Because Bart and I were riding together, we had a chance to talk before the fight. We agreed that whatever happened, happened. I knew that Bart used to do tough-man contests too, so I had my work cut out for me. Even though he'd never wrestled a bear, he was 6'5" and 260 pounds and I was 6'1" and about 220. That's a heck of a size difference but I wasn't about to back down from anybody. We went out there and laid into each other. It was brutal. He hit me so fucking hard, I ended up on the other side of the ring. I have no idea how I got there but he didn't knock me out. We went all three rounds and the judges gave the points win to Bart. It turned out to be one of the best fights in the tournament. We were still friends afterwards — we'd cleaned each other's clocks pretty good but neither of us was mad at the other. He told me, "I hit you with some good shots — it shocked me when you didn't go down." I had a black eye for a solid week after that fight but he never knocked me out. I got my five grand and I opened a lot of eyes in the back by showing that I was tougher than anybody had given me credit for.

Someone who wasn't as tough as they thought was J.R.'s boy, Steve Williams. I saw him fighting Pierre Ouellette in his first round match and he didn't look good. They were just swinging at each other and Steve barely survived. He didn't knock out Pierre, so it went to points and it was so clear they had gimmicked the score so it looked like Steve had dominated. I thought, "They're going to fix the whole thing and make it a work." I knew that if they didn't, Steve wasn't going to win.

Even so, Steve was up against Bart in the second round and I knew for sure Bart was going to knock him out. I'd just fought the guy and felt his punches. Steve was in trouble and he didn't know it. Earlier, when Bart and I were driving to a show, I told him, "You know they want Steve to win — you're fixing to throw a wrench in their whole plan." Bart said, "Yep, I'm going to knock him out." Later during the same journey, Bart decided to call Bruce Prichard to say, "Get ready to make that check out to me because I'm going to knock J.R.'s boy out." Bruce said, "That's great, man — if you do, you do." Bart knew Bruce wasn't taking him seriously. He said, "You think I'm kidding? I promise you, I'm going to knock him out . . ."

The night of the fight came. We were in Anaheim at the Arrowhead Pond and the TV monitor backstage was sold out. You could not get near that monitor; there was no room to move. Nobody knew what was going to happen. Steve and Bart started fighting — it was pretty even, punch for punch. I was counting the takedowns and it became clear that they weren't going to do it legit. Steve and Bart were even but the scoring onscreen had Steve with more takedowns. In the second round, Steve started gassing. Bart was outpunching him, staying on him and taking him down. Bart owned Steve in the second round but the scorecards came up and they still had Steve ahead. All the boys in the back were getting pissed. The third round was just like the second — Bart was kicking Steve's ass but we all knew that he was going to lose unless he knocked Steve out. With the fight nearly over, Steve was still in there and then, out of nowhere, Bart nailed him with a left hand and Steve just fucking dropped. Everybody in the back popped huge. The 60 or so people watching the monitor blew the roof off that place.

Terry Funk actually got upset with that because he felt the boys were disrespecting Steve, who is considered a god in wrestling, especially in Japan, but nobody popped because they hated Steve or wanted to see him hurt. They popped because they knew the judges had been fucking with the scorecards and the wrong man would have won. The feeling was, "Fuck you, you're not going to screw Bart out of this." There was no disrespect meant to Steve, just hostility towards the office for sending us all out there, telling us the whole thing was a shoot, and then trying to fix the outcome to suit their plans.

If I ever wanted any proof that I was right on this one, I got it that night. I was getting changed near the trainers' area. They had dragged Steve from the ring to the back and were checking him over. Steve's jaw was dislocated and his hamstring was torn. I heard Steve say to the guys who were working on him, "I don't know what they're going to do now . . . they already paid me the money to win this thing." Jim Ross was absolutely furious. For weeks, he'd been telling everybody that Steve was going to walk all over the competition, and now I had found out they'd paid him the prize money before he'd even won the tournament. I couldn't believe it.

Bart was up against the Godfather next. Godfather was a big, tough motherfucker but I knew Bart would take him. I was watching the fight backstage and 'Taker was there, sitting in a chair in front of the monitor. A lot of people were watching again and I said out loud, "This is gonna be interesting." 'Taker turned around, looked at me, and said, "That's your boy, isn't it?"

I said, "You're damn right it is."

He said, "Fifty bucks?"

We shook on it.

'Taker thought Godfather would take Bart out no problem. Bart ended up knocking his ass out in the third round. 'Taker didn't say a word; he just got up and walked off. I thought he was pissed but he came back later that day and handed me a fifty. Easy money. Bart went on to the final against Bradshaw and knocked him out colder than a well digger's ass. There were rumors that, after Bart knocked out Steve Williams, they told Godfather and Bradshaw to take a dive. Why would anybody drop their hands to get knocked out, especially when there's a lot of money on the line? Bart just knocks motherfuckers out; end of story.

In the office, they wanted Bart to get his ass kicked. J.R. was being vindictive because Bart fucked their plan up and fucked his buddy up. They paid Bart the prize money, they'd already paid the same amount to

Steve Williams, and they had to pay everyone else for their matches, so the whole thing must have cost them $350,000 in payouts, without giving them the result they wanted. Steve couldn't work with Austin now and they couldn't put Bart in his place. Bart had been around for six years as an underneath guy that nobody was going to buy against Austin no matter what management did. Even though J.R. was wrong about just "knowing" that Steve would walk through everybody, *he* didn't get any heat for it; Bart did. J.R. said he didn't have hard feelings towards Bart but he did for damn sure. The next thing you know, they'd talked Bart into fighting Butterbean at *WrestleMania.*

Butterbean was this huge, fat boxer who threw too strong a punch for anyone in the WWF to go toe to toe with (except Blackman — Blackman would have killed him). This guy was a pro boxer. I don't care who you are, you don't play someone else's game. None of us should have tried to box him but they got into Bart's head and brainwashed him into thinking that he could beat Butterbean in a straight-up boxing match. Bart bought into the hype. He didn't change as a person but he did start overestimating himself. If Bart had gone into it like a regular street fight, he would have shot in there and taken him down because Bart's a good amateur wrestler. If he was going to stand there and box the guy, he had no chance. Boxing is about angles. Fighting has no rules. Butterbean said that he didn't want fighting — just boxing. That was the deal for him to come in. The WWF still promoted the match as under *Brawl for All* rules but Bart was told it had to be a straight-up boxing match. They sent him off for 10 weeks to train with Danny Hodge in New York. Bart lost weight and got into awesome shape, but I don't care who you are, 10 weeks of training won't prepare you to beat a professional boxer. The whole deal was set up purely to humiliate Bart because he had humiliated Jim Ross's boy "Dr Death." The office knew he didn't have a chance. Even if Bart *had* beaten Butterbean, they would have found another way to screw with him.

When the fight rolled around at *WrestleMania XV,* everybody was watching the monitor backstage. The match only lasted 35 seconds and Butterbean nearly took Bart's head off. It looked like he broke his neck. Everybody's jaw was on the floor backstage. It was un-fucking-believable. I thought Bart was dead, Butterbean hit him that hard. The trainers brought him back around when he was in the ring. When they walked him to the back, nobody said a word. You could hear a pin drop.

That was basically the end of Bart's WWF career on TV. In reality, his career with the WWF had ended the moment he had knocked Steve Williams out. He didn't know the repercussions would be that big, and neither did I. We knew they thought Steve was going to win but we didn't know they'd planned a whole storyline based on his win, we didn't know they had paid him off already — nobody told anybody what the plan was. If they had sat us all down and said, "We need to make this a work but we want it to look like a shoot," that would have been fine. But because J.R. was so convinced that nobody could beat Steve Williams, he had everybody else in the office thinking it was a done deal too. The whole *Brawl for All* idea was a bad way to get a wrestler over. Wrestling is a work. If you want someone to get over in order to put him against the top guy, you better make sure everything is a work before he gets to that top guy. If you're going to make it a real shoot, you've got to be prepared to go with what happens. You can't guarantee a result from a shoot.

Steve Williams had no idea what he was letting himself in for; he didn't know Bart. I spoke to Steve about it later in the year and even he said it was a really bad way to do business. If the boys are told that they are going to go out there and fight for money for real, they're going to do what it takes to win. If management wanted a specific result, they should have told us what they wanted. Instead, they basically wasted nearly half a million dollars and ended the careers of both Bart and Steve Williams. A lot of the other guys got injured during the *Brawl for All* too, and it really didn't do anything for ratings. It just wasn't worth it. Everybody thought the whole thing was a very bad idea. The WWF learned from that and never tried it again.

Since they were now dead set on crushing Bart, they ended the New Midnight Express. That didn't bother me because we were going nowhere fast. I went to Creative after Bart won the *Brawl for All* and suggested that he and I do a rematch at a pay-per-view and base the build-up on the fact that he hadn't knocked me out. I thought it would draw a little interest because this guy had knocked out fighters who weighed 300 pounds or more, but he couldn't finish me off when I was only 220. I could have gone out and done promos talking about how the scorecards were a poor indicator and that, until one of us knocked the other one out, we had unfinished business. Then we could have gone out and done a shoot fight. I'm not saying you could have sold a pay-per-view on the match, but it would have been something to add to the presentation and help draw some money. It was definitely better than doing nothing with either of us — but doing nothing was the thing they went with and they pissed on my idea. They didn't have any plans for me and Bart.

Still, for me, the *Brawl for All* was a step forward — I was one of the only guys who didn't get hurt and I was the only guy Bart fought but couldn't knock out. That got me noticed and gave me a lot of credibility. It shocked a lot of people, who found themselves thinking, "Wow, Bob Holly is tougher than we gave him credit for." It planted a seed but it would take a while for that seed to grow. Until then, I was back in the job squad — and very literally, this time.

Since groups within wrestling were the in-thing in 1998, they put together a group under Al Snow, using an old gimmick of his from ECW. All the losers banded together and called themselves "The JOB Squad." They had Al, Scorpio, Gillberg, and me as the guys who never won but were now in a group that was somehow supposed to make us look better on TV. It doesn't make sense on paper but I liked it anyway. It was my only real interaction with Vince Russo, the head writer for the WWF at the time. A lot of people criticize him and say he ruined the business, but I thought he was okay. I was just disappointed that he never really followed through with things; he'd have a great idea one week, take it somewhere the next week, and then forget about it and go in another direction. You can't do that on episodic TV. You can't change the storyline for a soap character every three weeks, you've got to see them through or the viewers will lose interest and not buy into anybody. That's what Russo never understood.

The gimmick was a little confusing. We were meant to be this group of losers who did the job for everybody, but then we started to win matches and get over. After a month or so, Russo told us we were going to have a big night on *RAW* in November, and sure enough, we were all over the show. We went out and helped Mankind (not one of our group but also cast as a loveable loser) win his match against the Boss Man and

Shamrock, who were part of Vince McMahon's main event heel group. Gillberg won the WWF Light Heavyweight Title and Scorpio and I beat the New Age Outlaws, who were the tag champions, in a non-title match. That show made it look like The JOB Squad was going to be featured in a solid mid-card capacity.

But, just like everything else, it went absolutely nowhere. It was like nothing had ever happened. To say I was frustrated is an understatement. As 1998 turned into 1999, they stopped using Gillberg, Scorpio got released, and things were looking bad for both me and Al.

The popularity of the hardcore wrestling style in ECW had led to the WWF creating its own hardcore title, which had just been vacated. They decided to use Al in the division, maybe because of his ECW connection. Because his gimmick was that he was crazy, they sent him out on TV to have a hardcore match with himself. It was ridiculous. He was smashing himself over the head with weapons, throwing himself into the barriers . . . they sent me out to calm him down and then, when he took offense to that, we got into a fight. This was going to lead to a match between us at the next pay-per-view, *St. Valentine's Day Massacre*, for the vacant Hardcore Championship. I didn't think anything other than I was there as a body to put Al over, but I was happy to hear I would get to be on a PPV and hopefully get a decent payday out of it.

I didn't know it at the time, but this was the birth of Hardcore Holly.

PART 6: STAYING SANE ON THE ROAD

It can be pretty hard to keep sane on the road, so you've got to have some fun. Billy Gunn and I rode together a lot. When he rode with other people, he usually drove but for whatever reason, he was comfortable with me driving. That was until I had a little joke at his expense . . .

On this particular journey, he'd been asleep most of the trip. We were approaching the arena and he was still asleep. There was a train-crossing right near the arena, so I stopped the car right on the track, waited until a train was coming, and woke him up. Billy looked up, saw the train coming, and just about shit his pants. I had my hand on the emergency brake and wasn't letting go — he was yanking on my arm, yelling and screaming, "You're going to kill us, motherfucker!" But I didn't let go until that train was about 20 yards from us. I stabbed the gas and pulled in to the arena parking lot. Turns out some of the security team had seen what I'd done and were laughing their asses off. I was laughing like a crazy man myself. Billy didn't see the funny side. He drove for a while after that . . .

JBL liked to fuck with people too. One time, he pulled up beside me at a stop light and I knew something was up. At the next stop light, I was looking at a map when John pulled up behind me and rammed my car right through the stop light into the middle of the intersection. Cars were speeding through but John kept on pushing. I took off pretty quickly. Steve Blackman was in the car with me and he was pissed. I thought it was funny but wanted to get back at Bradshaw so, after he got ahead of us, I did 95 down the highway and hit his back bumper. After that, John stopped fucking with me because he knew I'd retaliate.

Steve did not like that sort of thing at all but we were good traveling partners. We had the same schedule — wake up early, eat, work out, and go to the show. We didn't like staying in expensive hotels. It's very important to be on the same page when it comes to where you want to eat and stay when you're traveling partners. I traveled with Sid, Billy Gunn, Scotty 2 Hotty, Kane . . . all great guys. But Steve was the most fun to fuck with. He could never stay mad at me. I can run faster than him anyway, and he can't kill what he can't catch.

As I said before, Steve is probably the most dangerous man on the planet. If you piss him off, you might just end up going missing. Somehow, though, I got away with it. When we rode together, I would drive and scare him on purpose. One time, we were heading to Chicago late at night in pouring rain. As we were crossing the Illinois state line, we came up on three semi trucks. It was hard to see because of the spray but I was fixing to pass them anyway. Steve looked at me and there was definitely fear in his eyes. He asked, "How can you see when I can't see?" I told him, "I can see fine on this side." The closer I got to the semis, the more worked up he got. It was a four-lane highway and I sped right between two of those trucks. Steve was scared to death. After we got past them, he said, "I couldn't see a damn thing." Then I told him I couldn't either. He was hot — I just laughed at him and said, "What, are you going to hit me? I'll wreck the car and we'll both die right here."

Steve got really mad at some other people though. At Kansas City airport, Steve and I were waiting around when Bradshaw came over. It was an early morning flight and John was still drunk from the night before. He started patting Steve's ass. Steve said, "John, I don't play that shit, knock it off." John patted him again. And again. Steve was getting brutally pissed. He told him, "John, next time you do that, I'm going to knock your fucking teeth out." So, of course, John did it again. Steve whipped around and backhanded Bradshaw, popping him with jabs in the face. John started swinging and missing, and his head was snapping back with each of Steve's jabs. Steve stepped back, planning to kick Bradshaw's knees out, but he got his leg caught in a bag handle. Al Snow and I grabbed

Steve, Ron Simmons grabbed John, and we pulled them apart. John was walking back and forth like a bandy rooster, looking to fight. Before we left, Steve told him, "I'm going to fucking kill you." He meant it too.

We got our car and got on the road. Ken Shamrock was riding with us. Me, Blackman, and Shamrock. That's a dangerous car, and I'm the warm one — a teddy bear compared to the other two. That whole journey, Shamrock was poking and prodding Steve, telling him that Bradshaw was going to beat his ass. Steve wasn't saying a word. And who did we see when we checked in to the hotel? Bradshaw and Ron were right there. The boys don't always stay at the same hotels, so it was a complete coincidence and not a good one for John. He came over to apologize and Steve said, "No apologies, I'm going to finish you later," then walked off. We found him in the gym, still boiling mad. Once we were in the arena and had sat down in catering, John walked in. Everybody went silent as Steve stood up. He said, "If you've got something to say to me, you say it now or I'm going to finish you in front of everybody." Bradshaw walked over, apologized, said "I shouldn't have fucked with you," and shook his hand. That was the end of it. Steve sat down and said, "Bob, if it wasn't for that bag, John would be in intensive care right now." Trust me, I believe it — if anybody can put Bradshaw in the hospital with one kick, it's Steve Blackman.

CHAPTER 18

GETTING SOME ATTITUDE

By the time I stepped into the ring with Al Snow at the *St. Valentine's Day Massacre* in February 1999, the WWF was on top again. WCW hadn't managed to keep up and we were red hot. "WWF Attitude" had caught on, especially with 18- to 30-year-old males, and we were cool. The cartoon days were long gone and the WWF was now playing to an older audience — and it was more popular than ever. We had The Rock, the Undertaker, and Mankind, and they were all over huge. Steve Austin was the hottest thing going, running around, giving everyone the finger, telling them to go to hell, and beating up the boss all the time. Hunter — now as Triple H — was the leader of a group called D-Generation X who acted like their name suggests, getting women in the audience to flash their tits. It was risqué programming for sure, but I had no problem with what we were doing. We pushed the envelope, got away with it, and sold tickets.

There were still kids being brought to the arena and watching at home but *RAW* didn't show anything worse than what you would see in video games and on TV. I actually thought our stuff was tame compared to some of the other things around at that time. Anyway, to my mind, parents should know what their kids are watching, but in the late '90s, TV and the internet were opening up a new world. Kids could get on the computer and see all kinds of sex-related stuff and the parents had no idea what they

were doing. It took a while for the adults to catch up and realize what their kids had access to, and that's because they weren't paying attention. If the parents don't have the time to care about what their kids are watching, that's on them, not on us. It's a damn shame when you see parents who are happy when their kids are watching TV or on the computer because that keeps them busy and the parents don't have to do their job. Kids should be outside playing.

The bottom line is that we put a product out there and didn't try to make it out to be something it wasn't. We were just one of many things of the sort that kids had access to so it's not like we were the only business making money off risqué TV. It was everywhere back then.

An example of the sort of thing management was putting on TV is the match between Val Venis and me. We each represented a woman and every time we got thrown out of the ring, the women had to take some clothes off. It ended up with me winning and Val's woman, B.B., taking off her bra. Hunter got in the way, though, so the audience didn't see anything. That's pretty tame in comparison to the other stuff you get on TV and on the internet, if you ask me.

Anyway, in 1999 we did a show in Tennessee, in which I was going to wrestle Al for the Hardcore title. I expected to give him a good match, put him over, take my check, and go to the back of the line, but when I got there they told me I was going over and winning the title. I was surprised to say the least. I got to talking with Vince about my name. After the Midnight Express, I'd thankfully dropped the "Bombastic" tag and was back to being plain Bob Holly. Vince said I needed something else. The seed that had been planted in the *Brawl for All* about me being tough had come through and now they thought I would be a good fit for the hardcore division, so Vince said that if I was going to be hardcore, I'd better be called "Hardcore" Holly. I was more than happy with that.

Al and I did our match, which ended up being a good brawl all over the arena, outside the arena, and even into the Mississippi River. It was wild and it helped get me over. People were surprised when I won but they went with it. I started wrestling Al on TV and house shows all the time, doing the hardcore matches with him. I thought they were fun. We'd mix it up and use all sorts of weapons in the matches to keep it fresh, but we'd limit what we used. You'd see other guys doing hardcore matches and loading the ring up with too many things, and it ended up being meaningless. We preferred to use two or three weapons per match and actually build a story around them. It made more sense that way and was still a wrestling match, not just two guys hitting each other with anything they could get their hands on. There's no skill in that. Just because it was a hardcore match, that's no reason for people to forget it was a wrestling show. The matches should have remained fundamentally wrestling.

I also got to do some hardcore matches with Brian James, the Road Dogg, who had managed to get away from Jeff Jarrett and become popular as part of the New Age Outlaws, a team with Billy Gunn, that joined D-Generation X. We were building up to a three-way match for the Hardcore title at *WrestleMania* with me, him, and Al. Then Billy screwed up and the plans changed. Billy was supposed to win the Intercontinental title from Ken Shamrock at the *Royal Rumble* but the night before, when he was drunk, he told everybody who would listen that he was going to win the title the next night, and then turned up to the arena with a massive hangover. Obviously, they kept the belt on Shamrock. Vince Russo then went and started switching everything around for God knows what reason and it ended up with the Road Dogg going into *WrestleMania* as the ic Champion and Billy going in with the Hardcore title. Billy wasn't happy doing the hardcore stuff; he felt like a fish out of water. I was just happy to be part of a featured match at *WrestleMania* at last. I opened the show at *WrestleMania XV* and won the three-way with Billy and Al. It was a good match that got the crowd going. I appreciated being given the Hardcore title at *WrestleMania* — I felt appreciated in my role in the company for probably the first time ever. I appreciated the paycheck too — I made $20,000 for that match. That was the biggest payoff of my career. I can't imagine what Austin and The Rock got paid for headlining that show . . .

The next few months carried on in much the same way — I worked the hardcore matches and I started to get over well with the crowd. They started reacting to me in a way they never had before. That's because my character finally felt right. It worked because I was comfortable. I was comfortable because Hardcore Holly was me, through and through.

I was never comfortable wrestling someone who worked really light. When they hit you, you're thinking, "Did they even hit me, and where?" I prefer it when somebody lays it in stiff so you know what you're selling. You don't want the crowd to see through your punches.

Now, you can pull a punch but you can't fake a chop. Anybody can do an overhand chop, but there's a technique to a backhand chop. They look good, they sound good. Flair was good at it, and so were Benoit, Shawn, and Jericho. I consider myself one of the best. Kevin Dunn, who is in charge of production, told me that his team always got a kick out of it when I'd chop — they'd even turn the sound up in the production truck. Benoit told me after one match, "You chopped me harder than Inoki — that was the hardest I've ever been chopped." That explains why he didn't chop me that often; he was worried I'd chop him back!

Vince took me aside at one point and told me I wasn't allowed to chop any more. Everybody was throwing chops and Vince wanted to save the move for Flair. They even put a sign up in Gorilla that said NO CHOPS. Shawn started doing them again anyway. I went to Vince and asked why I couldn't chop. He said nobody wanted to see that. I argued that everybody popped when I chopped. He came back with, "That's a cheap pop." I said it didn't matter if it was entertaining the fans. He replied, "If you were in a real fight, would you really chop somebody?" I asked him, "If I were in a real fight, would I really jump off the top rope onto somebody?" That sort of pissed him off. He just said, "No chops. Nobody chops," and walked off.

You have to adjust your style for different people. Shawn is smaller than a lot of the guys and a bit fragile because of his injuries, so you've got to be careful with him. He's not going to be a pussy and complain if you catch him with a shot here and there, but everybody knows to look after him. I liked working with the guys who gave as good as they got. Jericho, Benoit, Finlay, Undertaker — you don't have to worry when you're in there with them. They can take it.

Who was the stiffest wrestler I ever worked with? Bradshaw. Hands down. He held absolutely nothing back. If he knew you could take it, he gave it to you. I enjoyed working with John. When I was up against him, I knew I had it coming and I knew he was going to bring it. Believe me, any chance I got to give something back to him, I took it. One night at a TV taping, I was supposed to hit him with a chair. He found me backstage and said, "I know I've got it coming to me. . . ." I told him, "Yes, you do, motherfucker." I tried to rip his head clean off with that steel chair and he told me after that it about knocked him out. He loved it. It was give-and-take with us. Whenever he'd punch me or kick me in the head, he really *would* punch me or kick me in the head. He'd never do it full force but he'd lay it in there enough so that it fucking hurt. I never had to worry about John bellyaching. He wasn't afraid of a fight and he wasn't afraid to lose, either. He liked to screw with people until they wanted to fight him. That's just John. He got under the skin of Joey Styles — one of the announcers — so much that little Joey took a swing at him and knocked him out. It wasn't a big deal to John. He figured, "I fucked with him and he knocked me out, whoop-de-doo." He didn't like the guys who cowered in the corner and wanted to be left alone. He would fight a circle saw — he doesn't care if he wins or loses, he just wants to fight.

CHAPTER 19

OWEN HART

My run as Hardcore Champion came to an end on May 23, 1999, in the second match of the *Over the Edge* pay-per-view. Al put me through a table, pinned me, and went off with the title. I went to the back while they were clearing the debris out of the ring in order to do a big comedy superhero entrance for Owen Hart. They were going to lower him into the ring on a cable from a catwalk at the top of the building.

I got to Gorilla, shook Al's hand, and started discussing my match with the agent, talking about the mistakes we made, what we could have done better, and, all of sudden, we heard Bruce Prichard shouting, "Owen fell!" He went running off and I remember thinking, "Owen fell? What, did he fall off the stage?" Then it hit me that we were at a pay-per-view and we didn't have a stage. Oh shit . . . he fell from the ceiling . . .

Everybody scrambled, the paramedics ran out to the ring, Bruce flew past me with some other people. It was chaos and nobody knew what had happened. All we knew was that Owen fell.

The other boys were in the back and didn't know what was going on but I was right outside Gorilla. I didn't move. The paramedics worked on him in the ring for what seemed like forever. Eventually, they got him onto a gurney and wheeled him to the back. I was no more than 15 feet away as it went past. Owen's arms were hanging off the side of the gurney and the paramedics were pumping him the whole way to the ambulance. There was no bringing him back — I saw Owen's face and it was pure white. It was surreal. The paramedics loaded him into the ambulance, still trying to bring him back. He couldn't die at the arena — he had to die at the hospital. But I knew he was gone.

During the day, the word had been going around that Owen wasn't comfortable with the stunt. He'd been rehearsing it and he wasn't happy. He didn't talk to me directly about it, but I overheard him saying he didn't want to do it. The guy he was talking to said, "Just tell them you're not comfortable with it." Owen replied, "You know how it is if you tell them 'no' — they just end up firing you." He was right — the office *always* said, "Tell us if you're not comfortable doing something, we'll do something else," but we all knew that "something else" meant we wouldn't be working for the company anymore. You did as you were told or you were gone. Owen's back was against the wall and he had a wife and two young children to feed.

I know Sting had often done a similar stunt in wcw and never had a problem. I guess he had just been lucky every time he did it. Or Owen was unlucky. What we were all told was that Owen had accidentally disconnected himself from the cable. He was wearing a cape as part of his costume and when he flipped the cape back, he hit the latch that released the cable. So when he stepped off the catwalk, he didn't have anything attached to him and just fell. The cable was still intact in the ceiling. It was awful. The guy who hooked Owen up didn't do his job. If somebody is about to jump 80 feet, you keep your eyes on the cable. Owen couldn't see if it was attached because it was behind him. The stunt coordinator must have taken his eyes off Owen when he flipped his cape back and the cable unhooked. In my opinion, he should have gone to Owen and checked that everything was hooked up the moment before he jumped. If somebody had just double-checked Owen, it never would have happened.

Despite Owen's death, they kept on going with the pay-per-view. I didn't agree with that. Vince should have canceled the show out of respect for Owen and his family. Regardless of how many tickets got sold, how many ppvs had been bought, I don't think there'd have been a scene if the show had been canceled. Everybody would have understood. A few weeks before I wrote this chapter, I watched an IndyCar race in Las Vegas — a couple of laps in, there was a crash in which Dan Wheldon died. It was the final race of the season and IndyCar made the decision to stop the race. All the fans understood. Even though a lot of money was on the line in that race — millions of dollars spent by the race teams to get their cars and crews there and their million-dollar race cars prepared to run the final race of the season — but Indycar still canceled the race out of respect for the driver. Even though there was far less money for the WWF to lose at *Over the Edge,* Vince kept the show going because he was afraid he was going to have to pay everybody back for the PPV. Somebody's life is more important to me than some money.

After the fall, you could have heard a pin drop backstage. It stayed like that for days. We did a tribute show to Owen the next night on *RAW*. I wrestled Ken Shamrock for about 90 seconds. They only had so many positions for so many guys and I just happened to be one of the guys on the show. Without wishing to seem disrespectful, it was just like any other show to me. I had a job to do and the show had to go on — but I didn't forget about Owen. I thought about him and his family. It bothered me. I knew Owen. I wasn't close to him but I was friendly with him. We talked a lot. Many people remember Owen as the guy who ribbed everyone. He never messed with me, never got me with any of his ribs. I wouldn't have minded if he had though — they were all in good fun. Owen would rib himself in order to rib someone else. He was one of the true good guys of the wrestling business and it's a shame he had to go so early. It's just one of those things — it happened and you've got to move on, but you can't forget about him.

I don't know how it affected everybody else in the company. Everybody reacts differently. Once you're in the wrestling business, you've got to learn to shut things off pretty quickly or you're not going to survive. Everybody wears a mask and stays stoic. You won't make it if you let things bother you. Sometimes, you have to be almost inhumane, shut your feelings off, and go on. That's what happened.

CHAPTER 20

BIG SHOT & FAMILY MAN

Over the summer, I ended up doing an angle with both the Big Show and Kane. These are two big, tough guys — both around seven feet tall, very strong, very heavy. So I went out there and declared myself a "super heavy-weight" too. One time with Kane, they had me knock him out and beat him, 1-2-3, and then stand over him, jawjacking and talking a bunch of BS to him. He sat up, grabbed my throat, and choke-slammed me. It was a good angle and I couldn't believe they were putting me over upper-level guys like Kane now. I was getting paid well, I was respected in my work, and I was finally going somewhere. They let me start cutting promos too — that was fun. I developed this cocky, no-bullshit, don't-back-down character. I told Show that, if he was the Big Show, I was the Big Shot. The name stuck. I was getting over more than I'd ever been before. Sure, I got my ass handed to me a lot by those two monsters but I got to look competitive with them, like I was on their level, and it was damn entertaining. Even Chris Jericho, who is pretty hard to impress, told me that he loved that gimmick. If you can entertain Jericho, you can entertain anybody.

The most memorable moment of the run was probably a hardcore match I did with Show in Memphis. We fought outside of the arena and ended up by a wall. A car was parked above us. Show slammed me against the wall, then went up to that car and pushed it over the edge, right on top of me. At least that's what the viewers saw! They did it with camera angles. When he went up to the car, I rolled out of the way. He pushed it off the edge and I crawled back into position to make it look like I was underneath the car. It was great TV, very entertaining. They ribbed me about that angle when we talked about it in advance; they said, "We want you to lay right here and Show will push the car over, but don't worry, it will probably miss you!" They got a laugh out of that. Hell no, I wouldn't have done that. I'm not *that* hardcore . . . and not that stupid! I was having too much fun with my new gimmick and getting squashed by a car would have literally killed everything. As it was, things were going to get killed soon anyway.

Everything was going great. The Big Shot had come out of nowhere and it was getting over. Ed Koskey helped me with the gimmick; he had a lot of ideas for me and ended up writing a lot of my stuff. Management assigns someone to write for specific talent; for example, Brian Gewirtz wrote for Edge and Christian. Ed was my guy. Typically, when something gets over, they run with it. For some reason, even though the Big Shot thing was working, they pulled the plug on it. It seems to be a curse that follows me — as soon as I do anything that gets over, the plug gets pulled.

I showed up in Milwaukee for a TV taping and Bruce Prichard came over. "You're not the Big Shot anymore — now you have a cousin." I thought it sucked that they hadn't called me in advance to let me know, especially since the Big Shot deal was getting over. At least we kept doing something with the "super heavyweight" thing — my new cousin, Crash Holly, was a small guy who looked like Elroy from *The Jetsons*, but we would go out and say we were both super heavyweights and could fight anyone, any time. Crash started carrying a set of scales with him and we announced ourselves as weighing over 400 pounds each.

It did puzzle me at first as to why we weren't going to carry on with the Big Shot deal but the cousins storyline was something to keep me going. I was easy to please as long as I was in a storyline. I wasn't one of the prima donnas who got pissed off because I didn't get my way. A lot of the other talent did and still do. They feel like they're bigger than the company and they basically get spoiled. I might have grown frustrated when something was getting over and then they changed the direction, but that was their decision, not mine. I was happy enough to be in a storyline. I learned to not ask questions because the only answer I ever got was, "That's the direction we want to go." You're never going to get a straight answer and it won't do any good to try to figure out why they do what they do — you'll go crazy thinking like that. You go with the flow, throw ideas out there, and hope they run with some of them. It's like throwing darts at a dartboard — you hope you hit the bullseye but it's almost never going to happen. You just keep throwing and hoping.

I still got to cut promos with the cousins angle — that made my job much more enjoyable. I enjoyed the wrestling but doing promos every week just adds to the enjoyment of your job. Back then, we had creative freedom as long as we hit the bullet points they gave you. Having Crash to play off was good fun. He was someone else to focus on and he became my whipping boy. I was constantly putting him down, belittling him, and using him for my own entertainment. We would end up fighting all the time and we'd beat the crap out of each other. One minute, we'd be tag team partners fighting against others wrestlers, and the next minute, we'd be fighting with each other. Everybody loved that gimmick and that ended up getting over too. Ed Koskey wanted to do a vignette at Christmas — "a Holly family Christmas" — with us in a trailer home. It was a great idea; we were going to get some people to play inbred family members and have a dysfunctional family Christmas. They didn't do it in the end. That's a shame because it would have been funny as hell and I know we could have pulled it off. That would have been great entertainment.

After a while, they stopped me and Crash fighting all the time and settled us down into a regular tag team. It sort of took the edge off our act. I wondered if somebody in the office had a problem with me, or if one of the top wrestlers felt threatened, or something like that. It seemed that every time anything I did was getting over, my direction got changed to make sure I didn't get over more than some of the other wrestlers. I didn't understand. Why would you take away a character that everybody loves?

Crash and I won the Tag Team Championship from The Rock and Mankind towards the end of '99. We lost it a week or two later to Mankind and Al Snow. Winning the belts wasn't a pat on the back to me or Crash, we were just in the right place at the right time. They needed to get the belts off Rock and Mick, and we happened to be the team in the middle. They were moving the belts around so much at that point that they had no value anyway. I didn't have any pride in winning the titles that time. Some of the other times I've won titles have been fulfilling because I knew that I was being used and I was in a storyline, but in the grand scheme of things, what had I really won? It's pure fantasy — I didn't beat anybody, they let me win. I was told to be champion.

Don't get me wrong, there is value in being a champion sometimes. If you become the WWE Champion or the World Champion, you get paid a lot more because you're carrying the company. Getting one of the big belts is the big payoff. If you are IC or US Champion, you get a little extra money. Not much, but something. Getting the tag titles means absolutely nothing, money-wise. It's just a label and something else to carry through customs. That's why I don't feel any sort of pride for winning a title from The Rock or any sort of shame for losing a title to Al Snow; the people losing the titles are told to let the other guys win. So what did you win exactly?

Crash and I winning the titles was, for the most part, the end of our storyline. We were going to go our separate ways and do away with the whole super heavyweight gimmick. I could have acted pissed off, resentful, or whatever else, but they were going to do whatever the hell they wanted to do. We still worked with and against each other over the next year or so, but our "fighting Holly cousins" story was finished and it was time for me to do something else. I'd been on most of the pay-per-views and been used pretty much all the time during '99 so I wondered what was going to happen next. This time, it seemed that I was going to be fighting a woman.

Triple H's former bodyguard and girlfriend-at-the-time Chyna had been working with my old friend Jeff Jarrett. Jeff had returned to the WWF after having a poor run in WCW and Vince let him come back in order to humiliate him on TV. Vince is a businessman and signs people because he wants to make money with them but I think he also likes to set them up to humiliate them if they've wronged him. This time, Jeff ended up with the upper hand.

Jeff's contract was coming to an end and Jim Ross was told to sign him to an extension. For whatever reason, it slipped through the cracks and Jeff kept quiet about his contractual status. They had been building a match between Jeff and Chyna for weeks. It was one of the featured matches at the *No Mercy* pay-per-view and Chyna was going to make history by becoming the first female IC champion. The PPV was on Sunday and it turned out that Jeff's contract had expired the day before. He walked into the arena for the PPV without his gear and went straight to Vince. Backstage, we all could hear the yelling in Vince's office. Jeff was demanding that Vince pay him all the money he was owed from previous events and the money for the match he was going to do that night or he wasn't going to go to the ring. Shane, Vince's son, was really vocal — he was cussing Jeff out and was ready to beat the shit out of him. Jeff is a mild-mannered guy who wouldn't fight anybody, so he just sat there and held his ground.

Vince said he'd make sure Jarrett was paid, but Jeff said he wanted the money wired into his account immediately before he brought his bag and the IC belt in. Otherwise he was getting on a plane and going home. I thought it was wrong to do that. I sort of understand where he was coming from because it sometimes took up to six months to get our checks from a PPV. He was owed a lot of money and I guess he was worried that Vince wouldn't pay him. Even so, you don't hold somebody up like that. Management had spent so much money building up that match as one of the main events that they couldn't turn it around. They had to deliver Jarrett vs Chyna, and since Jarrett was the IC champ going in, he had Vince over a barrel. When Jarrett confirmed with his wife that the money — over $300,000 — had arrived in his account, he brought his bag in, got dressed, and stayed away from everybody. Road Dogg, being the loyal friend he is, stayed by Jeff's side. Before his match, Jeff took his bag, set it by the door of the arena, and went to the ring. He did his job and put Chyna over in a match that involved lots of household objects, including a big bag of flour. He came back, covered in that flour, walked past everybody, didn't say a word, grabbed his bag, and was gone. He went straight to the airport looking the way he looked. He got on a plane, flew home, and was back on *WCW Nitro* the next night.

Even though we had been beating WCW in the ratings wars for a long time, they were still trying to come back and sign people from under

Vince's nose. J.R. was told to secure us all. He almost lost his job over the Jarrett oversight. He got reamed out huge for that.

With Jarrett gone, Chyna moved into a program with Jericho. After about a month, they decided to throw me into the mix. They didn't really explain why they were using me, and I figured they were putting me in there so that I could do the job in a three-way match and neither Chyna nor Jericho, both featured wrestlers, would have to lose.

WRESTLING JERICHO AND CHYNA. (PHOTO BY GEORGE NAPOLITANO)

PART 8: WOMEN IN WRESTLING

I don't care for women wrestling, especially what they do in WWE. They put these women out there who can't wrestle a lick and it exposes the business. Sure, we all know it's a work, but this is a step too far. Fans don't want to see women wrestle. They want to see tits and ass. When Alundra Blayze was the women's champion, people didn't care about her. When Sable came along and added the sexy side to it, using women in the ring started to evolve and sell tickets. Sable was a huge draw. She turned the corner in wrestling for women, not Sunny. You put them side by side; Sable might be older, but Sunny shouldn't even be in the same room. Sunny was over but once Sable came in, everybody was like, "Who the fuck is Sunny?" Sable is the one who raised the bar.

They added some more scantily clad women because sex sold. They made the mistake of trying to get them to wrestle though, and that was like trying to get blood from a stone in some cases. Lita was horrifying. She thought she was so much better than she really was. Trish Stratus was all right but wasn't that great a wrestler, nowhere near as good as everybody makes her out to be. She got her push because she was somebody in the fitness world, so Vince wanted to capitalize on that. I'm sure her relationship with Rocky didn't hurt either. She needed people to help make her look good. Look at her *WrestleMania* matches in back-to-back years. When she was supposed to lead Christy Hemme at *'Mania 21*, it was terrible. The next year, Trish had a pretty good match against Mickie James and that was because of Mickie. In her position, Trish should have been able to lead and she couldn't.

Mickie is good. Molly Holly, Victoria, and Michelle McCool were good. Jackie Moore was a really good wrestler. She was the Steve Blackman of women — she'd hurt somebody in a second.

All the boys liked her. She looked good and she could wrestle. Her stuff looked believable. Her only drawback was that she was very short and couldn't talk well. Beth Phoenix is really fucking good. Everybody respects Beth. The boys treat her as part of the family because she works her ass off. Gail Kim is really good too. I respect women like that, who get into the business, learn how to work, go out there, and bust their ass.

Some of them can't wrestle so much but they're game to get involved where they can. When I was working with Cody Rhodes against Santino and Carlito, they had Maria in their corner and the agent wanted her involved. We did a spot where we were all on the floor and Maria walked in front of her guys and started shaking her ass to distract me. I looked at the crowd, paused, and came back from left field with my hand wide open. It couldn't have been a more perfect smack. It sounded like a shotgun going off. Carlito's eyes got as big as saucers. The crowd blew the roof off that place — it was the highlight of the match.

When we got to the back, I checked with her and she said she was fine. A while later, she came out of the women's dressing room, said to me, "You've got to see this," and pulled her skirt up. Well, I wasn't going to tell her no! Right on her ass, there was a perfect print of my hand in purple and blue. You could have taken a fingerprint off it. She thought it was great fun. Maria wasn't the best wrestler, but she was always fun to work with and did the best she could.

The girls who are only there as eye candy are harder to respect. The boys tend to ignore them unless they are after a piece of ass. Some of those girls think the sex thing will get them all the way. The Kat flashed her tits on pay-per-view in the Attitude era. She was just trying to get over. It got a good reaction, sure, but it didn't help her in the long run. She got chewed out as soon as she came backstage from that one. They were all over her, asking, "Why the hell did you do that?!" She just said, "Because I wanted to," but I'm betting Jerry Lawler planted that seed and put her up to it. The only reason she was there in the first place was because of her relationship with The King. She had no business in the WWF whatsoever. Terri Runnels acted out all the time. Melina was the most hated girl in the locker room at one point — she thought she was the best wrestler and the best-looking female and she was neither. Kelly Kelly was there for years but she never learned to work a lick. None of the boys respected her. It is women like that who take away from Beth, Gail, and all the women who have worked hard to earn respect.

CHAPTER 21
THE ROCK STAR AND THE NINTH WONDER

When Chyna first came to the company in 1997, she poured on the charm — introduced herself, talked to everybody. I thought, "Wow, what a nice person." She wanted the job really badly. She said she'd sweep floors, put up the ring, do whatever it took just to get a job with the WWF. She was an impressive specimen back then too, close to 200 pounds and absolutely no fat. Damn, why *not* hire her? What made her interesting was that you don't usually see women who look like her. How many women do you see day to day who are almost 6 feet and 200 pounds of solid muscle?! Of course she was going to draw interest.

They brought her in as Hunter's bodyguard and he got over so much more with her in his corner. Nobody really cared about him before Chyna showed up. With her there, he looked like a coward because he was letting a woman — no matter how big she was — stick up for him. It worked and the crowd hated them as a couple.

She was very nice for the longest time — until she started dating Hunter and the WWF started building her and building her. They created a monster.

By the end of '98, the DX gimmick had taken off and you couldn't get close to her. The only people she would bother to talk to were the top guys. Anybody from the mid-card down, she wouldn't have a thing to do with. She would still talk with me a little now and then because I'd been there since she started, but she blew hot and cold. For example, she knew I liked Twix candy bars, so she'd always bring me a Twix and even nicknamed me "Twixy." Then, other times, she would completely ignore me. She could be either the sweetest person on earth or the biggest bitch on the planet. I didn't like the way she treated other people, even though she was still decent to me. You don't mistreat the people who make you what you are, in my opinion. By the time our program rolled around, she wouldn't even talk to me anymore because I was just a glorified jobber to her. I didn't want anything to do with her at that point. I wouldn't even attempt to say "hi" to her backstage because she'd be wearing the sunglasses all the time and acting like she didn't even hear me.

At airports, when the cameras were on, Chyna was the first one to sign an autograph. As soon as the cameras disappeared, it was a different story. We'd have group flights and the fans would come over to us all, looking for autographs. She and Hunter would refuse to sign anything, while Steve Austin, the biggest wrestling star in the world, signed everything. That tells me that Steve's grateful to have fans and is giving back. Hunter and Chyna would just sit there with their sunglasses on and ignore everybody. I saw a similar situation one time when we drove to Baltimore for a show. Hunter and Chyna pulled in right behind me when the valet was parking our cars. Some fans came running over for an autograph and the first words out of Chyna's mouth were "Hey, you're not supposed to be here, get out of here." The two of them refused to sign anything. They were right that the kids weren't meant to be there but even so . . . these people are the reason you have a salary! They came over to me and I signed and talked with them. This group of kids even said to me that Chyna and Hunter had a lot of fans and it was pretty sad that they would act like that. I had to agree. If the fans had been rude to them, I could have understood, but the kids just wanted a moment of their time and an autograph. But that's just who Hunter and Chyna were then — whenever the cameras were on, they'd act like the big babyfaces they were on TV but as soon as the cameras stopped rolling, it was a different story. They were really the only two who were like that. All of the other boys were respectful and giving to their fans. We were told that we should always sign autographs because the fans are the ones who make it possible for us to get a check and pay our bills. I saw Chyna some years later when I was doing *Tough Enough*; she was doing something for MTV too, so we were both in the green room and she was very friendly to me. I always wondered if her behavior when she became a big star was because somebody had "brainwashed" her into thinking that she was superior to the other talent and didn't need to talk to people "beneath her." I knew that wasn't her deep down. The Chyna I knew was and is a very good person.

For any difficulties I had at the time working with Chyna, I didn't have any whatsoever with Chris Jericho. Chris had come in from WCW but he'd wrestled around the world and learned a lot in Japan, where he'd been taught to lay it in there. A lot of people in the WWF had a hard time coping with him at the beginning because he was so rough. He was a good worker but a lot of the guys didn't like working with him because they were pussies who couldn't take it. I had no problems working with Chris — he'd lay it in there, you'd hammer him back, and he'd never say a fucking word. I could clean his clock and he wouldn't complain — he'd just clean my clock right back. A lot of people had a problem with the way he worked, but Chris's priority was to make sure people didn't see through his stuff. Trying to make his work look realistic was getting him into hot political water but he tried not to let politics dictate how he was going to operate. He's always thinking, always coming up with new ideas for himself and for other people. He'll give as much advice to other people as he can. I learned a lot from Chris just by listening to him, how he articulates and how he lays out a match. When he's putting together a match, he'll be moving, walking around — in his mind, he's running through all the moves, thinking how the match is going to flow. He pays attention to detail. The only drawback with him is that, if you're not careful, he'll take 99 percent of the match for himself. It's not a selfish thing and he's not trying to get one over on you, he just gets carried away and sometimes you have to intervene and calm him down. If you ask him, "What am I getting from this match?" he'll stop and go, "Oh right, yeah!" I absolutely love Chris. He's a great guy and he's got so many great ideas for the business.

Working the program with Jericho and Chyna was a blessing and a curse. It got me plenty of TV time, it got me onto a PPV, and it got me working with Chris. It also meant I had to work with Chyna so not only did I have to think about what I had to do, but I had to think for her as well. I figured I would be the one losing so that they could both stay strong. I was going to be the sacrificial lamb, so to speak. It wasn't working with a woman that bothered me, it was having to work around her in the ring that was frustrating, having to make up for her lack of ability. I didn't have to worry about her burying me because I had nothing to lose — I wasn't in a spot where they could do much to hurt my standing.

For the lead-up to the match at the *Royal Rumble 2000*, they had me go over Chyna in a match on *RAW* so that people might think I had a chance to win the three-way match. I don't think anybody really thought I might win that match but it was nice to get a win on TV. I put Chyna over in another match — some people might think I would have had a problem losing to a woman but I was fine with it. She was different from all the other women because they'd built her up as a monster. If they'd asked me to lose to Trish Stratus, for example, I might have had a problem with that. Chyna? That was fine.

I was happy that I got to do some interviews in the build-up, including what was probably my favorite-ever promo. I mentioned before that, back then, we had creative liberty with our promos but if you were going to say something about someone else, you would usually go and run it by them first out of respect. You wanted to make sure they wouldn't have a problem with what you were planning to say. I ran this one past Chyna and she said she was fine with it. It was a sold-out arena and the show would play on live TV. I went out there and said that women don't belong in a wrestling ring. The crowd reacted and I carried on: "I know what everybody's going to say, that I probably think they should be barefoot and pregnant in the kitchen but no — let me tell you something, Chyna, women don't belong in the ring — women belong in the bedroom, face down, ass up." I got a reaction like I never had in my life. 20,000 people just roared. Chyna came to the ring and I told her that she knew where I stood and so she had two choices — she either got her ass out or she got her ass up. That place blew a gasket again. I was told later that all of the boys in the back popped but Linda McMahon, Vince's wife, had this shocked look on her face, like "I can't believe he said that" and walked off. After I'd flown home,

I got a call from Bruce Prichard telling me that I couldn't say things like that. Why? He said, "It's just going a little too far . . . You offended a few people." I told him that worse stuff was said elsewhere on TV. I said that somebody must have been upset because I got over a little more than they did that night. Bruce told me to run any more "questionable content" past the office before I said it on live TV.

The match we did at the *Royal Rumble* ended up being pretty good. Everything went well except for a spot where I was down. Chyna and Jericho were fighting and their minds went blank. That was very rare for Chris. Chyna did listen when we'd go over matches but she had a tendency to be forgetful. She wasn't too worried about it since she knew that people would cover for her. They were just standing there in the ring, trading punches, backed up against the rope and trying to figure out what to do. I crawled around on the mat and shouted, "Drop behind, nutshot." They got back into the groove and we finished up the match with Chris pinning Chyna. I could have sworn I'd be the one to get beat but they put Chris over Chyna clean. For a seven-minute match, it was all action and looked great. When we got to the back, Chris took me aside and told me he was glad I remembered what they had to do because that was fixing to get ugly!

That was pretty much the end of any interaction I had with Chyna, although something from that program did come up again a while later. Hunter was out in the ring, cutting a promo on Vince and talking about him going to jail for whatever reason. He said that Vince was going to end up in jail "face down and ass up." All right, so Hunter can say that and I can't? I guess being so far up Vince's ass that he can see exactly what Vince had for dinner comes with certain privileges. I also guess that Hunter had heard the reaction I got for using that line and thought he'd take the pop for himself. "Questionable content" my ass, Hunter just didn't want anybody else getting over. If he heard a good line, he'd put the kibosh on it and stop it from becoming a money-maker for anybody else. That pissed me off. But, as always, if I didn't like how things were going, I could have left. That wasn't going to happen. No matter what, my loyalty was with Vince. It always has been. He gave me my break in the big time and he always looked after me financially. At one point, WCW got wind that my contract was expiring in April or May, so Eric Bischoff gave me a call. It was a quick conversation and we didn't even get as far as how they might use me. He told me that wcw would double whatever Vince's best offer was to keep me. I told him what I was making and, sure enough, Eric offered to double it. I thanked him for the offer but told him I was going to stick with the wwf. He said he understood and respected my loyalty, and that was that. I sat down with Jim Ross to work out a new contract with the wwf and he asked what sort of guarantee I wanted. I threw out a figure that I thought wasn't unreasonable. J.R. said it "wasn't exactly what they were thinking" but he'd see what he could do. They came back a few days later with the okay and we got the new contract signed. It ended up being an extra 40 percent on what I was already making. I was fine with that. Sure, Eric had offered me double what I had been making but as far as I was concerned, loyalty means more than money. I've always felt that way. The thought of going to wcw never entered my mind. It wasn't an option — I was staying with the wwf no matter what.

PART 9: PUTTING ON A SHOW

It's an incredible production — a WWE show is like pulling together a Hollywood movie in one night instead of over several months. No rehearsals, no second chances — you've got your mark, you've got your time cue, and you'd better hit it. It takes so many people and so much more work than anybody realizes. Once you take the wrestlers out of the equation, you still need to make sure you've got the best of everything to put on the best show.

Vince was always in Gorilla, micromanaging the show from there. He doesn't miss a beat and that's why the ship sails so smoothly. If you run over your cue and go into commercial time, that costs the company money. You don't want to be the guy who does that because Vince will cuss you out in a second. I don't understand why a lot of people tolerate that behavior. To me, once your boss yells at you and you allow it, you've just made yourself a doormat. A man has to keep his dignity. The more somebody lets Vince walk over him, the more Vince'll do it because he can. That's why he continually makes fun of Jim Ross. I wouldn't care if my job was on the line, I wouldn't stand for it. Jim Ross is one of the best commentators in wrestling history, and he shouldn't be subjected to that, but I guess he's worried about losing his job.

A good commentator is vital to helping get the wrestlers over. They can make or break a match or a star. Jerry Lawler is one of the best but how he acts towards the women takes away from that. It gets old listening to him sound like a pervert. A lot of people hate Michael Cole but he is good. So is Matt Striker — he knows the history of wrestling, everybody's background, every hold. He could turn out to be as great as Jim Ross. I like Josh Matthews but he's too soft-spoken. You've got to have a commanding voice to be a good commentator, as far as I'm concerned.

A good ring announcer is important too. Howard Finkel is the greatest ring announcer of all time and they pulled him from the road, then took him offscreen. I don't know why because he loves the business. He'd be on the road 365 days a year if he could. Tony Chimel got heat because he replaced Howard — what was Tony meant to do? Say, "No, I'm not going to do the job you gave me?"

There's no place for managers right now. Back in the '80s and early '90s, you could just put anybody with Bobby Heenan or Jim Cornette and the fans would boo them. Now, the only time that works is when a clear connection exists between manager and talent — you've got to compliment the guy you're managing or people won't go for it. Like Paul Bearer and the Undertaker — they fit together logically and brought something to each other's act. When 'Taker started talking more, Paul wasn't needed so much, so they were going to groom him to be the timekeeper in Gorilla. It's an important job and Paul would have been good at it but when they were trying him out, he made fun of the head of production, Kevin Dunn. He didn't know Kevin could hear him in the production truck. Things didn't work out too well for Paul after that. It's a damn shame that someone who has been with the company for years ends up losing their job because someone can't take a fuckin' joke, but that's how it is. After Vince, Kevin basically controls the whole company. Or at least he did before Hunter got in there.

A good ref can give you a hand out of a sticky situation and help the match flow. If you forget something or make a mistake, the ref can cover for you. He is just as important as the wrestlers. Not all refs need to know how to wrestle but they need to understand every aspect of the business and how everything works in the ring. Earl Hebner was the best, which is why he always got the main events. Jack Doan and Scott Armstrong are really good too. I had some fun with Jimmy Korderas and Mike Chioda; whenever they would referee a tag match I was in, they would have to waistlock me to get me out of the ring so I would hang on and struggle as much as I could to blow them up! Great guys, great refs, both of them.

Other people get put in the wrong job sometimes. I love Teddy

Long to death but he's not a referee. He *is* a great character though, and works well in his role as an onscreen authority figure. Vickie Guerrero is also great in her role — Eddie would have been so proud to see how good she is. She is one of the sweetest women you could ever meet and everybody loves her backstage. I can't say enough about her; she is a great woman.

Using former wrestlers as agents or producers is a good move because they know what it's like to be in there and they know how to put a match together. Everybody has a lot of respect for the agents. All of the agents I worked with knew their stuff. Arn Anderson, Dusty Rhodes, Michael Hayes, Finlay, Barry Windham, Ricky Steamboat, Jamie Noble, Jerry Brisco, Mike Rotunda — all great at their jobs. When they told you to do something, you didn't question it.

I was asked if I wanted to become an agent at one point. I said no because Vince has a habit of screaming at them if something doesn't go to plan. The first time Vince screamed at me, I know I'd knock his fucking teeth out. You can't control what happens in that ring, all you can do is lay out what you want and hope your guys deliver.

CHAPTER 22
THE GOLDEN AGE

During the Monday Night Wars, lots of people went back and forth between the promotions. It didn't ever occur to me to go to WCW and, as I've said, the only conversation I ever had about it was initiated by them and lasted a matter of minutes. I didn't want to start again. I was comfortable in the WWF locker room, with the people I worked with, the agents, and management. If I'd gone to WCW, I would have been starting all over, having to get to know a whole new team. In the WWF, people knew me and my capabilities. I felt like part of a family. As frustrated as I might have been at times because I wasn't being used to my full potential, I'm big on loyalty. I'm not someone who sits there and whines about being a job guy. Maintaining loyalty and making a stable living is more important to me than winning in a fake sport. To some of the guys, it's the other way around.

I heard a lot of horror stories about Eric Bischoff and how he behaved when he was managing WCW. Rumor had it that he was pretty rough with people and treated them badly, but he was very polite to me in our conversation. When he came to WWE years later, he was fine to me. I have nothing bad to say about him.

A few people who had bad experiences with WCW ended up falling into the WWF's lap in early 2000. Chris Benoit, Eddie Guerrero, Perry Saturn, Dean Malenko, Shane Douglas, and Konan all walked out of WCW, unhappy with how things were going. The WWF wasn't interested in Shane or Konan. I heard that Konan had heat with a lot of people although the one time I met him, he seemed like a good guy. Douglas had already had one run with the WWF and the Clique had squashed that. Shawn and Kevin weren't around anymore, but Triple H now had that power, so I'm sure he had something to do with squashing any thought of Shane coming back. Eddie, Chris, Dean, and Perry all got signed. I thought it was a good move — they were great talents, all of them excellent workers. The political bullshit in the locker room was still there though. Even though we'd just got four of WCW's best guys, they all lost their matches on their first night, including Benoit losing clean to Hunter, just to prove a point. I don't know what the reasoning behind that was, if it was Hunter's ego, or if management wanted to put the new guys in their place, or even if they just thought these guys were too short to do anything with. It didn't make sense to me to cut off their momentum right from the start.

Of the four of them, I became close to Benoit first. Our styles of wrestling seemed to go hand in hand and that's what brought us closer together. We each had a mutual respect for the way the other worked and that made us bond. He wasn't an ass kisser; if he had something to say, he'd say it to your face. Eddie was the same. He wouldn't talk behind your back. In wrestling, you've always got guys who will kiss somebody's ass to get somewhere — the politicians. Jericho, Benoit, and Eddie worked their asses off to get to the top. They didn't do it the cowardly way. I always liked the stand-up guys who would tell you what they thought to your face. You knew where you stood with them.

I thought Dean was a great worker and it was such a shame that he showed no personality in the ring. In the locker room, he shows all kinds of charisma — that man is a funny motherfucker and if he'd done that out in the ring, he would have got over. I've got no idea why he didn't. Perry Saturn was a hard-nosed, "I'm going to kick your ass" kind of guy. His downfall with the WWF was when he took advantage of an extra named Mike Bell. The guy made a couple of mistakes and it pissed Perry off, so he roughed this extra up more than he should have. He threw Bell out of the ring and just about broke his neck. They didn't use Perry after that. You can't ever take advantage of your opponent because he's trusting you with his *life*.

I was sometimes rough on guys out there, sure, but Perry went way overboard. Benoit, Eddie, Jericho, me . . . we were all rough but we never hurt anybody so badly that they couldn't come back the next night and work.

It's one of the things that kills me about the people on the internet who write about me being a bully; there are plenty of other wrestlers who are just as rough as I am and I've never hurt anyone so badly they can't come back. It's like the Steiners, the Road Warriors, and the Powers of Pain — they didn't take pleasure in hurting people, they were just rough. It's how they were brought up in the business and how the business was. Some of the newer kids just couldn't take it because they didn't have enough heart and they weren't tough enough to be in wrestling. Anybody who wants to complain about getting hurt in the ring because Eddie or Jericho or I roughed them up a little needs to pay attention to the next story and they'll learn about what heart is and stop whining.

Mae Young and the Fabulous Moolah are two of the sweetest ladies you'd ever meet. All the boys respected the hell out of them and everybody rolled out the red carpet whenever they were on the show. By 2000, they'd already got over 100 years of in-ring experience between them, so that tells you how old they were. But they would still get in the ring now and then when they were given the chance. On one show, Crash and I were booked to do a tag team match against them, so we sat down in catering together to go over the match. Out of respect for them, I took myself out of the equation and told them that we would do whatever they wanted to do. Mae planned out a spot where she would be in the ring with Crash and I'd sneak in behind her. She would turn around and I'd clothesline her. I said to her, "Mae, I've got all the respect in the world for you but if you're asking me to clothesline you, you need to know that I lay it in there." She said, "Sure I know that, I want you to clothesline me." I said, "No, you don't understand — when I clothesline somebody, I try to rip their head off. It's TV, I don't want it to look bad but I don't want to hurt you." This nearly 80-year-old woman just looked at me and said, "Bring it, motherfucker."

In Gorilla, just before the match, I gave her a hug and thanked her in advance for the match, then asked if she was sure about the clothesline. She said, "If you don't bring it, when we get back, I'm going to kick your ass." Hell, I didn't want to get beaten up by an 80-year-old woman, so I was going to do what she said and lay that clothesline in there nice and snug. We started the match and I locked up with Moolah, grabbed her in a headlock, and took her over. I landed right on top of her. I was 235 pounds at this point. She was 77 years old and she was taking everything I could throw at her. Unbelievable.

The time came for the spot with Mae. She had her back to me as I was getting ready. When she turned around, I charged — she didn't have time to prepare for it and I threw that clothesline from left field like I was hitting Bradshaw. I ripped her head off so hard that the poor lady cut a flip. I felt so bad! I asked her if she was all right and she said, "Yep, I'm fine," and carried on. When we got to the back after the match, I went over to thank her and asked, "Mae, are you okay?" She patted me on the chest and said, "That's how you lay a clothesline in, right there," and kept on walking. Why the hell can't some of the boys be like that?! That match was great fun and good entertainment.

I always liked the hard-hitting wrestling matches. I found those fun. Some of the other guys had different ways of amusing themselves. We were doing a circuit of house shows in which they had Crash and me against Mick Foley and Al Snow and we were keeping it to pretty much the same every night. One spot always got a weird reaction though, and it confused the hell out of me because I couldn't figure out what was going on. I would grab Al and lift him up above my head in a delayed vertical suplex, and for some reason the audience would start laughing. Well, I came to find out that Al had been amusing himself at my expense. I had one of my hands around his head, the other holding him up by the side of his singlet. One of his hands was around my head but his other one was hanging around my waist. One night I saw that even Mick and Crash were laughing at this spot, so I asked Mick what the hell was going on. "He's jacking you off," said Mick. That son of a bitch had been making a hand gesture at my groin like he was jacking me off! I thought it was pretty funny but I wasn't going to let Al get one over on me. I told Mick that I'd find a way to get Al back. Mick was all too quick to point out that Al didn't wear any underwear under his singlet. That was all I needed to hear.

The next night, we were in a sold-out Montreal arena. We did the

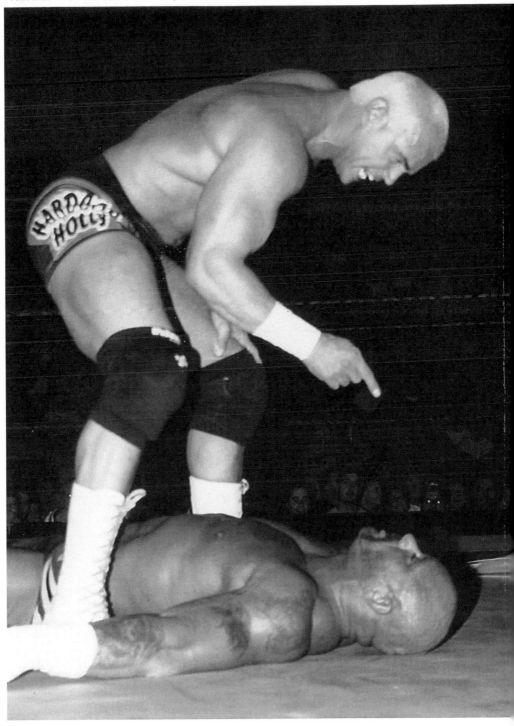

same match, the same spots. I grabbed Al for the suplex and I suppose he thought he was about to be a smartass again with his hand gesture. Boy, was he in for a surprise! I hooked his head, yanked the singlet so his private parts were on display for 20,000 screaming fans to see, and lifted him up high above my head. I held him up there for what seemed like forever. He was squirming and trying to get down but I wasn't about to let go. I made sure each side of the arena got a good look. And let's just say it was a cold arena that night . . . or that was Al's excuse!

That wasn't enough to stop Al fucking with me for his own amusement. I was doing a hardcore match with him and Steve Blackman on one show and Al had obviously talked Steve into helping him get me back. Steve probably jumped at the chance to rib me because of the number of times I'd scared him with my driving. This particular hardcore match went the wrong kind of hardcore; Steve got me in a headlock and held on tight. I was going nowhere. All of a sudden, Al came up behind me and stuck his thumb up my ass. I have no idea what he thought he was doing on that one.

I got them both back when we did other hardcore matches. One time, I switched the cookie sheets out from under the ring. They put these lightweight sheets under there that you could hit somebody with. They would make a hell of a noise and it would look impressive but it wouldn't really hurt. I arranged a spot in the match where I would use a cookie sheet and then replaced the lightweight ones with some heavy-duty sheets. In the match, Al whipped Steve towards me and I smashed him with one of those things — it had no give and Steve looked like he was out on his feet. You could literally see the bump immediately appearing on his head. He was still with it enough to tell me he was going to catch me and kill me after the match but I guess he thought better of it. Maybe he just didn't want to find someone else to drive him from town to town. Steve hated to drive.

Al was more easy-going than Steve. He hung out with Mick Foley a lot and the two of them loved going to carnivals. There was one particular carnival in Austin, Texas, that led to a really interesting situation. We had to go to Houston for TV the next day and Al suggested that I drop my rental car off and jump in with them. I didn't want to go to the carnival so

I told them I'd keep my rental and travel alone. Al and Mick kept asking me until I agreed. We would eat, drop my rental car, and go to the carnival for a little bit. Then we would drive on to Houston. Hell, I like roller coasters as much as the next guy, so I wouldn't have minded going. They jumped in their car, I jumped in mine, and we headed to the airport. They took off but I couldn't keep up because of the traffic. I got to the airport in the end, returned my rental, and stood out in the 40 degree cold, freezing at the curb, waiting and waiting. No Al. No Mick. I waited for over an hour before I gave up. I had to re-rent my car, so it cost me even more. I got to the arena in Houston the next day and Al came over to apologize. Mick didn't. He said, "I thought we were going to the carnival first!" I told him that wasn't what we'd agreed to — why would I keep the rental car longer just to go to a carnival that he was going to go to anyway? And when they didn't see me pull up at the carnival, didn't they figure something was wrong and that I must be at the airport? Mick said, "Oh, I didn't think of that." So they just went into the carnival without thinking about me freezing my balls off at the airport. Mick still didn't think he had done anything wrong.

Road Warrior Hawk overheard all of this and he blew a gasket. He was about ready to kill Foley. He went off on him, telling him you never leave your boys hanging, and least of all for a fucking carnival! He was so furious, I thought he was going to jump on Mick and beat the hell out of him. Even I told Hawk to calm down and he kept shouting, "Fuck him, he doesn't do the fucking boys like that!" 'Taker got word of this and all of a sudden, there was a call for Wrestlers' Court.

Wrestlers' Court was already in the WWF locker room when I got there. It doesn't happen anymore because they're too corporate, but in the '90s and early 2000s, it would happen now and then, only at TV or PPV. If one of the boys screwed up and got a lot of heat, they would get called up and chewed out in front of everybody else. It was just for the boys, no office staff or officials. Undertaker was the judge, usually with Bradshaw as prosecutor and Ron Simmons as the defending attorney. Ron, as a man of few words, wouldn't really ever try to defend anyone. It's a humbling experience, a humiliation. I would definitely not want to be in Wrestlers' Court.

Al didn't want any part of it so he tried to get Mick to apologize. Al hadn't really caused the problem; he was guilty by association. Apparently he'd kept saying to Mick, "We've got to find Bob," but Mick wasn't worried about it. Hawk told Mick, "You need to pay Bob back the money for the rental car, his hotel, his food, and his gas." In the end, Al convinced Mick that he didn't want to be in Wrestlers' Court so he gave me $500. Mick is so tight that you couldn't drive a pin up his ass, so it must have killed him to pay me that money. And when he did, he said, "I still don't think I did anything wrong." That was quite something.

Edge and Christian ended up in Court one time because they were buying gifts for Brian Gerwitz. He was writing all their stuff so they wanted to keep him sweet. They knew he collected these science fiction action figures, so they got him stuff like that. It said explicitly in our contracts that we are not allowed to buy gifts for any office staff, so the two of them got hauled up in front of 'Taker. The verdict: to make amends by getting a fifth of Jack for 'Taker, some cases of beer for Ron and John, and since I was the next senior guy there, some protein powder for me because I don't drink. If you break the locker room protocol, you have to pay for it. The penalty was never physical. Unless, of course, you really pissed everybody off.

The Public Enemy came in for a couple of weeks. These guys acted like they were superstars when really they were nobodies. They were working with Ron and John and told them that while they weren't prepared to go through a table, they still expected Ron and John to do it for them. That pissed Ron and John off like you wouldn't believe. They went to the ring that night and beat the everlasting shit out of The Public Enemy. That was basically the end of The Public Enemy in the WWF. You don't tell Ron and John what to do, and you don't say, "I can do this to you, but you can't do it to me." It just doesn't work that way.

As for me, I was working regularly and getting paid well but at times I felt like I was getting lost in the shuffle. They were starting to push Crash on his own and he was getting over doing the hardcore stuff. The Hardcore Title was now defended 24 hours a day, 7 days a week, and Crash became the guy who had to keep fighting anybody at any time because they wanted the belt. People tried to attack him after matches or backstage at first, but they got a little too creative with it and started filming clips of him getting attacked at a grocery store or in a romper room. I thought that was a little ridiculous and that the Hardcore Title lost a lot of credibility. I'm not saying that the belt was important, but it was a useful title that we'd worked to build up and now they were treating it like a joke. Some of the managers and some of the women would sneak in after Crash had been knocked out and win the title from him. I could just about cope with Jerry Brisco winning the title because he was actually tough in real life, but Terri Runnels winning the Hardcore Title? Really? Anybody walking down the street can apparently get that belt, and here we're meant to be an elite group in which only the toughest win that title. It didn't annoy me but I thought they were going to ruin something good. They do it every time, stretching the creativity more and more until they go too far and ruin it.

WrestleMania that year had me working in a hardcore match with a 15-minute time limit to fight 12 guys. Crash was going in with the title and whoever was the champion at the end of the time limit was the winner. They told us to go out there and beat the crap out of each other but have Crash win at the end. The idea was that I would be just about to beat him and the buzzer would go off before the ref could count three so that Crash escaped with the title by the skin of his teeth. The match was an absolute clusterfuck. So many people were out there and nothing made sense. It was just people hitting each other with anything they could find. No one was wrestling. The last minute was good though, when it came down to me, Crash, and Tazz. Crash was the champion at that point and Tazz had him about to pass out in a submission move. I grabbed a candy jar from the announcer's table and smashed it over Tazz's head. He went down, Crash was out, and I covered him. As the ref, Timmy White, made the count, he said, "We nailed this perfect." Timmy couldn't look at the screen so somebody backstage counted him down over his earpiece. Crash stayed down and Timmy pulled his arm just before he was about to hit three, because the bell was meant to ring to signify time had expired. The problem was that the guys backstage who were counting Timmy down weren't in synch with the clock on the screen, so it looked like I'd pinned Crash with two seconds left. They made a snap decision backstage and had Howard Finkel announce that I won the match, not Crash. They had Crash's music cued up and played that, but they lucked out since he and I used the same music. I was still confused about what had happened. So was everybody else. Crash didn't know what was going on. He thought he was supposed to win, then grab the belt and get out of there, so he did. Timmy had to go get the belt off him and bring it back to me. Crash wasn't upset because he didn't go over as planned; he didn't care about that. He was just glad to have a job and enjoyed what he was doing. Backstage, management said, "We'll fix it on *RAW* and switch the belt back to Crash," which they did. Even so, the agents and Vince himself chewed Tim White out. That seemed unfair to me. The blame should have gone to the people in the truck who gave him the wrong information. Tim was just going off their cues. It was a big old mess but I got paid $9,000 for that match, so I was happy enough.

The main star of the show that year was The Rock, who had become the top guy in the business. My hat is off to him because pretty soon after he started with the wwf, they were going to stick a fork in him and call him done. The fans didn't give a crap about him and he was on his way out the door.

When he first came in, I thought he was terrible. He couldn't cut a promo to save his life. There was one in particular in England, when he was the ic Champion. He cut the most generic promo ever, along the lines of "I'm the champion and I'm going to beat you and walk out the champion." It was the godawfullest promo that I'd ever heard. We made fun of him over it in the locker room and he laughed at it too. He was fixing to sink, then he pulled a rabbit out of the hat and started doing all of his promos in the third person. It was brilliant, and he came up with it himself. It saved his career. He ended up getting really good at promos and got over huge. It was purely a confidence issue when he started out. He still wasn't the greatest worker but what he could do, he did well. He just got better and better and went on to become one of the greatest entertainers in professional wrestling.

As he became a bigger and bigger star, Dwayne himself changed. He didn't become an egomaniac though; he became more confident in himself. If you were to walk up to him and say, "I've always wanted to meet you," he'd shake your hand, take a picture, sign an autograph, and say, "Thank you for being a fan." He's one of the kindest, most genuine people you'd ever meet. He doesn't have a big head, he's just very confident in what he can do and who he is. Even after he became the hottest act in wrestling, we'd rib him about his old promos and say, "Do you remember that one you did in England?" and he'd laugh and say, "Yeah, that was fucking awful." I guarantee that, to this day, even as a big movie star he is still down to earth. The last time I saw him was at the WWE Hall of Fame ceremony in 2008, when he inducted his dad and granddad. I talked to him for a while and I could tell he was the same person he always was — over-the-top nice to everybody, just a class act.

I'll be honest, I haven't seen many of his movies. I saw *The Other Guys*, which he did with Samuel L. Jackson, where they were smart-ass cops. I thought he did a good job. It wasn't a big part but he was as funny as hell. That's who he is though — if you get to know him, you find out he's hilarious. I can see how Dwayne is a great actor. Steve Austin became a good actor too. I tried watching *The Chaperone*, which had Hunter in it, and I had to shut it off because it sucked. It wasn't Hunter's fault — he's a funny guy, as he proved on *Saturday Night Live*, but they need to find a role that suits him. I think anybody could become a good actor if they're put in the right roles. Being on TV as a wrestler can open acting doors, but if you work for WWE, they control who does what. I know for a fact that a lot of the boys have had opportunities to be in TV shows and movies but never even knew because the producers called the office and the office has told them, "No, he can't do it . . . but we have *so-and-so* available instead." Then they try to give the role to one of their top guys. They play favorites. We found out one time that somebody had called in and asked Test to be in a movie but the office had blocked it, saying that they were using him that weekend and had plans to put him in an angle on TV. He would have received a good payoff for the movie and they blocked it. When he got to TV, do you think they used him? Fuck no, they didn't. That's the kind of thing that goes on with the office sometimes. It's awful — they don't want anybody getting over without them, I guess because then wrestlers might think for themselves or something.

They did let me do a movie at one point. We were in Louisville and I was in catering when Kevin Dunn came up to ask if I wanted to do a movie titled *Operation Sandman*. It was going to be filmed in Mexico and was going to star Ron Perlman. I said sure. Why not? I guess they came to me because nobody else wanted to do it. It probably wasn't a big enough role for the top guys. Whatever, I thought I'd take the job and have some fun.

I loved doing the movie. It was a made-for-TV thing and I thought it turned out pretty good. It was easy work, a lot of "hurry up and wait" — you have a lot of time on your hands on a movie set. We would shoot from six at night until six in the morning in an old GE warehouse in Mexico City, so there were long days, strange hours, lines to learn, and a lot of waiting around. But it was a lot easier doing a movie than wrestling. On a movie, they take 20 different shots from different angles, so you have a chance to perfect your character. In wrestling, it's in front of a live audience, so you don't get a chance to do things over. They say, "You'd better go out and nail it because we're not going to give you another chance." The movie people took care of me while I was there — my hotel suite was as big as a house and had three bathrooms. It was crazy!

I honestly didn't think twice about whether it would lead to other acting jobs. We were so busy on the road with the WWF and were making such good money that I was fine with what I was doing. If the opportunity came up, I'd love to do more movies. I never used my wrestling experience to make contacts or get an agent though. Just like anything else, getting into movies is about who you know, and I absolutely hate to know people in order to use them. I don't want to make people feel like they're being used. Hell, I could have kept in touch with Ron Perlman but I didn't. I got on great with the other actors but I didn't keep in touch with them. I had wrestling, I was keeping busy — I didn't want to feel like the only reason I was keeping in touch was so that later on down the line, I could use them. It's sad that, nowadays, to get anywhere, you have to use somebody. I've met so many people throughout my career who could have given me opportunities to do other things, but I refuse to use people. I don't regret that. If I want something, I want to have to work for it. Sure, it's nice for somebody to hand it to you but where's the achievement in that?

CHAPTER 23
AN UNFORTUNATE BREAK

Another guy who wasn't ever handed anything is Kurt Angle. He won a gold medal at the Olympics and then joined the WWF in late 1999. Kurt excelled so fast, it was scary. Over the years, I had some of my best matches, bar none, with him. Anyone who has ever worked with Angle knows that he doesn't work light. You don't have to tell him twice to lay it in there; he will clean your clock in a New York minute. It's funny that people on the internet bitch about how rough I am but are fine with Kurt. He goes balls to the wall and isn't going to apologize for anything. That's the way I like it. He really was a wrestling machine in the truest sense. I've got no idea how his mind operates anymore now that he's in TNA, but when he was with Vince, he kept growing as a wrestler in terms of being smart in the ring, learning how to work well, and telling a story with the best of them. At his peak, I could have almost put Kurt on the same level as Shawn Michaels. He should have been the top guy in WWE from 2002 onwards but, of course, it had to be Hunter. I didn't get it — by that point, Kurt was much more over than Hunter.

In June of 2000, they were still building Kurt up and pushing him hard, so I was one of the guys who helped get him over and make him look really good. We were at a TV taping for *Smackdown* in Hartford and were going over the match backstage. He was still pretty green, so I was calling the match. He was making suggestions and that was fine; I don't have a problem with a new guy suggesting something as long as it fits what we're doing and makes sense in terms of when we do it. Kurt had this spot he did in a lot of his matches where he went for a moonsault and missed, so I told him, "You need to hit the moonsault." If he didn't hit it sometimes, it would become too predictable when he went up to the top rope for it. Everyone would know he always missed. He said, "I don't know if I can do that — I've never landed on anyone." I told him he would be fine and that it would be a good swerve. Everybody would be expecting him to miss so why not nail it this time?

We got to the ring and the match was fine. When the time came, he slammed me and started to climb the ropes for the moonsault. I was laying there, thinking, "He's put me too far out." But I decided that he was a good athlete and he had pretty big legs so he'd be able to jump far enough and make it. As soon as his feet left the buckle, I knew he wasn't going to make it. I could see his legs were going to land on my ribs so I rolled towards the ring post to protect myself. As I turned in to him, his shin caught me on my forearm and it sounded like a damn shotgun had gone off. I rolled over, saying, "You broke my fucking arm!" Kurt didn't know what to do, so I said, "Cover me!" That was what we'd planned to do. I guess he figured I'd just stay down but that wasn't what we'd called, so I kicked out. The expression on Kurt's face was of total disbelief.

"What the fuck are you doing?!"

"Just hit me!"

"What?!"

"Fucking hit me, Kurt!"

In his book, Kurt said that once he'd broken my arm, he had to take over and become the ring general. No, sir, he did not! He was freaking out, so I told him to just keep going. I called the rest of the match. It was my decision to keep going, not his. Even the ref asked me, "Why are you still going?" I didn't answer him, I just got on with the match. At one point, I was supposed to lift Kurt's legs to do a stomach stomp and I couldn't even grab his right leg. My arm was just dangling there. We got through the rest of the match as planned and I went to the back for the doctor to check me out. I was wondering if maybe it was just a bad bruise. After all, I had finished the match and if I had a broken arm, I wouldn't have been able to do that. About 15 of the boys were circling me, checking on me. I actually felt bad for Kurt because he felt so bad. They took me to the hospital to get it x-rayed.

I was waiting for the doctor to come back with the results when Kurt walked in. I was surprised that he came to visit me — he hadn't needed to do that. It was appreciated though. I told him that I didn't think my arm was broken, just badly bruised. He dropped his head and said that he'd seen the x-ray as he was coming in and it was definitely broken. My heart sank. I'd just signed my new contract, and I felt that I was in a good spot and that they were going to start pushing me seriously again. I had been working my ass off, I was making plenty of money, and everything was going great. I was happy. Now my arm was broken.

They fixed me up with a temporary splint and sling and Kurt drove me back to the hotel. He made sure I got up to my room and got me settled before he left. A while later, there was a knock on my door. It was Kurt — he'd brought me up a bunch of food. When he left, he asked what time my flight was in the morning so he could help me get to the airport. I said he didn't have to do that but he insisted. That's what kind of guy Kurt Angle is. I didn't even know him that well, he'd only been around a few months, and he was doing all that? It says a lot about his character. Just turning up at the hospital to check on me was enough, but the next morning he showed up at 4 a.m., brought me breakfast, helped me pack my bags, carried them for me, checked me out of the hotel, checked in at the airport — he went above and beyond.

I went home and had surgery. They put a 10-inch titanium plate in my arm. Vince called me up after the surgery and commended me on working through a broken arm, but told me to never do that again. He explained to me that the broken bone could have cut an artery or something and I could have bled to death. I hadn't realized that could happen. He said if something like that ever happened again, I would have to stop the match. I know he was looking out both for me and his company when he said that but stopping a match because I get hurt just isn't me.

When I was home recovering, Kurt called me for the first couple of months on a weekly basis to check on me and make sure things were going well. He and Karen, his wife, sent me care packages and went way beyond what was necessary. They were so thoughtful and I really appreciated it. I was just looking forward to getting back because they had a ready-made angle: me going after Kurt to get revenge for my broken arm!

Being off as my arm healed was awful. I couldn't do anything. I still worked out but I was limited in what I could do. I couldn't ride my dirt-bike or work on my race car. It was a killer. I just had to wait, and I was fit to be tied. I went to a lot of NASCAR races during my time off and hung out with Hermie Sadler because his younger brother Elliott was racing on the circuit. I practically lived with Hermie while I was off. I'd get to hang out in the pits with the drivers. I enjoyed it but it was quite boring when the races started. When you're in the infield, you can't see anything apart from a split second of the cars and then they're gone again. I would watch a lot of it sitting in Hermie's motor coach. We also built a new race car together, which was good fun. It was ready to go around the time the big full-arm cast came off my arm so guess what I was doing?! Even though the doctors told me to take it easy, I was back behind the wheel and racing, even though my arm was broken and I was still in the forearm cast. We had some problems with the motor on that car so didn't do great in the races, until we finally figured it out in time for me to finish 12th in a 28 car race. I thought that was pretty good, considering I got spun out twice during that one! It was good to be back doing the extreme stuff. Unfortunately, on the next race, we blew the motor and that was that — it was time for me to get back on the road for the WWF.

I had been working out hard to get ready for my comeback. Most guys who are out with injuries do vignettes to promote their returns and built up the anticipation. They didn't do any of that for me.

Sure enough, for my first night back on TV, Kurt was in a match with Crash, and after he'd won, Kurt was putting the boots to Crash. I ran out to make the save. It was a way to get me back onscreen as a surprise rather than by building up a return match for me. I don't know why they chose to do it that way. You would have thought that the revenge angle between me and Kurt would be a starting point. It wasn't. The next night, I was tagging with Crash against Test and Albert. Nothing was done to follow up on the run-in on Kurt, nothing was made of the broken arm. It was another opportunity for building me up and they dropped the ball. Kurt was the WWF Champion

at the time I got back, so it would have been a good way to elevate me in a feud with the champion. At that point in my career, I would have been credible as a challenger and Kurt needed some good wins. I don't know why they didn't do it. It wasn't because of my work, and it wasn't because I was out of shape. It puzzled me, but I never questioned it. It wouldn't have done me any good to ask questions. Mouth shut, eyes forward. I show up, they say this is what you're going to do. That's just how it was.

I had suspected there wasn't going to be a program with Kurt because I had talked with Bruce Prichard a few times while I was off and suggested different scenarios for my return. After two or three calls, I realized they weren't really making any plans for me and Kurt to work together. It was a shame because I would have made that much more money if I'd done a program with Kurt but it wasn't the end of the world. At that point, everybody was making shitloads anyway. I went back to putting people over and was still making a ton of money. That year was the only year in my career that I made more than my downside guarantee. All in all, I made double what I had the previous year — and I didn't have to defect to wcw to do it.

CHAPTER 24

THE END OF THE WAR

Rather than getting a run against the wwf Champion, I got another cousin. Crash came up to me in catering one day and said, "We've got a new relative. Her name is Molly Holly." I didn't have a problem with that — if they were going to introduce someone new to my onscreen family, that just meant more TV time for me. I thought she was a very good worker, a hell of a lot better than Trish Stratus ever thought about being. She was smart too. A few years later, when the company was building up to *WrestleMania XX*, she hadn't been scheduled to be on the show so she went to management and suggested that she should do a match with Victoria for the women's title. But if she lost — and she was going to — she would have her head shaved bald. She sacrificed her hair for a spot on that card and got the *WrestleMania* payoff. I was never particularly close with Nora (Molly) but I respected her as a worker. She ended up in the traditional Holly role of doing all the hard work to make other people look good. I was much closer with Mike (Crash) — he and I had a decent relationship and I ended up liking the little fucker. He grew on me, so I wanted to look out for him and protect him.

Moving into 2001, the three Holly cousins did a few things together here and there, including a program with the Dudley Boys that went nowhere. For the most part, we did our own separate things. I got to work with both Benoit and Jericho as a sort of middle-man, bringing them together to move their program along. It was great working with those two. All our matches were good fun — especially the ones with Benoit. I had some of the best matches of my career with him and always looked forward to them. He knew what my role was but, despite that, he would always make sure to go out with me and put on a main event–level match and deliver something special for the fans. To be honest, I didn't like the matches where an enhancement guy had to put me over; I preferred the ones with guys like Jericho, Benoit, Eddie, and even Hunter, where I would put them over but we'd put together a good, hard-hitting match. I would look strong even though I got beat. I'd rather lose three or four of those matches than win 100 squash matches.

I did my thing with Chris and Chris, Molly went off to be a workhorse in the women's division, and Crash floundered. He got a quick run as the Light Heavyweight Champion but that wasn't anything to write home about. Over the next few years, Crash began to struggle and complained a lot backstage. He was having a bad time outside of work because he had a kid with a woman in California who was giving him a hard time. He wasn't a drug guy but he drank like alcohol was going out of style. He became his own worst enemy. I told him to keep his mouth shut loads of times, to stop worrying about other people and start worrying about Mike Lockwood. He didn't pay attention to my advice and ended up getting released in 2003. It was a shame but what was I going to do? We lost contact and I didn't hear much about him until Stevie Richards called me later that year. Mike had been staying with Stevie out in Pensacola after his life fell apart. Stevie told me that Mike had died. He choked to death on his own vomit. The court ruled it a suicide from an overdose of alcohol. I felt awful for Mike. He'd lost his job, he found out that his girlfriend was screwing one of the boys, and he had kept on drinking like a fish. I hated that it all happened, but just like with Owen, I shut off my feelings to protect myself.

After having been in the last three *WrestleManias,* I was disappointed that I got passed over for *WrestleMania XVII* in 2001. I wasn't in a storyline at the time, so I didn't get in. The biggest story in wrestling had just kicked off, however — wcw management had finally thrown in the towel and sold the whole promotion to Vince. There's a lot of hearsay about what brought down wcw. Some people say it was Bischoff, some say it was Russo, some say it was Hogan. It wasn't one person; it takes a bunch of people to bring a company down. In my opinion, it was a lack of leadership that brought wcw down. They had too many Chiefs and not enough Indians. The wwf had one boss — Vince. Everything was run by him, every match, every storyline, every idea, every piece of merchandise — everybody answered to him. In wcw, people had no idea who their boss was. If Ted Turner had known the wrestling business and had been at tv every week, that's who everybody would have answered to, but he gave control over to too many people. wcw ended up being about who you knew, not how talented you were. Eric Bischoff definitely took advantage of that, just like he took advantage of Ted Turner's money. He wasn't spending his own money, so he didn't think hard about his investments. Vince was spending Vince's money — that meant Vince had to be smart and care about all of his decisions. Bischoff didn't care the same way because he was playing the big man with someone else's money.

So after over five years, the wwf had finally won the Monday Night War. A lot of people started speculating that Vince was going to keep wcw running and have two different crews.

I think Vince's idea was always to shut them down and kill the competition, because he hates competition.

We didn't hear anything in advance. Nobody said a word. We found out what had happened when Vince went live on air and announced it. Everybody backstage thought, "We're going to have way too many guys now . . ." We were worried that we would get lost in the shuffle but we weren't job-scared. The guys who were job-scared were the ones who had walked out on Vince to go to wcw.

Wrestling fans were excited by the idea of a big wcw invasion on wwf tv. It didn't work out too well. I truly believe that Vince sacrificed a great idea and a huge money-making program in order to get his revenge and bury some people who had walked out on him . *Us vs Them* done properly would have been great tv. We needed to have the major stars from wcw in order to make it work, but the guys who came across just weren't at that level. Sting would have been ideal but they didn't sign him. The same with

Goldberg. I would have put my hand in my pocket and brought them both in. Business is business. Sure, it would have cost a huge amount of money to get a Sting or a Goldberg, but the way I look at it, if they're going to bring in a guy who sells tickets, that's fine because he is going to make everybody more money. If they pay that guy ten times what they pay me, that's fine as long as he sells tickets. Back then, they could have paid Austin $10 million a year and I wouldn't have cared because I knew he was going to make me more money. That was the way I looked at it, but Vince wasn't willing to pay the money to get all of the big names, so we were left with whoever came over in the buyout. At least we got Booker T, but he was the only real star who came across. Diamond Dallas Page was a pretty big star in WCW and he came over too, but he wasn't as big a deal as he thought he was.

Don't get me wrong, DDP was a good worker. He had star potential and he could have been a lot bigger in the WWF than he ended up being, but he screwed the pooch for himself on that deal. He was so particular about his matches that it pissed everybody off. He would sit down and write out the whole match in great detail, three to four pages of writing . . . he would actually write things like "we circle each other to the left" and "we lock up and I take your arm. I'll punch you and you'll sell my punch and grimace." He would actually write facial expressions in his match plans! It was unbelievable. He even tried to dictate what 'Taker should do in the ring at one point. That's why he ended up on TV getting pinned by 'Taker's wife. Unless you're Vince, you don't tell 'Taker what to do. Ever.

I had the pleasure of working with Page for his last WWE match. I got to the arena in Texas and was talking to Benoit when the agent came over to tell me I was with Page that night. Benoit started laughing and said, "Have fun with that one." I'd never worked with Page before that, so I asked what was so funny. Benoit said, "He's gonna annoy the fuck out of you all day long about that match." Benoit told me about the times he had worked with Page in WCW and how Page would present him with a seven- or eight-page detailed outline of the match. Because DDP was in tight with Bischoff, Benoit had to go by this book that Page had written for the match and it had driven him nuts.

"As soon as he knows he's working with you, he'll come find you and he'll want to go over the match with you right there and he'll go over it again and again and again."

I was like, "No the fuck he won't!" Chris just laughed. "He'll find you!" I hid for a while before going into catering so I could eat before all the food was gone. Sure enough, Page saw me and rushed over. "Hey, brother, let's go over the match . . ." he said. I told him to hold on because I had a couple of things to do but I'd meet him at the ring in a while and we'd go over it there. I never went to the ring. Page sat out there waiting for me for God knows how long. I went to get dressed about an hour before the match.

"Thank God I found you . . ." Page was sweating now. "I've been looking for you all day, brother, we need to get this match down."

I said, "Don't worry, I've just got to go do something." He looked nervous and said, "You're gonna come right back, right?" I nodded.

"I'm gonna come right back."

He fucking bought it again! I showed up at Gorilla about 20 minutes before the match and started warming up. He was already there, pacing, saying, "Oh my God, thank God, how come you didn't come back?" I said I tried to find him but couldn't and I guessed we were just like a dog chasing its tail. He was panicking now.

"I'm fucking sweating this . . . we've got to get this . . . I usually go over the match earlier in the day so I can get it down . . ."

I said that I just usually went over a couple of ideas in the last few minutes and then went out and did it. He didn't like that one bit. We talked about the match and he said he would prefer to not take my finish because he had a bad neck so I arranged to beat him with a dropkick. It ended up being a pretty good match, so it goes to show that maybe DDP didn't need to script everything as much as he thought.

Booker was completely different when he got to the WWF. He had respect for everybody when he walked in the locker room that first time. He was somebody in the wrestling world, a five-time World Champion, one of WCW's top guys, and he came in as if he were just another new guy starting out. That got him a lot of respect. He introduced himself to me like he was brand new in the business. We became good friends. When he had his wrestling school years later, he asked if I would help out, so I went and did a show for him for free. I stayed with him and his wife, Sharmell, and they are two of the kindest people you could ever meet. I always felt like Booker was one of my best friends in the locker room. I thought he got a fair shake with WWE and had a good run. He worked for years to make it to the top of that promotion because when he came in, they made him go back to square one. He took his ass-kickings and he did what he was told to do. He deserved every bit of working on top in WWE and I was so glad to see him get the World title eventually, because he earned it.

There were some other guys who came across in the WCW invasion who could have been built up more than they were. Hugh Morrus was a good talent, one I felt they could have used better. Lance Storm was a great worker, although as a character he was very plain. My in-ring personality has been criticized, but I was *told* not to smile and *told* to look like I was miserable. Believe me, I was not — and am not! — a naturally miserable person. But I think the Lance you got on camera was the Lance you get off camera. They tried to give him a fun, dancing character a few years later and it went nowhere. It just didn't feel right and Lance couldn't pull it off. Sean O'Haire had a fucking great look. He was a big bastard at 6'6" and very agile. They could have made him a killer, but instead, they dropped the ball with him.

I remember chasing O'Haire and his partner, Chuck Palumbo, through Madison Square Garden. The two of them had just interfered in a match and beaten up the WWF guys, so a bunch of us went out there to chase them off. They tried to escape into the crowd but we blocked their way, got them back in the ring, and beat the hell out of them. It was the first time any of the WWF guys got their hands on these invaders and I'll tell you something — in that ring that night, it was one potato, two potato, three potato more. . . . The agents said, "It's TV, just lay it in there." We knew what that meant. It was seek and destroy. Those two were the sacrificial lambs and the beating they took — and they took a hell of a stiff beating — was a message to the rest of the new WCW guys to know their position. There was no real reason why it was O'Haire and Palumbo specifically who took the beating, at least not a reason I ever heard of.

I kind of ended up as one of Vince's enforcers during the invasion. I was told to go out there and beat the shit out of a few of them. They needed the legit tough guys there just in case something happened, so Vince turned to me, Ron Simmons, and Bradshaw a lot. We wanted to make sure the wcw guys knew that they wouldn't be coming into *our* locker room and taking over. In wcw, everybody had an ego. They were going to have to get used to leaving their ego at the door or they were going to get their asses handed to them.

The biggest jerk by a mile was Buff Bagwell. He had a horrendous attitude and he got what he deserved. He messed up by not getting that he wasn't in wcw anymore. He showed up to house shows when he wanted to show up. He wouldn't shake anybody's hand and wouldn't change in the same place as everyone else — he wanted a room to himself. Sometimes, when he decided he didn't want to come to the house shows, he had his momma call in to the office for him to say he was sick. Somebody took him aside and smartened him up, telling him, "This is the way it is, this is our procedure." But he still refused to play along with it and he paid for it dearly. Jim Ross got Ron, Bradshaw, and me together and told us to go out to the ring after Bagwell was done wrestling and, in Jim Ross's words, "Kick the shit out of him." That's what we did — we hit the ring and we took turns with him. I didn't beat him hard enough to break his nose or knock his teeth out, but I hit him pretty hard. Bradshaw and Ron did a lot more damage than I did — they were competing to see who could beat him harder. I was a distant third in that competition. I would say Bagwell wouldn't speak to me after that, but he refused to speak to me even *before* we did that. That pissed me off.

They ended up sending him up to Connecticut to the wwf tv studio so that he could learn how to work properly and fit in. I guess he smarted off too much while he was up there because Shane Helms blasted him with a water bottle and knocked him out. Bagwell got fired pretty soon after that. It was never going to work out with him because he thought he was too much of a superstar. Most of the others got it pretty quickly and knew where they stood in the locker room; they knew they had to start fresh.

I saw the whole invasion thing as another chance to show people what I could do, get people over, and get myself over, and I hoped that maybe they'd give me a spot at the next *WrestleMania*. That's how I looked at everything along the way. Every new chapter was another opportunity to build towards 'Mania. I didn't get many chances to be on pay-per-view that year though and didn't have as good an earning year as the previous one. I didn't get on the 'Mania card either. I was pissed off that after the whole invasion angle had fallen apart and been forgotten, they brought back fucking Kevin Nash and Scott Hall, two of the guys who had been the most disloyal to Vince, and gave them spots at *WrestleMania*. By this point, Kevin was washed up and couldn't work anymore, and Scott was a wreck because he drank too much. They paid these guys all this money and gave them big programs leading in to 'Mania. Within six months of their coming back, Hall got fired and Nash tore his quadriceps off the bone because his body was done.

That was really the end of Scott Hall in wrestling. He's a first class bully — I've seen it first hand. He'll walk into a restaurant when he's drunk, he'll find a guy who has his family with him, and then he'll belittle the dad in front of his kids. It's awful. Scott is a great guy when he's not drinking, but if you add alcohol, he's a sorry motherfucker. They brought Nash back when his leg healed and tried to get him over. It didn't work and he disappeared again. They tried this all again just recently. It didn't work again. You'd think they'd learn, but I guess if you kiss Triple H's ass, you get an opportunity quicker than if you can actually wrestle.

PART 10: COMPETITION

I think wrestling today would be better if Eric Bischoff had managed to buy out WCW and keep it going. Competition is good for the industry and was definitely better for the wrestlers. For a few years, we were in a position to get paid better. I still don't feel we were ever paid entirely fairly. Both companies were making so much money that they could have afforded to pay the boys a lot more.

TNA isn't competition for Vince. They take guys who didn't make it with Vince and make them their top guys. Nobody is going to get behind that. All the while, they've got their own guys who are damn good, like A.J. Styles and Daniels, and they never get behind them properly. I don't think Hogan is helping them — he should have got out of wrestling a long time ago but I guess he's been on a stage all his life so he's finding it hard to step off.

It's going to take something huge for WWE to take off again. I honestly don't see it happening. Without competition, there's nothing to push them. They're making so much money off merchandise that TV ends up as nothing but a platform to help sell it. Maybe if the ratings drop to a level where Vince has to start paying for his air time again, that might kick their asses into action, but for now, they'll keep on throwing two guys out there without a storyline, just for the sake of having matches and filling TV time. The commentators will talk about the main event guys and pay no attention to the match in the ring, and you go round and round and only end up with about eight stars.

CHAPTER 25
TOUGH TIMES

To accommodate all of the guys they had on the roster after the invasion, WWE split the company in two and put the guys either on *Raw* or *Smackdown*. I ended up on *Smackdown*, working under Paul Heyman. I loved working with Paul — that guy is such a damn genius with such a great mind for the business. He was the man behind the original ECW back in the '90s, and that was one of the best wrestling shows ever. I had a lot of interaction with Paul. We came up with a load of ideas for me, but they all got blocked by the higher-ups. For what reason, I don't know. I guess I was good enough to get other people over and that was all. Any good idea for me that Paul took to the writers got squashed.

At least I got a finisher at this point. I hadn't had a real finish up until then. I used something off the top rope back when I was Sparky Plugg: either a cross body, a splash, or a kneedrop. After I'd become "Hardcore," I usually won matches by using foreign objects. I did use a pump-handle slam sometimes, but Vince Russo came to me around the time they were starting to push the hell out of Test and asked if I would mind giving the move to him. "Do I have a choice?" I asked. He replied, "Not really." So why fucking ask me?! I tried the Falcon Arrow for a while but didn't really like it. It didn't help that Russo wanted to call it "the Hollycaust." That got stopped quickly when the office decided the name would offend a lot of people. After I watched a whole bunch of documentaries on the subject, I understood. It's something people don't want to be reminded of. To try and shock people, Russo probably would have pushed for me to use it to beat Bill Goldberg, Billy Kidman, and all the other Jewish wrestlers . . .

I came up with my finish when I was watching a match on TV. They did an up-and-over in the corner and the guy charging in caught the legs of the guy trying to jump over him. They struggled and ended up going into a sunset flip, but I thought to myself, "What if I held onto the legs and then whipped the guy over my head?" So next time we got to TV, I asked one of the extras I knew if he'd mind taking the move. We got to the ring and tried it. It was a simple flat back bump, but he was hanging down my back so far that whipping him over meant he went further and it would hurt more. I told him to push up off my hips so he didn't have so far to go and we tried that. It was a much easier bump, so we went with that and, the next time I got to go over on somebody, I used that. One of the announcers came to me after the match and asked what they should call it. So I went back to them and said, "Why don't we call it the Alabama Slam?" Vince seemed to prefer the "Alabama Slammer," but the commentators usually just went with my suggestion.

I thought it was a very convincing finish and people like Spike Dudley and Paul London made it look devastating when they would emphasize the bump; I always appreciated guys like that who did their best to get my move over. Those guys get it — if you're going to lose, lose to something that looks like it about knocks you out. If *I'm* going to lose a match, I'd rather get beat clean with a guy's finish instead of having him roll me up and sneak a win. A number of times over my career, an agent would come to me and say, "We're going to do a fuck finish and make it look like you got screwed." And every time, I'd tell them that unless they needed a cheap win for storyline reasons, I'd prefer to lose to the other guy's finish and make my opponent look strong. I appreciated them trying to protect me, but I never liked cheap finishes as a fan or a wrestler.

As far as I'm aware, I never hurt anyone with the Alabama Slam. I *nearly* hurt Rico with it one time, because he didn't push off my hips like I told him to. I had to whip him hard to get him over, and it must have stung to say the least when he landed. He was fine after though. When

I asked him why he didn't post off my hips, he said, "I just forgot," so I replied, "Well, don't or you're gonna get hurt!" For all the rumors that went around out there that I liked hurting people, the fact is it would have been real easy for me to break somebody's neck with that move. I could have held on to their ankles and pushed up when they were coming down. They would have over-rotated and landed on their neck. These guys were putting their lives in my hands, so I was damn sure going to make sure they were safe. Nobody had a problem taking it because they knew I'd look after them.

I never found any of the boys were sloppy with their finish. Some moves were stiffer than others but I always liked those. They looked more convincing. The stiffest of all was Bradshaw's clothesline. A man could literally be knocked out by that because he swung that arm from left-field. I always looked forward to our matches because of the physicality. He knew I liked to work stiff, so he brought it, and I knew I never had to worry about hurting that big bastard. If I could have worked with guys like that every night, I would have been happy. But when he came at me with that clothesline, I knew he was coming to try and take my head off!

Even though I had a finisher at last, I wasn't in a program on TV and was just putting people over, so they found a use for me as one of the trainers on the second season of the WWE reality show *Tough Enough*. Hunter apparently didn't like the show because he felt the business shouldn't be exposed any more than it already was. Hunter doesn't like anything that doesn't benefit Hunter. Reality TV was starting to go everywhere and our business had already been exposed as a work, so what else was there to expose? The whole concept was to find some new talent, put them under the same roof, and take them through an intense training process that would turn them into WWF superstars. They all were different personalities and it was a really interesting show.

My old friend Al Snow was the head coach on the series and I thought we worked well together. I work rough and he works light. We have two totally different styles but I think he's great. He did good cop, I did bad cop. *Tough Enough 2* was the highest rated show on MTV until the Osbournes came along, so we must have been doing something right. Doing that series was a wonderful experience. All of the trainers were good; we knew what we were doing. We had Chavo Guerrero and Ivory as trainers too. Ivory wasn't the greatest wrestler but she could work decently enough. She would get in the ring and roll around with the girls, showing them first hand what to do. I feel like she got a bit of a raw deal with WWE and they dicked her around, pushing people who couldn't work at her expense. She was always positive and upbeat — I don't think I've ever been around somebody who had so much energy.

The biggest problem with the show was that MTV wanted to control it. Each week, when we sat down to determine who was going to be eliminated, the MTV producers would try to intervene and tell us to keep certain people because they were "good for the show." We had to keep telling them that it was a competition to find the best fit for the *wrestling business*, not the best fit for the next week of their show. Of course we wanted good ratings but we weren't about to keep somebody who was useless just because they brought some drama to the show.

Out of everyone from season two, Matt Morgan went on to do the most in wrestling. During filming he tweaked his shoulder and had to quit, feeling he couldn't carry on. He got signed to a contract anyway and was later put on TV. He didn't get over. In his mind, he thought he was the best big man, above Kane, above 'Taker, above the Big Show. I didn't think he was any good, and if he had been, WWE would have kept him. They love big men. He looked good but he couldn't work and he couldn't get over. That's the bottom line. The fact that he quit *Tough Enough* because he got hurt just went to show he didn't have enough heart for the business. Jackie Gayda blew out her knee during filming but she sucked it up and got on with it. She finished the show, she was one of the two winners, and she got signed to a contract. I liked her; she was a good sport.

The other winner of *Tough Enough 2* was Linda Miles. During the show, she was a great personality and a really nice person but once they put her on TV and started giving her a push, you couldn't find a door big enough for her head to get through. She thought she was the whole show. We'd be on a tour overseas, three or four days in, and she would complain to anybody who would listen that she was worn out. She was so dramatic about it all. She had double standards in the ring too — she wouldn't hold back on anybody but complained loudly if anybody was the slightest bit rough with her. Her downfall came at an airport one day, waiting for our bags to come around the carousel. We hadn't been on the road long on this particular tour, but she already looked like she was about to pass out. When her bags came around, she told one of the newer guys to get them for her. He was *told*, mind you; she didn't ask. The guy asked her why he should get them and she snapped, "I'm too tired to get them, so *you* get my bags for me *now*." All the boys turned around and looked at her as if to say, "Who the fuck do you think you are?" The guy rightly refused and she got *seriously* pissed. Word got back to the office about all of this. Combined with her continual whining and diva-like behavior, they decided to get rid of her. She thought she was a huge star who deserved more than what she was getting. Nobody is bigger than the company, least of all Linda fucking Miles!

When *Tough Enough* got picked up for a third season, I asked to be a coach again but they told me they had plans for a storyline involving me, so I wouldn't be able to do it. They didn't tell me anything else about this storyline so I suspected they were lying to me. Meanwhile, they kept using me to help the new guys along. I was fine with that because I enjoyed it. I can lead somebody and I can help them learn. Being a coach on *Tough Enough* had showed me I was very good in that role.

In mid 2002, Randy Orton started with WWE and they asked me to work with him in his TV debut. They knew he was a hothead so they wanted me to test him. J.R. came to me and said, "We want you to beat the shit out of this kid, let's see what he's made of." They wanted to see if *he* was tough enough. I really worked him over to see if he was going to get mad. I was super rough with him. He never complained. Look at him now; he's one of the best in the business. Even back when he started, all the potential was there. He was green but he listened and he did what he was told. His attitude and his temper did get him into trouble elsewhere though. He got pushed fast and started making money for the company, so he got away with a lot. He failed several drug tests but wasn't really reprimanded. I think he got suspended a couple of times but nowhere near as many as he should have been. He probably should have been fired for his behavior at times.

We were in Spain at one point when he was World Champion and we were heading to Germany. Our flight had been delayed due to a hole in the fuel tank, so we were waiting at the hotel. Randy had been whining the whole trip about wanting to go home and wanting time off because his wife was pregnant. If you're the World Champion, you don't get time off — that's the price you pay for being World Champion! Considering the amount of money you make in that role, you'd better damn well stay because you've got to earn it. He lost his temper so badly that he destroyed a five-star hotel room, causing over $15,000 worth of damage. We were all in the banquet room, waiting for another plane while Randy was off wrecking everything he could get his hands on. Triple H left his credit card with the desk and told them to charge the cost of the repairs to him. Admittedly, I thought that was pretty damn noble. Do you think Randy got fired for his actions? Of course not. If that had been somebody at my level, management wouldn't have thought twice about it. They would have said, "Send him home, he's done." Hell, if I'd caused 15 *cents* worth of damage, they probably would have got rid of me.

Randy was still in a bad mood when he came downstairs. There was some kind of road rally, like a cross country race with exotic race cars, going on. There were 20 of these expensive cars all lined up and we were about ten feet away as we got on the bus. Randy got ready to kick in one of the doors — he reared up, but Dean Malenko grabbed him and told him to knock it off. Randy was way out of control at that point.

A lot of people on the internet have spread stories about Randy, many of which are true, but the bottom line about Randy is that he's a good guy who can also be an ass — and that's something you can say about almost anyone. He's had a baby since then, and that straightened him up, which it damn well should have. That baby made a big difference in the way he chose to make decisions, and he stopped the stupid behavior. Having a baby will change anybody — it opens your eyes. You've got somebody who depends on you now and you have to say, "Okay, I've got a responsibility and I've got to take care of it."

CHAPTER 26
PUSHING THROUGH THE PAIN BARRIER

Another new guy who came along in 2002 was Brock Lesnar. He was a huge monster who was also a great amateur wrestler, so management strapped a rocket to his ass and gave him the WWE Championship soon after his debut. He was still pretty green, so they put him with veterans to learn. They asked me to work with him on an episode of *Smackdown* in September of that year. It was just going to be your typical match; I go out there, make him look good, and then get beat. I came up with the idea that he would go to powerbomb me, I would sit out and land on my feet, and we'd go into the finish from there. He was cool with that — Brock was very easy to work with, willing to listen and follow instruction.

When the time came for us to go home, we set up for the powerbomb but when he lifted me up, our timing was off. I jumped at a different time than he lifted, so I didn't manage the rotation I needed in order to get up on his shoulders. I tried to correct it but we were both really sweaty — he tried to hold on to me but he couldn't, and I ended up coming down on my neck. If you watch the footage, it looks like he drove me into the mat. As soon as I landed, I knew something was wrong. Everything in my neck just crunched. My whole body went numb — it was horrifying. Brock knew something wasn't right, so he gave me a moment to come back around as the ref asked if I was all right. I said I wasn't sure. I figured I'd be fine as soon as I was able to move a bit, so I said we should carry on and finish. It was a taped show, so we did the powerbomb spot again, in case they wanted to edit out the first attempt that went wrong. We did it fine this time — I got the rotation, landed on my feet, and dropkicked him. It looked good. We went from there and ended the match with him beating me with his finish. When we got to the back, Brock was upset, saying, "Man, I'm sorry, I feel like shit." He was trying to blame himself. I told him it was all me because I hadn't managed to sit up on the powerbomb. He didn't drop me on purpose, I knew that.

I went into the locker room and lay down on the trainers' table. Johnny Laurinaitis came in and asked if I was all right before he went in search of Brock. The trainer brought me some ice and was looking at my neck when Brock walked in. He apologized again; I could tell he felt horrible. I told him that it was an accident. Wrestling ain't ballet! Brock said that Johnny had just chewed his ass out, telling him that he'd only been there for six months and he couldn't be hurting guys like that. I told him I'd speak to Johnny and make sure he knew Brock wasn't to blame for the accident.

I've heard a lot of people claim Brock dropped me on my head on purpose because I wasn't cooperating with him on the powerbomb — that I wanted to make him look bad, so I didn't bother jumping properly and that I got what I deserved when he dropped me. Where these people got this idea, I don't know. I think these people were happy to have seen me get hurt. It boggles my mind that there are people like that, and I guarantee that these people who started rumors from their computers wouldn't say a damn word to my face. Nobody ever asked me about what happened or tried to get to know me before passing judgment, they just went ahead and made assumptions. Anybody who has ever learned to wrestle can look back at that footage and see that our timing was off and the whole thing was just an accident. Nothing more, nothing less.

I went home after the taping and rested up. I thought I'd give it a few days and I'd be fine. It was when I went to the refrigerator and tried to grab some lasagna with my left arm that I knew something was really wrong. I nearly dropped it. It was a pretty damn heavy dish but I should have been able to lift up some lasagna, right? I was able to hold it with my right hand. I tried again with my left. Couldn't do it . . . something *was* wrong. I thought I'd give it another week or so and see how it felt.

I went back on the road later that week and got back in the ring, figuring this was just another injury I was going to have to work through. Time would heal me. I was doing a tag match when I took a bump and it felt like somebody nailed me with a sledgehammer between my shoulder blades. A regular bump shouldn't have hurt that damn bad, so I told the trainers and they agreed that something wasn't right. The next night, I was in another tag. The agents told me to stay on the apron and avoid hurting myself. I said I'd just do the comeback and wouldn't take any bumps. They were fine with that. We built up to it, I got the tag, I came in to do my stuff, and I threw a punch at one of the other team. It felt like somebody had drilled *me*. I did nothing but punch somebody and it hurt *me*? Yeah, something was definitely wrong. The next day, they sent me to get an MRI and that was when we found out that I had a ruptured disc in my neck, cracked vertebrae, and pinched nerves. They lined me up for neck surgery right away. I was definitely not going to be doing anything any time soon . . . or so I figured.

After I'd been booked for the neck surgery, I got a call from the office, saying that they needed me to fly to L.A. to do a cameo on *Tough Enough 3*. My arm was basically numb at this point and I was very uncomfortable but I said I'd do it. I went out there and met the guy in charge, "Big" John Gaburick. He said, "I know you're in pain and having surgery tomorrow, so I don't want you getting in the ring." I said we'd see and that if I needed to get in there, I'd get in there. But the plan was for me to be there in a purely advisory capacity. I was supposed to give the show's trainees some advice on the wrestling business, how the locker room is, and how to make it as a professional. I'd done some talking and given them some advice, and towards the end of the day I watched these guys in the ring. They were doing a round-robin thing where they would tag in, do some spots in the ring, and then tag out. They were laughing and joking around — that was it. I started to get pissed off with these wannabes. Wrestling is supposed to be serious! People can get hurt and these guys didn't have a clue what was going on. By this point, they should have understood that whenever you've got an audience, you've got to be serious. This was going out on TV and they were clowning around! I told Big that I wanted to get in the ring, so they stopped the whole thing and said to the cast, "We're going to do Bob, Al Snow, and Bill Demott in there against you guys — you all tag in and out against these three."

Since they hadn't listened to what I'd said earlier, I felt I needed to educate these kids physically. There's a time and a place for kidding around and having a good time, and it's not when you're in front of a television camera. I take wrestling seriously and wasn't about to let these little fuckers act like goofballs. When I got in there, I'm sure they could see in my eyes that I was not fixing to laugh and have a good time. I was there to work and teach these guys what the wrestling business is all about.

Matt Cappotelli happened to be in there when I got in. I knocked him down in the corner and started stomping on him — as I've said a million times already, I work stiff but I don't set out to hurt people. But he was flailing around and trying to move. I wanted him to stay down but he was not following my lead. Anybody who wrestles knows that if you are in the ring with someone more experienced than you, you go where he puts you and he controls what happens. Cappotelli should have known it too, but he still squirmed and tried to get up. He ended up getting a boot in the mouth, which busted him open. The producers from MTV wanted Big to step in and stop the match but he told them not to be stupid — it was part of wrestling! I guess reality got too real for MTV.

Sure, I got rough with him, I'll admit it — but I'm rough with everybody! I took it upon myself to teach him what wrestling is like. Wrestling is a rough business. I didn't bust his nose or do anything to him that hasn't been done to me — or that wouldn't be done to him at some point in his career. Big understood what was going on. Bill DeMott sided with me. Al didn't like it but he was the mother hen of the series — he coddled those guys. Whenever they were hurt, they went to him and he would nurse them back to health and make sure they were okay. That's not how wrestling works and Al wasn't doing them any favors. I was trying to introduce them to the real wrestling business because it's not laughing and kidding around. It's serious.

The next day, they filmed Matt Cappotelli crying like a little fucking girl, saying he wanted to go home because he'd been roughed up a little bit. He had a black eye and a busted lip. I can't tell you how many black eyes and busted lips I've had and not once did I ever complain about it. Here was this kid on a show called *Tough Enough* and he was ready to go home because he got a little hurt. They ended up talking him into staying — they should have let him quit, as far as I'm concerned. If he was going to go on TV and cry about me being rough with him, he had no business in wrestling. Years later, he ended up with a brain tumor and I felt really bad for him, but he would never have made it in the business. I knew it because of the way he carried on after his run-in with me. He didn't think getting hurt was part of the business. Are you kidding me? I was there with cracked vertebrae and a shattered disc in my neck, about to go into surgery the next day, and I was in there teaching him how to work, getting on with it. He got his lip busted open and he wanted to quit the business? Wrestling was definitely not for him.

To be completely honest, I was not much rougher on Matt than I was with anybody else. I'm pretty much the same with everybody. When I'm a little bit rougher with somebody now and then, it's to test them, to see if they can take it. I'd seen Matt in training earlier that day, and I thought he was decent enough for what skills he had, good enough to make it. My whole perspective on him changed when I saw him whining on TV. I lost all respect for him right there. I felt like saying, "Come on, grow up. This isn't fucking kindergarten . . ."

The only other guy who impressed me that season was John Morrison. He and Matt were the best guys by a mile. It's funny, but when John started for real with WWE after he and Matt won *Tough Enough*, he was wary of me, but after a couple of years in the business, he came up to me and said, "Bob, now I understand why you did what you did back then. I get it now. You didn't do anything wrong." He said he appreciated my help in training him and making him understand how wrestling was. He got it.

My neck surgery happened the day after I shot that session for *Tough Enough*. It went fine but I knew it was going to be a long time before I healed properly. Vince called me afterwards to check on me. So did Brock — he called a few times to apologize again. I kept telling him not to worry. The writing team called as well and said that the whole internet was buzzing about the thing with Cappotelli. The replay of that episode was the highest-rated replay MTV had ever had at that point. The writers said that it was a damn shame that I'd had to have surgery because there was a great story there! They said they could have used it to make me one of the top heels in the company but the timing was just horrible. I was like, "Well, that figures . . ."

At least I had a ready-made feud with Brock to come back to, providing the writers didn't sweep it under the rug like they did when Kurt Angle broke my arm. I wasn't confident of anything. I ended up spending over a year off TV. The company looked after me financially while I was off, paying me every cent that was in my contract, so that was one less thing to worry about. Still, I was itching to do something and be useful. I wasn't on *WrestleMania XVIII* or *XIX,* I damn sure wanted to be on the card at *XX.*

PART 11: GENUINE TOUGHNESS

People can talk all they want to about how certain wrestlers are too rough or don't work soft enough, but last time I checked, wrestling was a contact sport. I don't know what some people who get in that ring are expecting, but we sure as hell aren't going to go ballroom dancing. If they have a problem with getting hurt, then they're in the wrong business because they haven't got the heart for wrestling. Having heart isn't something you learn, it's something you're born with. Either you've got it or you don't.

Wrestling is a tough business. Some people talked about me being a bully — those people don't know a thing. Because I played the gimmick of being a no-nonsense, grumpy bastard, my critics just assumed I beat people up. If I'd been given the Doink gimmick, nobody would have accused me of being a bully. I still would have gone out there and done my job so well you couldn't have slid a piece of paper between my fist and the other guy's forehead. Sure, I was rough in the ring but I wasn't the only one. I accept I was one of the roughest out there — probably top 10% — but there were a few people even *I'd* think twice about fucking with.

Obviously Steve Blackman is top of the list — he is as dangerous as they come. Kurt Angle and Ken Shamrock are legit badasses too, but Blackman would take them out in a heartbeat. Steve is so quick — I rolled with him a couple of times in practice, and before I knew it I was on my back. I'm decent enough at amateur wrestling to roll with some of the guys but nowhere near Steve's or Kurt's level. I countered Steve one time and threw him. He didn't like that, so I got out of the ring in a flash. I didn't want to die . . .

Dave Finlay might actually be the toughest guy in the locker room. I'm a cupcake compared to him. We've talked about Bradshaw already. Ron Simmons is just as tough as everybody says. You don't fuck with Ron. Shelton Benjamin is legit tough too. He'll tie you in a knot and make you smell your ass real quick. Steve Regal can go too; he's a great talent and one tough motherfucker. Brian Kendrick would surprise you — he will take an ass-kicking and then fight back hard. If you try to kick his ass, you're going to be there for a while. He's so quick, he'll make you wish you never started in on him. Same with Paul London — those two might not look tough, but you don't want to mess with them. I wish they'd been given a better push, because they were two of the best WWE had. If management had given them a microphone and let them just be themselves, they would have made everybody a lot of money.

On the other hand, there are guys management wants you to believe are tough, but they're not. It's a shame because in MMA, the toughest of the tough are the champions. In the make-believe world of wrestling, some of the champions wouldn't do too well in a real fight. Cena can't fight. Triple H genuinely thinks he is a badass motherfucker and he really isn't. Kevin Nash picked his spots — he would only call out guys he knew he could take. He wouldn't have fought me because he knew I'd kill him. Steve Austin wasn't as tough as they made him out to be on TV. I like Steve but that's the truth. I'm not saying all these guys are pussies, but I wouldn't want them to be backing me up in a bar fight. I'd want Blackman, Bradshaw, and Ron Simmons. Those are the guys to have in your corner.

A few of the boys have tried their hand at MMA when they got done with wrestling. Dave Batista had a great look for wrestling but I wasn't sure how well MMA would work out for him. Once, when I was playing around with Dave in the ring before a show in Louisville, I tied his ass up. Kevin Fertig and a bunch of the other boys saw this go down. Dave started panicking and yelling, "Let me go!" Everybody laughed. He started in on Booker at another point and Booker knocked his ass out cold.

I really like Dave but I don't think MMA is for him. In his first match, he was lucky he won. He was on defense the whole time until he got a takedown. I don't know how far he's going to get in MMA because there's a difference between fighting some overweight guy and competing at the top level. Still, he said he was going to do it and he did, so people need to get off his back.

Obviously the most famous wrestler to go into MMA is Brock Lesnar. Before Brock got into MMA, I thought he might be the baddest man on the planet, but not any more. He may not be the baddest but he's still one tough motherfucker — you have to be to win the UFC title. I was surprised when Brock quit MMA but maybe I shouldn't have been. He seems like he's still trying to find his niche in the world and, once the fun is gone from something, he moves on. He has that financial freedom so he's not motivated to keep going once he loses interest. Brock was perfect for MMA until his opponents figured out that he didn't like to be hit in the face. It's a shame, because if he had been able to take a punch, he could have been the all-time best in MMA. I would have loved to have fought Brock. I don't know who would have won. You can never tell. If he wrestled me, I wouldn't have a chance. If we were to stand there and throw punches, I bet I could beat him. I've proved I can take a punch.

I wish I'd been able to get into MMA early in my career. It started getting big in the mid '90s but suddenly died. Then it exploded again about a decade later. By that time, I was too far along in my wrestling career, and my body was too broken to do it. If I'd have been 20 years younger, there's no question in my mind — I would have trained to go into MMA rather than wrestling. How would I have done? It's hard to say, but if I'd had decent training, I think I would have been good. It's become so technical now that you've got to be well rounded in everything. If you're not, you won't be fighting for very long. I'd definitely have trained for at least a year before having my first fight.

I think I would have enjoyed the challenge. As far back as I can remember, through my teenage years and my bar-fighting days, I've thrived on fighting. To this day, if anybody fought me, whether I won or not, I'd enjoy the challenge of the fight. But it's way too late for me to start MMA now. It's frustrating that my body is broken after almost three decades of wrestling, but it is what it is. When you get into wrestling, you know it's the price you will pay. You accept it and go on.

CHAPTER 27

COMING BACK FOR BROCK

They didn't really build up much for my return. They asked me to fly up to Stamford and record a promo, which was fine. I had no idea what they wanted until we got there, but at least they were definitely going to have me work with Brock. We did a 30-second vignette where I said that Brock had taken 12 months of my life and now I was coming for him . . . I wasn't coming for his title, I was coming to hurt him. It was a good promo but I thought they could have done a few more and built it up bigger. It was a good, real angle that could have drawn money.

Brock didn't want to work with me. That didn't help. He was fine with me when the injury happened and he was fine with me afterwards, but when our first match had happened, I was just somebody to get him over. When I came back, I was still not a top guy. They were going to put me, a mid-level job guy for about a decade, in there with the company's biggest monster? Believe me, I understood why Brock wouldn't want to work with me — he thought he damn sure wasn't going to make any money from that. I wasn't a draw, and unless they promoted the return really well, I wasn't going to be. As always, it was down to how they presented it onscreen. They didn't build me up enough to make me look like a threat to him. There was no reason why not — we had a solid, genuine reason why I would want to fight him and hurt him. That's easy for the fans to buy into. But rather than doing it properly, they hot-shotted the idea and threw it together too quick.

A couple of weeks after the promo aired, they had me tape a conversation with Paul Heyman, the GM of *Smackdown*. Then Paul banned me from the building, promising that if I left immediately, I'd be on the team against Brock at *Survivor Series*. After doing the promo where I said I was coming back to hurt Brock, here I was, putting my tail between my legs and behaving myself. It didn't make sense to me. We got to *Survivor Series* and they had me attack Brock before the match started. I got a few shots in before they disqualified me and sent me to the back. The idea was to stop us from having anything more than brief physical contact so that people would want to see us fight more. On *Smackdown* the next week, they had me run in from the crowd and attack Brock. It got a fucking huge pop and the crowd was into it. Then Heyman suspended me indefinitely. Even though the first promo hadn't been enough, this was starting to get good. A couple of weeks later, they had me do the same thing — this time, I dressed up as a fan with a mask, jumped the rail, and beat on Brock until officials separated us. Again, it got a huge reaction. We had the ball rolling now, they just needed to put me over some people to make me look like I could actually be a threat to Brock.

Heyman put a match together for which he would choose my tag partner and we would have to fight A-Train (a massive jobber) and Matt Morgan (the big rookie from *Tough Enough 2*). If I won, I would be reinstated. If I lost, I'd be gone for good. He gave me Shannon Moore, a guy who did frequent jobs, as my partner and we won. It was meant to help me get over but I beat one new guy (Morgan) and one guy who everybody beat (A-Train). That wasn't enough to get me to Brock's level. They figured then that they'd have me go over on the Big Show and *that* would be enough. But everybody beat the Big Show back then! We did two matches on *Smackdown* and, in the first one, I lost by disqualification because I kicked him square in the balls. This set up a no-DQ match the next week, and I beat him clean and bloodied him up. That was supposed to be what made me a threat to Brock, but it was too little, too late as far as I was concerned. I beat Big Show once and beat some irrelevant guys in tag matches. I told the writers that I needed to be beating guys who meant something, rather than being a jobber who was beating other jobbers. If they wanted to make something of me, they should have had me cutting through Heyman's guys and beating them clean, one on one. If it got me over and I was able to draw money with Brock, great. If it didn't, at least I'd be higher up the card and they would be able to use me to get some other guys over more. It seemed like a win-win situation to me, but what do I know . . .

We were set to have our match at the *Royal Rumble* — and it was a pretty big deal for me to be in the WWE Championship match on one of the three biggest shows of the year. It was definitely the highest up the card I had ever been. You could say it was the biggest match of my career. We had been given 15 minutes, including our entrances. There was enough time there to build up some drama and make me look like I might actually be able to beat Brock and win the title. I knew that nobody was really taking me that seriously as a contender but if I was able to look strong against Brock, that would really help me. We laid out a pretty good match — even though Brock hadn't wanted to work with me, he was very giving in the ring and unafraid to sell for me.

When we got to Gorilla to warm up, we were told, "You've got eight minutes now — including entrances." They halved the length of the biggest match of my career so that Shawn and Hunter, who were following us, could have the extra time and go long. I thought it was selfish as hell. They had both worked on top for years — including working together on pay-per-view four times in the past 18 months! They would go on to work with each other another four times on PPV in 2004. All main events. You're telling me they needed those extra seven minutes more than Brock and I did?

We had to throw out whole chunks of our match. A lot of the drama was lost. I thought it ended up pretty decent but at about six and a half minutes, I believe it is one of the shortest WWE title matches ever. Hunter and Shawn then went out and wrestled for nearly 23 minutes — and they had 29 minutes with entrances and post-match. 32 minutes if you include the video package before the match. With video package, entrances, and match, we had a fraction over 10 minutes. That was it — my run on top. One short match with Brock that played second-fiddle to Shawn and

Hunter working for the millionth time. Maybe management thought I wasn't over enough to deserve more time but I was what they made me. They treated me like an afterthought pretty much the whole way through my return and my run with Brock. I figured I would at least get one good payoff for my *Rumble* match. I'd heard that being in a world title match at the *Rumble* means about forty to fifty grand for the guy doing the job because it's an advertised championship match; it's one of the highlights of the show. When I got that check in the mail, I couldn't believe it. Five thousand dollars. You think Shawn and Hunter got five thousand dollars for their match?

Brock didn't stick around long after that match. He'd reached a point where he said, "This isn't for me." He got on TV, was heavily pushed for two years, beat almost everybody, and then decided he'd had enough. He was criticized for doing that but what was he supposed to do? He didn't ask to be pushed that much to get launched into stardom. He worked as hard as they worked him. WWE was always going to push him to the moon. He was this huge guy who had a great look and he could actually wrestle. He was going to draw, so WWE was going to push him. Brock was never arrogant or expectant. As successful as he got, he didn't change — he never acted like he was above everybody else. Once he realized that he didn't want to be there anymore, he couldn't be expected to stick around for six months to put over the people who made him a star. He had other opportunities and he took them. At least he was man enough to stand up in a production meeting and tell everybody he was quitting. How many other guys stood up in front of all the boys and said that? Brock is all right by me. WWE made money off the guy and continued to do so even when he wasn't working there.

Brock's last night with the company during that run was *WrestleMania XX*, a night that ended with two of my best friends, Eddie Guerrero and Chris Benoit, in the ring as WWE Champion and World Champion respectively. Eddie had won his title from Brock the month before. I was happy for him because he'd overcome his demons, worked hard to accomplish something, and reached the top of the industry. *'Mania* was Chris Benoit's crowning moment, with him winning the World title in the main event of the biggest show of the year. That's success right there. They both made it to the top, as far as you can go — I was so happy to see my friends succeed. I wasn't the only one. Everybody — from the fans in the arena to the boys backstage — had wanted Chris to win the title at 'Mania against Hunter and Shawn. Everybody wanted to see it but nobody expected that management would actually go through with it. Everyone was tired of seeing the same guys get the title over and over. The World title always seemed to stay with the same guys — Hunter's new Clique. If you go back and look at who had the World title from its inception in 2002 through to the beginning of 2006, in only six of those 40 months was that belt *not* around the waist of somebody in Hunter's circle. Benoit was allowed to have it for a few months, Goldberg was allowed to have it for a few months, but the rest of the time it was Shawn, Randy, Batista, or Hunter. Usually Hunter. They just wanted all the money for themselves. As I said before, it's selfish — just like when they cut back my one match at the top of the card, basically ending my comeback push. I didn't even get to work on the card at *WrestleMania*. They found 50 spots on the show that year. Fifty spots and after 10 years on the payroll, I wasn't in their top 50.

They put together a couple of 10-minute matches with eight or 10 guys in there to try and fit everybody on the card; the payoff those guys got would have been nothing, like a thousand dollars, but it was still a chance to gain exposure from being on the biggest show of the year. I paid my dues in that company, I crawled before I got a chance to think about walking. Other guys would come in, the company would invest money in them, and then they'd get fired or leave — and I'm not talking about Brock here, I'm talking about guys much lower on the card, guys who were no good and were never going to draw a dime for the company — and I was still there, not complaining, doing what I was told, working hard, and still being overlooked. It was hurtful. That year especially, I felt like I deserved to be in *WrestleMania*.

PART 12: WRESTLING FANS

Whether I won or lost — and I lost more than I won — the fans who supported me were loyal. You can't ask for better fans than that. I always wanted to go out and do my best for that guy or girl who paid to cheer me on. I might not have had as many fans as some of the other boys but I loved the shit out of the fans who supported me. There are some strange ones — I've been asked to sign bras and panties, a baby's arm, a diaper . . . but you treat all the fans the same. I like to treat them all like they're my only fan.

Even though I've now retired, I still get noticed in public. I'll see the look on someone's face, how they'll start eyeballing me and wagging the finger. "You look just like that wrestler," they'll say, ". . . like that guy on TV." Now, if I'm in a crowded public place, I don't want to attract a lot of attention. I'm always cordial to anybody who approaches me but I won't always admit who I am. It sort of depends how I'm feeling that day. A lot of the time, I'll ask them a trick question, just to see what they do.

"Hardcore Holly?" I'll say.

"Yes! That's him — you look just like him."

"Yeah, I get that a lot. Everybody tells me that. I don't watch wrestling, so I don't know. Is he any good? If I look like him, he'd better be good!"

Not once has anyone ever said, "No, he's terrible" — they usually say, "Yeah, he's really good." A lot of people say, "They should have done more with him." I leave it there but often I then feel guilty and end up going back to the person and saying, "Yeah, I'm the wrestler." If the person is a wrestling fan, they get a kick out of meeting a guy who worked for WWE.

One time, after I'd put my groceries into the car, I decided to go back and talk to a guy who had asked if I was "Hardcore Holly."

I went all over the store but couldn't find him — I actually felt really horrible about it because I think it would have made his day. A couple of months later, I was having some work done on my basement and one of the guys doing the work just happened to be that same guy! Needless to say, I apologized to him and told him that I had tried to find him that day to let him know he was right. He thought it was pretty funny, and after I'd given him an 8 x 10 autographed picture, all was forgiven.

At the arenas, some of the fans take it too far. They've bought a ticket, so it's their right to yell things and boo or cheer who they want, but there comes a point when they should watch their mouths and show some respect. At a house show back when I was on one of my heel runs, I'd just got to the ring and the crowd was booing and hurling abuse at me; it was a full house with about 13,000 people there, so it was pretty loud, but I could hear one guy about five rows back above everybody else. He was acting like a big shot, showing off in front of his buddies. I shouted that he should sit down before I came over there and beat his ass. Standard heel behavior. This guy wouldn't shut up though; he got louder, yelling and cussing, daring me to come over the railing and saying that *he* would beat *my* ass. I said, "Yeah, you dare me?" I'm not one to back down from a dare, so I jumped over the railing and walked right up to him. I got in his face and said, "You gonna beat my ass?" He didn't even look at me — he just sat right down and shut up. I don't blame him; this is back when I was gassed to the gills and ready to go! That whole arena started in on him, chanting, "You're a pussy!" Even his friends joined in. Suddenly I was the babyface. . . . That was pretty good.

Another time, a fan crossed the line at a show in Montreal. This was back in the Attitude era. Pretty much anything went, but I felt there were still boundaries of common decency. This guy in the crowd just stuck his camera right in my face, an inch or two from my eyes, and took a picture. I wheeled around and said, "You're not even gonna ask if you can take a picture?" He just laughed and said, "I don't have to ask you for shit." Well, I thought that was pretty disrespectful so I told him, "You take another picture and see what happens." He kept on laughing and said, "You ain't gonna do shit to me," and stuck the camera right in my face again. I smacked that sumbitch out of his hands so fast that he didn't have time to blink. It hit the ground and smashed into pieces. I don't mind people taking pictures, but if you're going to stick a camera right in my face, you'd better ask first and show a little respect. The guy wasn't laughing anymore. He said, "You can't do that!" I looked him in the eyes, said, "I just did," and walked off.

Sometimes, you get famous people coming to shows and thinking they're allowed to act differently because they're celebrities. I was wrestling D-Lo Brown in Detroit and we worked our way onto the floor so I could get a hockey stick from underneath the ring. Just as I was fixing to nail D-Lo with it, somebody in the front row grabbed it. I jumped over the railing to confront the guy and he got in my face — so I shoved that motherfucker back three rows. He had a whole bunch of friends with him who went over and picked him up off the floor. When I got to the back after the match, I was told that the group of guys were the Detroit Red Wings and the guy I'd shoved was considered the toughest of the tough in the NHL. Tough or not, he didn't do dick-all to me after I shoved him on his sorry ass!

I look at male and female wrestling fans as all the same. Some of the boys don't — they have a different view of the female fans. I never put myself in a position that encouraged any of the females to throw themselves at me and wouldn't have gone for it if they had. There are some crazy fans out there that end up stalking wrestlers, and if you give them an opening, they're going to take it. I never crossed that line. Sure, I took in a few strays here and there during my travels but they weren't fans, just women I met on the road — usually at a gym or a restaurant.

At *WrestleMania* one year, I was in the hotel gym with Steve Austin. I was on the StairMaster and he was working out next to me. There was this girl who worked there, a really good looking woman.

Austin decided to fuck with me so as she walked past, he blurted out, "This guy wants to meet you." We talked for a bit and Steve made himself scarce. I think he was trying to embarrass me a little but it didn't work. I ended up spending pretty much the whole week at the woman's house. Thanks for the assist there, Steve!

CHAPTER 28
BACK ON MY BACK

2004 saw Bradshaw win the WWE title after having been a mid-card guy for years. Two things led to him getting the big push. Number one, Eddie was finding the pressure of being champion hard to take and he pushed hard for John to be the guy to take it off him. Number two, John and Vince had become really close because John, who is a real-life investment expert, had given Vince a heap of great ideas on that front — they were in the stock market together and that brought him and Vince closer. They needed a new heel, someone they could depend on at the top of the card, and John was in the right place at the right time with the right connections. I thought it was a good move to put the belt on somebody different rather than just cycling through the same guys, but I wasn't sure it would work with John. I was happy to be wrong there because it ended up working really well! John knew how to get heat and be a good heel. They kept the belt on him for a long time, and rightfully so. I loved his new J.B.L. gimmick but I also kind of wondered why they still weren't trying to do something different with me. I'd been around longer than him and I felt I could be just as good as him in a character. Yet they went with him on top and I kept on working underneath.

After working against Brock, I found myself back in the familiar position of working with newer talent and putting them over. It wasn't like when Jim Ross asked me to test Randy out a couple of years before though. Johnny Laurinaitis was in charge of talent now and he never asked me to "test anybody out." Instead, he wanted me to go out there, make the new guys work, and see what they could do. He knew he could trust me to carry anybody to a decent match and that if a new guy could hang with me without complaining, they were worth keeping around. Over the next year or so, I got to work with almost everybody on the *Smackdown* roster. There were a few people I thought had real potential.

Kevin Fertig came in as Mordecai, a sort of anti-Undertaker, and the idea was to build him as an opponent for the Dead Man. I worked with him at a PPV and put him over — I liked that match. Kevin and I had good matches. That guy can go and he's as rough and tough as anybody out there. He's super nice and very respectful, even if he can be a huge ass-kisser. He went as far as he could to live his gimmick, wearing white clothes, white shoes, white shirt everywhere he went. He was working hard to get the Mordecai gimmick over but he could only go so far without the writers and Creative on board. They lost interest in him after a couple of months and sent him back down to the developmental territories, saying he needed to learn how to work properly. I don't know why they did that — that guy could work just fine. They brought him back as a vampire a few years later, got bored again, and then fired him. That blows my mind.

Orlando Jordan was also a great worker. He was doing fine until it became apparent that he liked young guys. He ended up losing his job because he had all these young boys hanging around with him at the hotels, and that wasn't good for business. We're not talking illegal young — but it's not great publicity. Management wasn't comfortable with it. Another shame, because he was a great worker and a great guy. Who cares about his sexual preferences? After all, Pat Patterson works there!

Mercury and Nitro (John Morrison) were good — you can't deny that. I had some great matches with them both when I was tagging with Charlie Haas and when I was tagging with Booker T on house shows. That was what they did with some of the singles guys when Creative didn't have anything for them — they dumped us in a tag team to keep us busy.

Charlie Haas was good too. He worked his ass off, especially when he and Shelton Benjamin were tagging. Very few people know this but

Shelton and Charlie would get to the arenas early and work on their tag stuff. They'd grab a couple of enhancement guys and head to the ring at about 1 or 2 p.m., where they'd sweat their asses off. Working with Arn Anderson, they tried to improve as much as possible. Charlie really wanted to succeed.

Another tag team they brought in was the Highlanders. Rory was very respectful. Robbie, on the other hand, was a smartass who had an attitude because now that he was in WWE, he thought he was a big star. Creative were going to go with them as one of the top teams but Robbie blew that. Rory knew his place in the locker-room pecking order but Robbie thought he was *the man.*

I was doing a match in Europe with them when they first arrived and I threw a few chops at Robbie. He didn't sell any of them. Then he grabbed me and tried to turn me so he could start chopping. I blocked him and asked what the hell he was doing. He said, "Fucking turn around!" Yeah, that wasn't going to happen. If he was a guy I knew and had worked with enough to trust, I probably would have let him turn me, but I didn't know these guys yet. I didn't know if they were going to hot shot me or take liberties or whatever. I sure as hell wasn't going to let this new guy take over the match. I grabbed him by his throat, threw him back in the corner, and started to pummel him. I told him right then and there, "Don't you tell me what to do ever again, motherfucker." I tagged out quickly after that because I didn't want to lose my cool for real. When Charlie and I got to the back, I went up to Robbie and said, "Who the fuck are you to tell me what to do out there? Who are you to not sell my chops? Are you our World Champion? I've been here a lot longer than you, you've only just come in so you ain't shit. Just because we're putting you over, it doesn't mean you're better than us." I explained that my job was to do what was right for the match, not what was right for me or him. That is something you learn with experience. He was just doing things for no apparent reason. I told him he needed to listen to me in the future because I worked for the match, not for myself. We never had a problem after that, but he got a lot of heat from the boys for disrespecting me. He went to watch a TNA show live and was shown on TV in the crowd while he was under contract to WWE. What a fucking dumb move that was. They both got let go for that.

For every decent worker they brought in who had potential, they brought in other guys who were trouble backstage, didn't work hard enough, or were just plain awful.

Jon Heidenreich was the biggest waste of money that company ever spent. That guy needs to be in a loony bin. He was a fucking maniac from the word go. He would show up late when they were trying to push him. We were supposed to report to the arena on TV days by 1 p.m. but he would show up about 7:30 p.m. When Johnny Laurinaitis told him that he'd get fined if he carried on showing up late, Heidenreich threatened to beat Johnny up, then go and beat up Vince. . . . Fucking idiot — he didn't have a clue what he was doing. Fuck him and the horse he rode in on.

I couldn't understand why they went with Carlito at all. He was boring, he was slow in the ring, he wasn't a good worker, he telegraphed everything he was going to do . . . I just didn't get what they saw in him. He would complain backstage all the time and threaten to quit — and for a while, they catered to him! He got a good mid-card push and made some decent money, probably more than his talent and attitude deserved. He should have been grateful for it but all he did was complain. There were guys at his level, like Shelton Benjamin, who were so much better at what they did, but they went with Carlito and he was still always unhappy. I never understood that.

Simon Dean was a stooge. Nobody liked him. Any piece of information he could find out that would get somebody in trouble, he stooged them off. He ended up in management but they quickly realized he wasn't cut out for the position and let him go.

Luther Reigns was a big, impressive-looking guy but he just couldn't get it. He didn't understand how to put a story together, the psychology of why you might do a headlock or an armdrag, or why a babyface should shine at a certain time. He was a guy from Venice Beach who dabbled in entertainment and grew up as a wrestling fan. He figured he'd give it a go and because he looked impressive, WWE tried to make him a major player. He just couldn't wrestle, period. It was the wrong industry for him.

The Bashams didn't have the "*It* factor." Mark Jindrak was too worried about being pretty. Nunzio was too small. Kenzo Suzuki couldn't work or understand English but they pushed him anyway.

I put every single one of these guys over. As I write this, not a single one of them works for the company. They all started with WWE in or after 2003, when I'd already been in the company for almost a decade. Of them all, only John Morrison and Carlito outlasted me. All the rest of the guys didn't last much more than a year each, if that. I wasn't the only one putting them over. The company wasted good talent like Jamie Noble, Rhyno, and Val Venis, to name a few, by making them do neverending jobs to get these new guys over. Then, when all these guys didn't work out, all the talent who had been losing week after week were now worth nothing. What could they have achieved if they'd pushed me or the other guys instead? We were good, we were respected backstage, we fit in, and we worked hard. We'd proved ourselves but they kept going with these new guys and hoping that something would stick.

You need people to go out there and lose, sure. Some guys were ideal for that role — Funaki and Scotty 2 Hotty, for example. Good guys who were good workers but just weren't credible at a higher level because they were too small and didn't look like they had any killer instinct. Jamie Noble was a pit bull out there, and funny too. They kept starting things with him and then stopping for no reason. Rhyno was a good worker who deserved a break. Val Venis was always over but they ended up putting him underneath for no reason. Even Charlie Haas was used as a glorified enhancement guy. He should have been kept in his team with Shelton. They could have drawn money against La Resistance.

La Resistance. Now, *there's* a story . . .

Sylvain Grenier was Pat Patterson's boy. Everybody knew why he got the job and a good push to start out. That relationship lasted a while, but Pat got tired of the taste of the same candy over and over, so he decided to switch flavors. Pat wasn't a bad guy or anything and we always got on fine, but I probably didn't do myself any favors with him later in my career. I bent to pick something up and he happened to be there. He said, "If you bend over and I'm behind you, you're fucked." I shot right up and said, "No, motherfucker, if you touch me, *you're* gonna be fucked." He looked at me as if to say, "Hey, I was just kidding."

I definitely wasn't kidding though.

All the boys in the locker room couldn't believe what I'd said because Pat had a lot of stroke. Once Pat got bored of Sylvain, the guy didn't go anywhere. To Sylvain's credit, he did actually get better in the ring. I think they should have kept him together with René Duprée as La Resistance because they had that French heel thing going. Whenever they walked into the arena, it was automatic — you couldn't help but hate them. It was a natural gimmick with natural heat and if they'd been up against a team who meant something, they would have drawn money for the company. Management decided to break them up and see if they would sink or swim by themselves.

René Duprée had a lot of heat in the locker room because of the way he acted. Nobody liked him. He was a prick to everybody. His biggest misdemeanor was against me. The internet picked up on some of this story and made me out to be a bad guy, but as usual, they didn't have the facts. Here's what happened . . .

It was in the middle of 2004 and René was traveling with me for the first time. We'd been working house shows together so we figured we'd ride together to the TV taping. I thought he was a decent worker as a heel — he knew how to get heat, so it was easy to work with him. This was around that time bad hurricanes had been hitting so I had to get back home. Before I left, René asked if I could leave my rental car with him in Spokane. I told him that was fine as long as he made sure to fill the car up with gas before he returned it.

A couple of months passed without incident. Bradshaw and I were on a layover in the Houston airport, eating lunch, when my mom called to tell me that I'd got something in the mail from the City of Spokane District Court. When I was on the road, I had all my mail forwarded to her. She then told me that my driver's license had been suspended because of an unpaid parking ticket and that there was a warrant for my arrest in Washington. I just about blew a gasket. As it happened, René was walking by just as I got off the phone, so I confronted him about it. He told me that he didn't know what I was talking about and he'd never got a parking ticket using my rental. He totally denied it. Both Bradshaw and I had a few choice words for him. I ended up having to fly to Spokane, and it cost me the flight and a whole weekend of missed work including a TV taping. This wasn't cheap to take care of. René still denied it. Whenever I confronted him about it, he'd deny it and refuse to make it right. That really pissed me off, so I decided to take matters into my own hands. I gave him a little warning on the plane the day before I was planning to get even with him. I found I was sitting behind him, so I tapped him on the shoulder and told him, "You've got 24 hours to learn how to fight." All the boys turned around and looked at him, and René just sat there looking like a deer in the headlights. If he'd owned up right there and admitted his wrongdoing, that would have been it. Everything would have been fine. I guess he didn't think I was serious . . .

Twenty-four hours later, he still hadn't apologized. We were in Rochester,

New York, and the match was me and Charlie against René and Kenzo Suzuki. I started hitting René, laying it in and telling him to hit me back because we were fixing to go. He ran away from me — just took off backstage, where he thought he'd be safe. I went after him and caught him, dropped him, and proceeded to beat the living shit out of him. Big Show grabbed me from behind and threw me off him and Dave Finlay, who was an agent at that point, came over and said, "What the fuck, Bob?" I said, "No, what the fuck, Dave? You don't know?" I told him about the parking ticket situation. Dave responded, "He deserved to have his ass kicked." I fucked René up enough that they had to take him to the hospital for a bunch of scans. I got a call from Johnny Laurinaitis that night at the hotel, asking what happened. After I told him, he said, "You can't be doing that," and then started laughing. He carried on with, "But who am I to tell you that when I used to do that sort of thing myself?" He told me later that

Vince wasn't mad at me, but he didn't want this sort of thing going on any more. By TV on Monday, Vince's mood had changed — or been changed.

Johnny came to me and said, "Vince wants to see you in a bit and he's pissed. Somebody got in his ear and said that what you did to René was bullshit." I said, "Let me guess, that wouldn't be Hunter, would it?" Johnny told me he'd come to get me when Vince was ready. He advised me to stay quiet and listen to what Vince had to say. I thought, "Yeah, like I'm just going to sit there and take it . . ."

I went into Vince's office later — Johnny came with me because there always has to be a third party present in cases like this for legal reasons — and as soon as I sat down, Vince started in on me. I threw my hand up and said, "Whoa, whoa, whoa — don't sit here and yell at me when you don't know the story because I will just get up right now and walk the fuck out." Vince was taken aback. He couldn't believe somebody was talking to him like that. He looked at Johnny, then at me, and said, "Okay, tell me what happened." He went from yelling to being as calm as could be just like that. It was the only time Vince ever yelled at me.

I explained what had happened and started talking about the sort of person René was. I told Vince how he acted towards people in public, how he would talk down to waiters in restaurants if his food wasn't fixed right. I told Vince that he wasn't the sort of person who represented the company well and that I had kicked his ass because he deserved it. Vince said — and these are the words out of his mouth — "I don't know René, all I know is that the guy kisses my ass every time I walk by." He went on to say that the majority of the people who worked for him only ever told him how good his hair looked or how nice his tie was and he couldn't stand the ass-kissing. I couldn't believe he was telling me all of this. He said that he understood why I did what I did to René but he couldn't have that going on at his shows, so he was going to fine me $10,000. I said he could fine me as much as he wanted because I believed what I did was the right thing to do. René had refused to own up to what he'd done. He'd cost me my driver's license and he could have caused me to be thrown in jail. Nothing Vince said or did could have changed my mind. Vince shook my hand and said, "Just don't be doing that anymore in my ring — if you're going to do it, do it somewhere else." I said, "No problem. Can I do it in the locker room?" He knew I was joking and laughed. We left it there.

Later that day, Johnny came up to me and said, "When you told Vince to be quiet, I thought you were done . . ." After the meeting, apparently Vince turned to Johnny and said, "I have a lot of respect for that guy." A lot of people are intimidated by Vince because of his stature. But he ain't no different from anybody else — anyone can walk up and talk to him. I have no problem with Vince — I like him. He's a businessman and one of the smartest men in entertainment.

About a week after this all went down, René came to find me. He apologized and said that he shouldn't have thrown the parking ticket away, and he shouldn't have lied to me afterwards. He said he knew it had cost me a lot of money and he promised to pay me back. I told him not to worry about that. All that mattered was that he'd owned up to it and apologized. That was good enough for me. After that, our relationship was great. I never had a lick of trouble with him for the rest of his stay with the company, which, just like all of the other new guys, didn't last long.

Although I didn't have any more problems with René, I think this incident caused me big problems in the long run. I heard later that Hunter did interviews where he said that what I did was inexcusable and I was lucky to have not been fired. I guarantee that if Nash had been the one to kick René's ass, Hunter would have been fine with it all.

Instead of properly using the existing workforce, WWE tried to create new stars with another season of *Tough Enough*. MTV wasn't interested anymore, so WWE did it as a weekly segment on *Smackdown*. It was horrible. The whole concept just didn't work. A guy named Daniel Puder won and he got immediate heat in the locker room because of something he did with Kurt Angle. In one of the segments, the contestants were going to shoot fight with Kurt. Only it wasn't a shoot. They'd been told backstage it was going to be worked but presented as a shoot. Kurt ended up wrestling with Puder and was taking it easy, leaving himself exposed because he thought they were just working. Puder grabbed him in an armbar because Kurt basically let him have his arm. It *looked* like Puder had Kurt in trouble, and Kurt took offense to this. If it'd been a real fight,

Kurt would have stretched his ass in a heartbeat. All of a sudden, Puder was going around, bragging on the internet that he could beat Kurt Angle in a fight. All of the boys took offense.

After Puder won *Tough Enough*, they put him in house shows — against me of all people. My first night with him was in Lowell, Massachusetts. Here was a guy who had only just won a reality contest for a wrestling contract, with absolutely no clue how to work, and I had to put him over. I kept it quick and simple — took him out there, chopped him up, and he beat me with a roll-up. It was fine. The next day, Jimmy Yang told me about something that happened when he and Puder had been riding together to the next town. Apparently, he called his buddies and said, "Guess who I beat tonight?!" and was bragging about beating me. Jimmy said he was making it sound like he'd beaten me for real. I didn't say anything to Puder about this and just got on with my job. I put him over again that night, three minutes and finish with the roll-up. Afterwards, I asked Jimmy to let me know what he did in the car that night.

We flew into Chicago the next day and I caught up with Jimmy.

"Did he do it?" I asked.

"Yes, he called everybody and said he beat you again."

"Did he tell them that it was a work?"

"No, he was talking like he really beat you."

That was all I needed to hear. Chicago is a town with die-hard fans who want to see violence — and that night they were going to get their money's worth!

I started chopping Puder like I had in our first two matches. The crowd kept chanting "more!" so I kept on going. And going. And going. I stopped counting after 20. His chest was black and bloody. I just kept on chopping because they kept on chanting — and because Puder deserved it. He won the match and the crowd booed; they knew it was bullshit. I went up to him backstage and said, "When you're riding down the road, go ahead and call your friends and tell them that I let you beat me, because if this was a shoot, I would have stomped a fucking hole in your ass." Jimmy told me the next day that Puder hadn't said a damn word to his buddies in the car. What happened with Kurt went to his head, and he convinced himself that he'd beaten me for real. He was his own worst enemy. WWE gets rid of people like him real quick. Even if they'd kept him, he'd never have been any good — he was too into himself.

Before he got released, we had some fun with him. In the 2005 *Rumble* match, Eddie, Benoit, and I decided that we were going to mess with him a little bit to put him in his place and let him know he wasn't in charge. It was all in good fun. For us, at least.

Eddie and Benoit started the match and Puder came out third. I was out fourth and we all laid into him. It got to the point where Chris and I were taking him from each other to have our turn. Eddie was just hanging back and laughing. We were all laughing about it afterwards. Eddie was in such constant pain in those days that it was good to see him laugh.

PART 13: DRESSING FOR SUCCESS?

It's important to look good in the ring and you won't find many guys from WWE who don't have great gear. When I was there, everybody was expected to get gear that reflected the promotion's standing as the top in the industry. That went without saying. Where I took issue with them was when they started trying to dictate to me what I could wear when I *wasn't* on their shows.

Sometime during 2004, we were told there was going to be a meeting about a dress code. This came about because Johnny Stamboli got on a plane wearing an offensive T-shirt. I believe the T-shirt had on it something along the lines of "I'm going to fuck your mother." Word got back to Vince and he was pissed — understandably. He would have been within his rights to discipline Johnny after that, but Vince decided he wasn't going to give anybody else the option of doing that sort of thing, and that what was needed to help make WWE look more credible and professional was a dress code.

Word got out among the wrestlers that management was definitely going to tell us what we would wear when traveling to shows, and they were just trying to decide whether to go with suit and tie, or dress pants and shirts. Everybody was pissed about this in the locker room. I was pretty vocal about it but I wasn't the only one. When I said, "I'm damn sure going to say my piece in that meeting," everyone else was jumping in and saying, "I'm with you, I'm going to speak up too."

At the meeting, Vince told us he was implementing the dress code effective next week and we were all going to have to wear dress pants, shoes, and shirt. No jeans. No T-shirts. No exceptions.

Except for the guys whose gimmicks wouldn't make sense for him to be dressed up.

Then he said Steve Austin, Mick Foley, and John Cena were exempt. Two top guys and one guy they were grooming for the top spot. I stood up and said, "Okay, Vince, look at my gimmick — Hardcore Holly, tough guy redneck. Is Hardcore Holly going to wear dress pants and a nice pair of shoes?"

Vince looked at me and said, "He sure is."

I shook my head and said, "But that's not my gimmick."

"Well, that's what you're going to be wearing."

I stood there for the next 20 minutes and debated it with Vince in front of all the boys and not one of those sorry motherfuckers said *anything*. I told Vince that we were traveling all the time and needed to be comfortable. He just shot back, "Businessmen travel and they wear a suit and tie. I can make you guys wear suits and ties if I want." I pointed out that businessmen didn't travel as much as we did, and that we were on the road 24 hours a day sometimes in the same clothes. "Bring a change of clothes" was his reply. Any time I brought up a point, Vince just shot me down by basically saying that "this is my company and this is what I want."

Back in the locker room, I was pissed. Everybody was thanking me for speaking up and defending them. I just said, "All you mother-fuckers do is talk for the sake of hearing your own voices. When it comes down to it, you're not going to say a damn word because you're so job-scared." I couldn't believe they were all thanking me for speaking up when they could have done it for themselves but didn't have the balls.

So we had a dress code. Hardcore Holly, angry redneck, had to dress up. Chris Jericho, rock star, had to dress up. Eugene, mentally challenged manchild, had to dress up. Even Kane, a pyromaniac, was sure to put on nice pants and a dress shirt before he went about his business. The Undertaker didn't have to — he chose to. That's the sort of man 'Taker is. If the boys are going to have to do something, he'll do it too.

We had to observe the dress code whenever we went out in public on the way to or from shows. This included if we were going to the gym, or even if we were going for breakfast at the hotel. I'd always worn track pants and a good T-shirt — I looked fine and like an athlete. Now I had to dress like a businessman, even though I was supposed to be an independent contractor? I was so against it. Every day, I would dress any damn way I wanted and pull up in my car about a mile away from the arena to change into my dress clothes. Then I'd go right to the locker room and change back into something comfortable. I did that for years and they never got wise to it.

The only time I got into any trouble was when we were on a European tour. I decided to not bother with the dress code at all because we were overseas and always traveling, so I wanted to be comfortable. One morning, when we were all checking in at an airport, referee Mike Chioda was still drunk from the night before and, when he saw me in my cargo shorts, T-shirt, and tennis shoes, yelled out, "Nice dress code, Bob" really loudly. I just stared a hole through him and Hunter grabbed him by the collar, saying, "Shut your fuckin' mouth, Mike." Word got back to the office on this because Timmy White had to mention it in his agent's report, so Johnny Laurinaitis took me aside and gave me a slap on the wrist. He didn't fine me; he just said, "Don't do it again." Hunter, to his credit, didn't say a word about any of this as far as I know. He told Mike, "You had no business saying that to him" at the airport and then let it drop. I know Hunter was reporting to Vince daily at this point, so I was surprised that he didn't say anything more about it. Sometimes he stuck up for the boys; sometimes he threw them under the bus. You never knew where you stood with him.

When it comes to any sort of dress code in wrestling, as far as I'm concerned, an athlete dresses like an athlete and a businessman dresses like a businessman. You didn't see Vince putting many of us in business class on the flights and you didn't see businessmen sitting in coach either, so the least he could have done with the amount we traveled was to let us wear comfortable clothes.

CHAPTER 30

EDDIE

Chris, Eddie, and I were pretty close. We rode together for a while, but I couldn't deal with Eddie's travel habits for long. He was always on his own clock. If we agreed to leave at a certain time, Eddie would show up 30, 40 minutes later . . . it was the same with going to the gym. Eddie did things when Eddie was ready. In the end, I told Chris that I couldn't deal with it and he understood. Eddie ended up riding with Chavo. That worked better.

It was obvious that Eddie was struggling with his health. He was run down when they made him WWE Champion. They work you to death when you've got that belt. You don't have days off. Time away from the ring is for public appearances and things like that. No matter how hurt Eddie was, he went out there and gave it his all. His body started breaking down. He had a ruptured disc in his back and asked for some time off — they wouldn't give it to him. They told him he was the champion and working hurt came with the territory.

One of the saddest things I've ever seen is Eddie backstage, lying down in the trainer's room on one of the tables, hurting so much that he couldn't tell if he had to go to the bathroom or not. He would just lay there backstage on the table at the house shows until 10 minutes before his match, when he'd take some energy drink or something with honey, then drag himself all the way to Gorilla. He would go out there and put on such a good show that no one could tell he was beat down and worn out but, as soon as he was back through that curtain, he came right back down again, walking slowly like he was a defeated man. He would drag himself right back to the trainer's table and lay down again. Nobody sent him home to get well because they didn't give a fuck. He begged for time off and they didn't give it to him. They took the belt off him, thinking that would take away the pressure, and then they went and put him against Kurt. A wrestling program with Kurt Angle is not time off!

Eddie kept struggling onward. He found it hard to cope. I remember talking with him in early November 2005 — we were in Kentucky at a show and he seemed unhappy. I asked him what was wrong and he went off on me. He was upset about something that would be going on TV and my question lit the powder keg — wrong place, wrong time. Hey, we were good friends, it was okay for him to vent to me. After he had finished yelling, he walked away.

I hate that this was the last time I spoke to him.

A week after that conversation, we were doing a show in Minneapolis. It was at the same arena where we'd had a problem with Eddie right after he'd joined the company. Back then, management had a big program lined up for him and he didn't turn up. Nobody could get in touch with him. He had finally arrived at 5 p.m. and he had been so wasted he could barely get out of the cab. Benoit and Malenko grabbed him and hurried him into a room to sober him up before anybody could see the condition he was in. He had his demons, which led to his release in 2001. He turned his life around, got himself clean, got his job back, and lived a good life. In November 2005, in Minneapolis, that life ended.

When I entered the arena for the show, everybody had long faces. They told me Eddie had died. I couldn't believe it; all I could say was "Are you fucking kidding me?" He was in so much pain and under such a lot of stress that his heart had given out. I was immediately pissed because I thought the company had treated him pretty fucking badly. Here was a guy who knew his own body, knew he was hurt, and had asked for time off. They bullied him to continue working. They pushed him and pushed him until he had a heart attack. I don't think it would be fair to blame

Vince McMahon personally for Eddie's death, but the business certainly had a hand in it. It's the reason Vince has made sure to look after Vickie, Eddie's widow. Of course, Eddie always could have just said, "I'm taking time off, I'll see you later." Believe me, management didn't want to lose Eddie so they would have done whatever he wanted. He was too valuable to the company and they had too much invested in him.

Eddie's death took the wind out of everybody's sails. While you couldn't compare it to Owen's death, it *was* a similar kind of mood. The company filmed two TV tributes to Eddie that night. I didn't work on either of the shows and I didn't record one of the backstage interviews talking about him. I didn't want to talk about it. I still don't. I shut myself off. I hated how our last conversation had gone. I couldn't even go to his funeral because we were on the road, heading to Europe. Anyway, I shouldn't have been going to Europe in the first place.

A few weeks before Eddie died, I was scheduled to have elbow surgery but I noticed a bump under my right armpit. I figured it was either a pimple or an ingrown hair. I can't leave anything alone, so I tried to pop it but it wouldn't go away. It was a really hard bump. I had no idea how I'd got it. The next morning, it was so painful that I couldn't pull my bag with my right hand. When I got home, my doctor checked me out and said that it was an infection, and we were going to have to wait for it to clear up before we did the surgery. I ended up back on the road. By the time I got to Minneapolis, I felt like I had the flu. Dr. Rios checked me out backstage and said I had a staph infection and it had spread to the forearm. He told Johnny Laurinaitis that I was really sick and needed to go to the hospital to get it taken care of. Johnny said that I was needed on the overseas tour, so the hospital would have to wait. I'm not one to complain but even I said to Johnny, "I'm as sick as hell, man." Johnny insisted I go overseas. I thought it was just another case of working hurt — you work through it and it goes away eventually. If I'd refused to go, they would have probably fired me. Maybe that's how Eddie had felt.

We finished filming TV and got on a plane at midnight. By the time we'd landed in Germany, my forearm was twice its normal size. Larry and Dr. Rios came to my room to take care of it. Larry held me down and Dr. Rios made an incision in my forearm to relieve the pressure. He started popping and squeezing and all of this green and red and yellow stuff came out. It smelled absolutely awful. They spent about 20 minutes trying to drain and clean my arm, then taped me up from my wrist right to my shoulder to make sure the infection wouldn't spread to anybody else. Even Dr. Rios said I shouldn't have made the trip to Germany, but I told him that Johnny had insisted that I was needed, so I figured they must have had an important TV match for me or something. I still felt like I had the flu but I went to the show, ready to work. I found out that I was in a battle royal at all the shows that week. They didn't need me for that! Anybody could have filled my spot, or they could have run the match with one less person and nobody would have blinked twice. I was furious with Johnny for doing that to me. They had to drain my forearm every single night and day and it still got worse. When we got to TV in England, I went to Johnny and insisted I go home. It was the last night of the entire tour at this point anyway but Johnny arranged for me to fly right out.

When I got back, my doctor took one look at my arm and said, "You need to go to the hospital right now." He called ahead so they knew to expect me. I ended up staying in the hospital for four weeks. They did surgery to get the infection out of the bone. It didn't work, so they brought a disease specialist in to talk to me who put me on Vancomycin, which is one of the strongest antibiotics out there. It's basically a last resort. If that didn't work, he told me, they were going to have to amputate my arm from the shoulder down. That just about ruined my day, right there. Thankfully, the Vancomycin worked and my arm started to get better. They put a PICC line in me and let me go home. After two weeks of home visits from a health care worker who took my blood, did tests, and changed my PICC line, I went back for a check-up. The doctor said that if I'd gone to the hospital when I'd originally been told to do so, we would have avoided the whole thing. I told him that Johnny had insisted I work through it. The doctor said, "That man is the reason you ended up in the hospital and nearly lost your arm."

Because they'd gone against Dr. Rios's orders, the company was very liable and they knew that they had set themselves up for a huge lawsuit. I could tell because they were kissing my ass the whole time I was off, telling me not to worry about anything and that they'd get me anything I needed

. . . I just wanted them to give me a decent push when I got back! I figured if I hadn't deserved it for all my hard work, I definitely deserved it now for what I'd been through.

I hadn't been in a great mood on that European tour. I'd been with the company long enough to be considered a locker-room leader, one of the veterans who unofficially helped run things and kept the boys in order. I was pissed off because I was sick as a dog and had just been dragged all the way across the ocean to be in some irrelevant matches, but when I thought the guy who was going over in those matches wasn't grateful, that was the straw that broke the camel's back. They were busy giving Ken Kennedy a good starting push and he was winning these battle royals. One night in Italy, we got back to the locker room and Ken didn't thank the guys in the match for putting him over. Thanking the guys who put you over is the very first thing you should do after a match because they just made you look good. I gave Ken several minutes to do this and nothing happened. I called him out on it in front of everybody. He said he would have gotten around to it. I told him you don't go and do whatever else first, you thank the people who put you over and shake their hands. The next night at another arena in Italy, when Ken came in, I marched right over, grabbed his bag, and threw it in the hallway, saying, "Get the fuck out of my locker room — you're not changing in here until I say you can."

It seems pretty harsh when you see it on paper but I was the veteran teaching respect to the new guys. Hell, Benoit made The Miz change in the hallway for six months because he caught him eating chicken over Chris's bag and making a mess he didn't apologize for. The veterans supported each other on this sort of thing. You all had to band together to make sure the new guys stayed in order. Kennedy was the only person I ever threw out of the locker room.

A couple of days went by before Benoit came to talk to me. Kennedy had started riding with him back in the States, so Chris knew a few things I didn't. He told me that Ken had just lost his dad. Chris knew Ken was going through a rough time, and said that he respected and supported my decision to throw Ken out of the locker room, but suggested that I should go and talk to him. I found him and said "Why didn't you tell me about your dad?" Ken said that he didn't feel like it was something he needed to tell people but, yeah, he was having a tough time. He started crying. I felt bad for him, I really did. It broke my heart to see him crying like that. I told him to get his ass back in the locker room and apologized for upsetting him. From that moment on, we became good friends.

We all had plenty on our minds at that point, anyway. We were all coping with Eddie's death in our own ways and the office had just announced that they were going to introduce a "Wellness Program" to make sure nobody else slipped away like Eddie did. At the very start, it looked like something that Vince was putting in place to help everybody out. It took a while for people to see it as the crock of shit it was.

CHAPTER 31

STEROIDS

The Wellness Program was a political move in response to Eddie's death to make WWE less of the "bad guy." This new program was going to enforce much stricter testing for prohibited substances, including steroids. Eddie was a small man naturally, so I'm sure he took something to gain size and get as big as he did. That said, I don't think steroids were entirely responsible for his death; it was more to do with how much stress he was under and how exhausted he was. Benoit was concerned about this new testing policy. He told me he was worried about having to get clean because the steroids helped him recover and he was in such constant pain. He was going to do whatever he could get away with. We left it at that.

I get asked a lot if I used steroids. Hell yes, I did. I'll be the first to admit I was on the gas. So was almost every single person in that locker room in the '80s, '90s, and into the 2000s. I'm not ashamed of it. The real question is did I *abuse* steroids? No, I do not believe I did. There is a big difference between steroid use and abuse, just like there is a big difference between drinking alcohol and abusing it.

I started taking steroids after the New Midnight Express finished. Oddly enough, that was when I started to get noticed more in the locker room and to get used more in matches. Go figure, right? It just goes to show what you need to do to get used. People don't pay to see a wrestler who looks like your everyday guy walking down the street. They pay to see larger-than-life characters. The office never dropped hints though. It was an unwritten thing that you had to do what you had to do to keep your spot. Nobody ever told me to take them. You just had to look around the locker room to know what had to happen. It was like we were all racing cars and everybody else was using racing fuel while I was using regular unleaded. Wrestling is a competitive industry, plain and simple. After four years underneath, I knew what I needed to do. I took Deca Durabolin and testosterone: one cc of Deca every 10 days and a shot of testosterone every seven to ten. Honestly, that was probably more than I should have been taking but not by much. I never felt that I was abusing it like some of the other guys. They were taking so much of the stuff.

Some people think that if you take steroids, you'll automatically get huge. That's not the case. Steroids help you heal faster. Given the nature of what we do and all the bumps involved, they help a lot. They allow you to work out harder and recover faster, and that is where you see the growth. If you don't work out, you're not going to see a damn change beyond looking bulkier because steroids increase water retention too. In the '80s, some of the guys were just bulky because they took a lot of steroids. Then there were guys who were big *and* shredded because they took steroids and did everything else properly too. You've got to diet, eat right, and work out, otherwise you might as well not bother. The steroids just help you along. Because I wasn't really overdoing it, I never had any side effects that were noticeable. Taking a synthetic testosterone stops your body from producing its own testosterone naturally. Deca is one of the cleanest steroids you can use and you can stay on it all year. I cycled on and off the Test but once I was on the Deca I stayed on it until I came off for good.

When they brought in the Wellness policy, we were told by management that tests were going to be random and regular, everybody was eligible to be tested, and anybody who tested positive for any banned substance would be suspended unless they had a valid prescription. We were also told that the office had no say in who would be suspended; that would be down to the company running our testing. But the whole program was a joke. Certain guys started losing weight and muscle mass, but other guys stayed the same size. Go back and look and you'll see who was on and who was off.

Right away, I started phasing out the Deca. I got a prescription for the testosterone, because I still needed that and it was medically authorized and all above-board. I kept working out hard and I don't think coming off made that much difference. I lost about 10 pounds or so but I didn't lose much size. It was more difficult for a lot of the other guys. Some probably lost their jobs because of the testing. Rob Conway, for example, was a guy who needed a little chemical assistance to present the expected image. They used him quite a bit because he looked great but once they started drug testing, Rob didn't know what he was going to do. He told me, "If I can't be on the gas, I can't wrestle." He was going to be like a stick figure without the steroids. He got smaller, he got less TV time, he wasn't over, he ended up getting released. I felt bad for him.

Wrestling is an image industry. WWE marketing has always exaggerated the stats on their guys to make them seem more impressive — telling people they're taller or heavier than they are. I'm legit 6'1" like I was billed, and I'm taller than a lot of guys who were billed at 6'3". Likewise, when I was at 228 pounds for real, they were billing Christian as heavier than me, and he's about 180 pounds soaking wet! A while ago, Vince insisted that he wanted people announced at their legit weights but that didn't last long. Having Rey Mysterio at 150 pounds wrestling for the World Heavyweight title didn't look too good, so they went back to billing him heavier — it's all about image. There is a lot of pressure in that company about image and people get let go over it all the time.

It became clear to me that something was not right with the policy when Ken Kennedy got suspended for steroids. Around that time, Ken was riding with another guy who was on the gas. Ken would call the guy in Florida he got his stuff from and would then hand the phone over so his buddy could put in *his* order. They ordered at the exact same time, got tested at the same time, but only Ken got suspended. Ken was floating around in the mid-card. The other guy was being groomed for the top. That right there told me that it wasn't the lab that was handing out the suspensions.

The policy is there so that WWE can show Congress that they're doing it, but there's a huge double standard when it comes to the results. The guys who don't draw money are the ones who get suspended and made examples of. If any of the top guys get caught violating the policy, they get off light because they make money for the company. Undertaker and Flair refused point blank to take the test. They wouldn't do it — they told management that they would sooner walk out. Triple H, John Cena, and Batista all got tested. I can guarantee that because I stood in line with them, but I've got to question their results, since they were the only ones who didn't shrink in size. Look at Chris Masters — he shrank to about half his size when they brought steroid testing in. It didn't help that Hunter kept bringing attention to how much Chris had shrunk and fucking with his head about it. That was pretty low, if you ask me.

Go look at the guys who didn't shrink once they brought in the testing — top guys earning top money. Like many things, if you're able to throw money at a problem, you can usually find a way around it. The WWE's Wellness Policy has blood tests every six months for specific things; the blood goes off to a lab and gets tested for HIV, hepatitis, and conditions like that. It does *not* get tested for steroids. The drug testing is done by urinalysis and by a completely different lab. Urine testing can show testosterone, Deca, and a host of other steroids, but my understanding is that it can't show human growth hormone. If you've got a legal prescription for your testosterone and combine it with HGH, that's a great combination for building muscle and getting around the Wellness policy but it costs. HGH runs to a couple of grand a month, so only top guys can afford it. Deca was $150 for a 10cc bottle that would last a few months. That's the sort of thing that the underneath guys can afford. When I was there, it was hard to get to be a top guy without being on *something*, so a lot of people had to take their chances with the cheaper stuff and hope they didn't get caught.

It was different with smoking dope. Vince told us that we would not get suspended if our test results showed marijuana in our systems, but we would get fined. It was $1,000 when I was there. I believe it's gone up to $2,500 since. That puzzles me because marijuana is just as illegal as steroids. If you get pulled over by the police and they find you've got pot in your car, you're gonna be in trouble. I thought it was strange that they'd suspend you for steroids but only fine you for pot. Then I figured it out — most of the top guys smoked pot and had no intention of stopping. If Vince had to suspend everybody who tested positive for marijuana, his roster would have basically been me, C.M. Punk, and a handful of others. In any other form of athletics, if you're caught smoking pot, you're gone. WWE basically gave you a slap on the wrist for pot and a kick out the door for steroids. That strikes me as a huge double standard.

Personally, I'd much rather be in the ring with a guy who is gassed to the gills than a guy who is high as a kite. Trevor Murdoch and Lance Cade were two of the biggest repeat offenders for pot; they were constantly being fined. I had to work with them a lot and I did not like it one bit. They would smoke on the way to the arena and fly high through our match — they could have seriously hurt me. Don't get me wrong, I've got no problem with a person if they want to smoke pot; I just don't think they should smoke it right before they go in the ring with me and I put my life in their hands!

I got suspended for steroids one time. I had a call from Dr. Black, the man they had in charge of the whole Wellness program. He told me that they had found Deca in my system and asked me for my prescription. Even though I gave it to them and everything was in order, they suspended me a month without pay. I asked him who was making the call on the suspension and he flat-out told me it was Vince. WWE had told us all that the decisions on suspensions were out of their hands but Dr. Black told me that everything went through Vince. I asked him about the pot fines too and he said those were also Vince's call. Dr. Black told me that if he had it his way, all of the pot smokers would be suspended too. I guess I was just another underneath guy set up as a scapegoat so the top guys could get away with it . . . it pisses me off, because if Congress decided to investigate WWE's policy and tested properly across the board, they'd get very different results.

People always make a big deal about steroids. I never understood the judgmental attitude. Drinking alcohol is far worse for you than doing steroids and almost everybody drinks. I don't judge people if they want to do that. You do your thing and I'll do mine. How many people do you hear about who die from steroid abuse each year? Very few. How many people die from alcohol abuse? Many, many more. If you watch those reality jail shows, most of the people are drunk off their asses. People make stupid, fatal decisions when drunk and not in the right state of mind.

People die every day from drunk drivers. And consider the effect alcohol has elsewhere on the body. Sure, steroids can weaken the heart when taken in excess. Alcohol in excess weakens the heart, the liver, and the kidneys, on top of hugely affecting the brain. People die of alcohol poisoning, cirrhosis of the liver, and so on. Alcohol is far more easily available than steroids and more socially acceptable, so people drink it every day without a second thought. They look in the mirror and say, "Yes, I have a drink but I don't abuse it." That's the same as me saying, "Yes, I took some steroids but I didn't abuse it." People don't see it that way though. The way I see it, it's my body, I'll put whatever I want in it. I don't drink alcohol but if you want to put that in your body, it's your call. I'm not going to look down on you for making that decision.

Because of what steroids are and the sort of people who usually take them, the deaths that can be connected with steroid use tend to be of high-profile guys. You don't get laymen dying from steroid abuse but you damn sure get them dying from alcohol misuse. Look at the statistics — alcohol is one of the biggest killers in the world. Not steroids. It's just so easy to point at steroids whenever anything goes wrong and claim "'roid rage" but I'll tell you this — I never got mad because I'd taken steroids. I got mad because I'm human and I get mad sometimes! Everybody gets mad. If an old guy is driving down the highway and gets pissed off because somebody cuts him off, does that mean Grandpa is on the gas?! Everybody blows a gasket from time to time; if the guy happens to be on steroids, it's just an easy excuse.

PART 14: WORKING OUT AND EATING RIGHT

When I started going to the gym, I kind of skipped around and didn't have a routine. It didn't get me very far. If you're going to spend time in the gym, you need to learn how to work out properly. I learned this when I started working out with Sid. I still do the workouts now that I did back then. I've never lifted particularly heavy weights; I've focussed more on reps. I used to bench over 400 pounds but it made no sense to me, so I cut back to 225. A wrestler's body gets abused night after night — heavy lifting puts pressure on your joints, so why abuse your joints more than you have to? You can still grow and look big lifting lighter. You've just got to make sure you are pushing yourself to the point of struggling on the last rep.

I lift for 45 minutes to an hour, maximum. I work out fast and superset everything. I do one exercise, then go straight into another one. So, for example, on chest day I would do 15 reps with 185 pounds on the bench press, jump off, grab some dumbbells, and do a set of 15 flies right away. Rest for 45 seconds and do it all over again. Four or five sets of that will wear you out. Then I would superset incline dumbbell presses and dips, and finish up with cable crossovers into push-ups. That's a damn good chest workout. Some days, I'll change it up to shock the muscles into growth. You've got to try different things to find out what works best.

I'll work out five days a week and split my week so Wednesday and Sunday are rest days. I focus on one main area per day in my lifting. I do chest one day, then back, then shoulders, then arms (biceps and triceps together), and then legs. When I'm done lifting, I do 45 minutes to an hour of cardio on a stepmill.

It's all about what you eat. You can work out as much as you want but if you don't eat correctly, you're going to look bad regardless.

You've got to eat regularly to keep your metabolism going. If you don't eat, your body shuts down and starts storing fat, so you need to eat small meals regularly. I'm lucky — my metabolism is fast, even now that I'm 50 years old. I can eat almost anything I want and stay lean. It's crazy. I eat every three hours or so. If you eat squeaky clean, you can lose weight without working out. Alcohol is one of the worst things you can consume; it'll put weight on you in a heartbeat.

Generally, I eat a lot of chicken, fish, turkey, red meat, eggs (including the yolks), quinoa, couscous, brown rice, roasted asparagus, sweet potatoes, spinach, and protein shakes. To lean out quickly, I don't eat carbs. No pasta, no white rice, and no bread. If you are not taking in any carbs, the only thing to burn *is* fat. Your body always burns carbs before fat, therefore if there are no carbs to burn, you will burn off fat. If you follow a high-protein, high-fat, no-carb diet for a few weeks, your body will burn fat and lean you out. This should only be done for short intervals at a time.

The best time to work out is in the morning, but you should always fuel your body before you go. It's like a car — if you don't put gas in, you can't go. If you go to the gym with no fuel, you're going to peter out. You need something that gives you energy. I'll eat turkey and eggs in a wholewheat tortilla, then have some oatmeal with protein powder and I'm good to go. There are enough slow-burning carbs in there to get me through my workout. I also recommend drinking plenty of water and having some coffee in the morning — that helps with metabolism too.

Above all else, don't overcomplicate things. People think getting in shape is complicated but it really isn't. You've just got to be smart. The truth is that you are what you eat. If you eat bad, you'll look bad. End of story. Eat sensibly and work out, and you'll look and feel better.

CHAPTER 32

BOB'S BACK... NEEDS 25 STITCHES

I was home for the first half of 2006, recovering from my latest elbow surgery. After the staph infection had cleared up, we'd been able to go through with the surgery. But I needed both of my elbows taken care of and the surgeons wouldn't do them at the same time. I had to let my left elbow heal before they did my right elbow. Just like the time I broke my arm, I was so limited in what I could do that it was driving me insane. I wasn't supposed to lift anything. I basically wasn't supposed to *do* anything, or so it seemed. My doctor knew I loved riding dirt bikes and specifically said, "No riding." I told him no problem, but do you think I listened to him for long? I was so tired of lying around, doing absolutely nothing, so as soon as my elbows felt decent, I loaded my dirt bike up and headed out to the motocross track. It was during the week, so I was the only one out there. I was feeling pretty good, going fast and jumping. I came up to a "table top," which was about a sixty or seventy foot jump. It was designed so that when you hit it, you'd sail through the air and try to land on the downside, avoiding the dirt wall, and then go about your business. The left side of the takeoff had a lip on, which kicked the back tire up. It would make you nose-dive before the landing, and that was an uncomfortable feeling. I moved to the right on the jump to correct that.

A couple of other guys showed up when I'd been riding for about 45 minutes. One of them started racing me. "All right then — let's do this," I thought. After all those months of nothing, it was great to be doing something again. The wind was picking up, I was going faster, and this guy was coming up behind me when I went up the table top jump. I hit the ramp at a good clip but I hit it too far to the right. That big dirt wall was right there, and I knew I was in trouble. I bailed off the bike in mid air — just let it go — and slammed into the side of that dirt wall with the elbow I'd just had surgery on. I tried to push myself up and found I couldn't do it. I thought I'd broken my collarbone. The guy behind me had almost landed on me. He stopped to help me when he saw that I'd wrecked. My collarbone wasn't broken but my elbow wasn't looking too spiffy — my stitches were ripped wide open. My bike wasn't doing much better — the forks were bent, the handlebars were twisted. They helped me load the bike into my truck because I couldn't do it by myself. When I got home, I took some sterastrips and closed up the gashes where the stitches had come out. I wasn't about to go back to the doctor and admit I'd hurt myself riding! It probably set my recovery back a little bit but WWE never found out about it. I just enjoyed extreme sports, and my return to TV was about to get extreme too . . .

I got a call from the office in mid 2006, telling me that I was going to be working with the ECW brand from now on. They were, trying to make a buck by resurrecting Paul Heyman's promotion from the '90s and running it under the WWE banner. I thought it was a good idea because it would give everybody on the roster a chance to be on a program. Some really talented guys had been sitting in the back doing nothing and I thought this would be a great avenue for them to get regular TV time and be used in storylines. Some WWE guys who were ECW originals got moved across, including Tommy Dreamer and Rob Van Dam, both of whom I liked. They signed some guys from the original ECW roster too — I thought the Sandman was a good choice, even though he couldn't work worth a damn, because he was still so over from his run in the '90s ECW. I was a little disappointed in Sabu because he wasn't who he used to be. Some of that was politics, some of that was age. They brought Andrew Martin — Test — back and I thought he was great. And I guess they figured, since ECW had been an anything-goes sort of environment, it could use a guy like Hardcore Holly.

Management didn't ask me if I wanted to be part of ECW — they just told me. I didn't care. All that mattered to me was that I was on TV again. I'd been off-screen for nearly a year so I wanted to get back in front of an audience. ECW was filmed on the same day as *Smackdown* was so it didn't affect my schedule. The biggest difference was that it was live TV rather than taped. That's one of the reasons why they shifted me onto that show. I'd always been told that I was really good at hitting time cues, and the agents appreciated that. Timing is important even on the taped shows, because although you can edit the footage, it costs a lot of money. It's better to just get it right the first time. When you're doing live TV, it's critical that you have guys who are experienced with tight timescales or it can screw everything up. They knew that they could tell me, "You've got seven minutes" and seven minutes later, guaranteed, someone's hand would be raised and we'd be ready to move on to the next match or segment. They had a lot of guys there who weren't used to working on live TV and even with the referee constantly telling them how long they had, they still couldn't figure it out. So having someone like me out there to control the pace of things was useful.

I thought ECW would be a perfect fit for me. I was excited, thinking I'd get to be one of the top guys, get a lot of TV time doing matches and promos, and be involved in a mixture of things. I was half-right — I definitely was in a prominent role as one of the main players on the show. But when it came down to the important matches, they used me to get other people over again. I picked up some wins along the way but I was still pretty much a glorified enhancement guy. It all goes back to what they want to do with someone — it doesn't matter how good you are, it only matters what they want to use you for. Still, I did what I was supposed to do: worked hard, pitched ideas to the writers, and hoped that maybe something would happen. It never did.

The big plan was to base the group around Rob Van Dam. He was still very popular (even though Hunter had been burying him for years), so they had him win the WWE Championship and then declare himself the ECW Champion too. It was going well until he screwed it up for himself. Rob is Rob and he's going to do what he wants no matter what. He just wanted to wrestle and smoke his weed. He didn't care about anything else.

They had just built a pay-per-view around him winning the company's top title and were building a new brand around him, and then he got busted by the police for smoking pot. He got suspended and they had him lose both the WWE and ECW Championships over the next week. When he came back from suspension, his momentum had slowed, so they wanted to get him back on track. As usual, they turned to me.

It didn't bother me that I was asked to put Rob over. That was my job. I always liked Rob. He's one of the best guys you'd ever meet. I loved working with him. A lot of the guys complained about him when he first joined WWE in 2001 because his kicks were too stiff, but I never had any problems with him. I took everything he gave me and didn't try to shy away or put my hands in front of my face to block his kicks because I wanted it to look believable. Sure, a few of those kicks connected pretty hard and rang my bell, almost knocked me out a couple of times, but he didn't do any real damage. I work like that so who am I to complain? When he does that Rolling Thunder move though, that fucker lands on you full force and he is *heavy*.

We worked together a bunch on the road and had a lot of great matches, but the one that really stands out, the one people still talk about, aired on live TV in September 2006. It ended up being probably the best match I ever had.

The instructions were pretty simple — go out there and get Rob over, help him look good, and have a good match. Just another day on the job. This was all about Rob. We were told to make it about 12 to 15 minutes and that a two-minute commercial break would be in there. We would have to plan something pretty spectacular so we could down-sell for that amount of time. Since we'd worked together so much on house shows, the match was easy to put together. I focused on making sure it all made sense and that, by the end, Rob would get over the way they wanted. When we got out there, everything was going great; the crowd was into it and the timing was just right. About seven minutes in, the referee told us that we had 30 seconds before we went to commercial. We had a big spot planned with a folding table that we'd set up beside the ring earlier, so we got into position for that. The ref gave us the 10-second warning; we were in perfect position. I was on the ring apron, outside the ropes, and Rob was in the ring. We faked the suplex one way. I went up for it but came back down on my feet on the apron. Then I lifted Rob up for the suplex to the outside and we both came crashing down through the table. The crowd erupted — all I could hear was them going nuts.

In the middle of all that noise, laying there on the floor in the wreckage of the table, I was thinking, "That stung awful damn bad." It felt like I had a sunburn and somebody had slapped me hard on my back. It wasn't anything like some of my dirtbike accidents, it just stung, like I'd been badly scratched.

When the referee came over and told us we had a minute before we came back from commercial, we started moving. I rolled over onto all fours and suddenly saw a puddle of blood. I recall thinking, "Holy shit, where did that come from?" I had no idea if it was Rob's blood or mine. It looked like somebody had been shot. Rob wasn't bleeding. I glanced under my arm and saw all of this blood running down my side. I thought, "What the fuck have I done now?!"

I got up onto the apron. The guys with the handheld cameras could see the blood, which meant everyone in the arena could see it on the big screen. The crowd let out a big gasp. Everyone in the back apparently went scrambling to get the doctor and the trainer. I just wanted to get on with it. The referee was wearing an earpiece, and he was told from backstage that I should wait on the apron because Dr. Rios was going to look at me before we went back on air. The ref said that Vince might want to stop the match. Oh, hell no! Nobody was going to stop that match as far as I was concerned! I had no idea how bad it was and I didn't care. The ref told me it was pretty bad but I was moving around a bit and thinking, "How bad can it be?" Turns out it was pretty damn bad! Dr. Rios and Larry — the trainer — came running down and checked it out. Larry said to me, "I'm going to tell them to stop it." No way, I thought. It was too good of a match. I said, "Motherfucker, you tell 'em to stop it and I swear to God, I will punch you in the mouth right now." He looked at me dumbfounded and said, "Bob, come here and let me look at it one more time." I told him to get the fuck away from me and rolled back in the ring. I didn't give them a chance to stop the match. I was feeling pretty stubborn that night. I didn't realize how bad the injury actually was until I was in the ring and happened to look up at the big video screen — they had a shot of me from behind, and I could see a huge gash about halfway up my back. It was at least a foot long and pretty deep. Blood was dripping out of it — it looked fucking brutal.

As nasty as it looked, it didn't actually hurt that much. I thought it added to the match, made it that much more interesting for the fans. The rest of the match felt good and the people were into it. I wrestled another eight minutes with that injury and, as I said earlier, I think it was probably the best match I ever had. I earned a lot of respect that night. You're never going to make everyone happy all of the time, and there are always those fans who just don't like you for whatever reason. That night, I earned a lot of respect even from those guys. The audience gave me a standing ovation when I left the ring. That was nice — I was a heel at the time, so for them to respect me and what I'd done in the ring that night was appreciated. When I got backstage, Vince shook my hand, gave me a hug, and said, "You're one tough motherfucker — thank you for a great match." I just went out there and did what I'm paid to do the best I could, and I gave the fans what they wanted. I'd never quit a match because I was bleeding!

They led me to the trainer's room and put 25 stitches in my back. I felt fine. I was just happy that the match was good. Over the next few days, once the adrenaline had worn off, it was a little more painful but still not that bad. It hurt to be touched and I couldn't lie on my back but other than that, it just felt like a regular cut. The most annoying thing about it was that it was in a spot that was literally a pain in the backside. Everything I did, I felt it right there. It affected the way I sat down, the way I worked out. I had to take two weeks off from training to let it heal. It was more of an irritation than anything else.

Rob was very grateful after the match, like he always was. He's grateful whenever you work with him. That can be a rarity in this business. We had become really good friends because we'd been working together so much, so I'd wanted to do the best I could for him in that, give him 100 percent and really help get him over as best I could. I felt bad for him when he blew his big shot earlier that year, but that's on him. I hated that WWE decided to change directions and didn't push him back up to the top when he got off suspension. He went out every night and did what he was supposed to do. The fans liked him, they bought tickets to see him, they bought his merchandise, and he delivered good matches. It pissed me off that they saw him as a liability and wouldn't roll the dice on him while they protected a guy like Randy Orton who, back then, was way worse than Rob ever *thought* about being. That just goes to show that if you make the company a ton of money, they'll change the rules for you. If you're not making them money — and often it's because they've not put you in a position where you *can* make them money — they will treat you as expendable and get rid of you at the first sign of trouble. It's a big double standard.

After that match with Rob, I was probably the most over I'd been in five years. It was a great chance for them to capitalize on that and put me in a position where I could make money for them. I was a veteran, I knew what I was doing in the ring, I could cut a decent promo, I had credibility with the fans, and I'd proved beyond a shadow of a doubt that I was loyal to the company. They were lacking in good heels at that point so it made sense to me that they would use me as a no-nonsense heel in ECW. The Big Show was the top heel but he was always complaining because he was in such bad shape. When he had to take some time off, there were no other heels left.

It seemed to me that I might finally get a break and what did they do? Because the fans cheered me at the end of my match with Rob, the office decided to turn me babyface. I thought that was dumb. They assumed the audience would want to cheer me just because that one crowd gave me respect for working through a sliced-open back. There's a difference between one audience showing respect for a wrestler who has gutted out an injury and the fans being ready to take to me as a permanent good guy. Turning me babyface was a mistake, which they realized a few weeks later. They turned me back heel, and you can't do that — if you turn a guy too much or too quickly, the audience stops caring. All that momentum I had after the match with Rob vanished. They really blew that opportunity.

The big plan for ECW after Rob got busted was to bring Bobby Lashley over from *Smackdown* and make him the top guy for the brand. If Lashley was going to be a good draw as top babyface, he was going to need a good heel to work with, somebody who knew how to work with his limitations — and there were a lot of them because he was so green — somebody who could get some heat on him and make it look believable. I looked around that locker room and knew nobody was a better fit for that position than me. Problem was that I'd lost so much momentum after that asinine face-turn that they didn't feel I would work in that role. That was their own damn fault for turning me babyface!

Instead of using me as the top heel, they went with Test. He had a good look and his promos were okay but could stand to get better. I'll say this — he was vicious. People talk about me being stiff in the ring; I was nothing compared to Test. He was rough. I didn't have a problem with him but I thought I deserved that spot.

Still, they thought enough of me to use me in one of their main events, even though I wasn't originally advertised for it. We were going into the first official — and what ended up being the only — ECW pay-per-view, *December to Dismember*, which turned out to be a horrible night. Most of the guys in ECW at that point were undercard guys who had been losing on *RAW* and *Smackdown* but were pushed as top guys in ECW — and none of the fans bought it. For the main event, they used this thing called the Elimination Chamber. A huge enclosed cage surrounded the ring: inside were four pods, with a wrestler locked in each pod. Six wrestlers in total were in the match: two starting in the ring, with a pod opening every five minutes to let a new guy into the match. You could get eliminated at any time. Since it was meant to be hardcore wrestling, they called it the Extreme Elimination Chamber and put a weapon in each pod. One guy had a crowbar, one had a barbed-wire baseball bat, and so on. I turned up at the arena that day and they took me aside right away to tell me that Sabu failed a drug test. They were taking him out of the match and I was going to replace him. That was just fine by me.

I was one of the two starting guys and was working with Rob. Even though it was a new environment for us, we were so comfortable with each other that we just called things on the fly. We knew what to do. I enjoyed that match but it was probably the most painful thing I've ever done in my career because that chamber was solid steel. It had no give whatsoever. Rob and I did a few moves using the chamber and I took a couple of bumps on the steel floor. They tickled, to say the least . . .

I stayed in the match quite a while, which was a surprise, given I hadn't been advertised. I enjoyed working the match, and I thought it turned out pretty well. I made the best out of the situation and got some good screen time in. They paid me $1,000 — for a match on pay-per-view, that's terrible. The other guys probably got more because they were advertised for it and I was put in at the last minute, but even so, it's still terrible. Still, I didn't complain. Big Show was complaining enough for everybody at that point. He was backstage that night, whining about having to do the match. He was miserable because he was so out of shape but he only had himself to blame. He liked his cheeseburgers and cigarettes. It's difficult sometimes, but you can still eat clean on the road — it's what you make of it and all Big Show was making was a bunch of excuses. He dropped the ECW title to Lashley in that chamber match and then took a year off to get healthy. When he came back, he was lean and looked great, but gradually he put a lot of it back on again. It's a shame to see.

The thing about Paul — Big Show — is that he's a really great guy and I've always thought he's a good worker for a big man. He's easy to work with. WWE didn't use him the way they should have. When he first came in, they had him lose to Steve Austin in the first month, but Steve was already over so it made no difference to him. They should have been establishing Show with the WWE audience so he could make money further down the line. Then they started flip-flopping him from heel to face all the time, making him lose credibility. They just couldn't figure out how to use him properly so I can't blame him for being pissed off. He was always good to me though. We rode together sometimes and he was easy-going. He didn't want to work out but that wasn't a problem for me; I just took the car and did my thing. Like Sid, he never let me pay for anything — he would insist on paying for the car, the gas . . . if he wanted to stay at a particular hotel and I'd say, "That's out of my price range," he was quick to say, "Don't worry about it — I'll pay." He's just a really gracious guy, which makes it all the more unfortunate that Hunter made fun of him behind his back all the time. It was ridiculous and sad, because Paul liked Hunter and looked up to him.

I got to work with C.M. Punk in the Elimination Chamber and afterwards in ECW. I thought he was a good worker and he was always polite to me. He always said he was happy for me whenever management started to use me. I always liked him. During his undefeated streak, they had me be the first guy in WWE to beat him in a singles match. But the office didn't make it mean anything, so they didn't do anything with him or me as a result. He bounced around a bit after that but has since become one of the top guys in the business. He was the hottest thing going over the summer in 2011 but then Hunter got his hands on him and that was that. They had a match and Hunter went over. Hunter didn't need that win. Punk got to kick out of Hunter's finish but he still lost, so what does that do for Punk? Not a lot.

A few years after I left WWE, Punk brought my name up in a promo on *RAW*, saying that he was in an arena where I'd hit him so hard that I'd given him a permanent blind spot in his eye. I have no idea why he brought me up in that promo but I doubt he meant it as a negative thing or a complaint. I can't even remember the match he was talking about because I worked with him so many times. You get all these little injuries, you get hit here and there, and they all blend together. It wasn't a one-sided thing either — Punk kicked me in the face a bunch and just about cracked my skull with his finisher a few times, but that's just part of wrestling. You don't whine about getting hurt or about somebody hitting you too hard. If you do, you're in the wrong business. Punk never complained that I was working too stiff with him and I don't remember him going for medical aid after any of our matches, so it couldn't have been that bad. If he was really that pissed about it, he would have tried to bury me in that promo by saying something more negative about me. I was glad to hear he brought up our match — we had some good ones. Maybe he misses me, misses the physical abuse . . .

After I finished working with Punk, management told me I was going to work with Lashley, who was now the champion. They'd tried using Test against him and that didn't work out too well. Their matches were terrible, so they decided to give me a shot after all and told me that I'd win the ECW belt. I was happy to hear that and thought we could have some good, hard-hitting matches. I liked Bobby and enjoyed working with him — he was green, sure, but he listened well and learned quickly. The road agents always told me how much they thought he improved when he worked with me. I thought hell, if you're that impressed, use me properly in a decent program!

I was working through some pain at this point because my elbow was all busted up again. There were so many pieces of bone floating around that I'd pinched a nerve, which was affecting my hand so badly it was starting to atrophy. I had scheduled a surgery to take care of it but cancelled when Vince McMahon came and said he had big plans for me.

The company was building up to *WrestleMania* and was going to do a match with Vince and Donald Trump each choosing a wrestler to represent him and the guy whose wrestler lost would have his head shaved bald. It was going to be a really big deal, heavily publicized as one of the main matches on the show. Vince took me aside and told me he was going to go with Bobby representing Trump and with me representing him. He said that he would greatly appreciate it if I would put my surgery off until after *WrestleMania* so I could work that match. I said sure, no problem — hell, I was going to be in a main event match at *WrestleMania*, I could tolerate being uncomfortable for a little bit longer!

Then, close to *'Mania*, I had a cage match with Bobby on ECW TV in which he had to beat me in less than five minutes or he would lose the title — and he was going to go over. I thought that was sort of fucked up to have him beat me in less than five minutes on TV in the build-up for a big match on pay-per-view. It didn't make me look like I had a chance. I soon discovered that it wasn't meant to. During the match, Umaga came down to the ring and after Bobby had beat me, he did a running jump into the cage wall. He busted it down and made the whole thing collapse on Umaga. Right there, I knew I was out and Umaga was in. They didn't even have the decency to let me down in advance. I wasn't angry, just disappointed. Given how many times they hadn't done anything with me before, I probably shouldn't have been surprised. I have no idea why they ended up going with Umaga. I guess they just thought it would be a better program.

When I saw Vince after the cage match, I asked him what happened. He said that things had changed but he promised me that I'd have a match at *WrestleMania*. I said, "As long as I get to be in the show, that's okay." I'll bet you can see where this one is going . . .

I showed up in Detroit for *WrestleMania* and my name wasn't on the sheet. I wasn't in any of the matches. There was another ECW match there, an eight-man tag team match. One of the teams was made up of four new guys who, combined, hadn't been with the company a fraction of the time

I had been, and they were going to get on the pay-per-view? I was fucking furious and management knew it too. They knew they'd done me wrong but Vince never apologized.

That was my breaking point. I felt so hurt. I had been so loyal to the company and worked so hard night after night. I'd worked hurt, I'd done everything I could to make the up-and-coming stars look good, and then had my hopes built up and broken down like that. It was such a letdown. After all the years of working hard because it might be my time soon, I realized it just wasn't ever going to happen for me. The next day at TV, I went to see Dusty Rhodes and his writing team and told him that if he wasn't going to use me, I was going to go home and get my elbow fixed. So that was that — they never did give me the ECW title. Instead, they wrote me out of the storylines with an injury. That was the end of my run in ECW. Another wasted opportunity.

What made that whole situation even more disappointing was that Bobby didn't stick it out. He got hurt and ended up quitting. They had put so much time and money into marketing him and building him up as one of the next big guys and he bailed on them. He would have been a World Champion on one of the two main shows but, like Batista and Goldberg, he was never a wrestling fan. He didn't love the business, he was just a big, strong guy who said, "I'd like to try that," then got pushed because of how he looked. So Lashley came in, worked for the company for a couple of years, was heavily invested in, put in a main event at *WrestleMania,* and then turned around and said, "This isn't for me." Meanwhile, I'd worked hard and stayed loyal to the company for 13 years. I think my frustration is justifiable.

To put it all in perspective, the guys they pushed instead of me in the first half of 2007 were Lashley, Test, and Umaga. Lashley quit because he didn't care about wrestling. Test and Umaga both died from drug overdoses in 2009.

I got my elbow fixed, got back in training, and told WWE I was ready to come back but I really didn't care anymore. If I got a break, great — but I wasn't expecting it.

The travel was always a major pain in the ass. Sure, I got to see a bunch of countries, but so much traveling got to be pretty tiresome. Despite the long flight, I did enjoy Australia whenever we toured there. The weather is great, the country is beautiful, and it's so clean with such pleasant people. Once, we all had a day off and nothing to do. Hunter arranged a bus to shuttle us the two hours to Steve Irwin's zoo. He paid for the bus and the zoo entrance fees out of his own pocket. I'm a huge animal lover, so I enjoyed it hugely. We were all offering some food to the kangaroos when one of them picked me out of the group and hopped over. I squatted down to feed him and this kangaroo took a sniff of the food, then leaned in to me and bumped his mouth on mine. Ken Kennedy just happened to get a picture at that exact moment so it looked like I was kissing a kangaroo! It was a fun day, even though it was raining. Believe it or not, Hunter bought us all raincoats too. The whole thing was nice of him. He's a strange guy — I could never figure him out.

Montreal is completely the opposite of Australia — there seems to be a lot of rude people in Montreal. Several times when I stopped to ask for directions, the French Canadians just looked at me funny and walked off. I never did like going into Canada, period. Not many of the boys did. It was always such a hassle at customs. We entered other countries without a problem but getting into Canada could be brutal. They'd take forever with us; it was torture. Any time we worked there, we'd get paid in Canadian dollars, so when the exchange rate was bad, we lost money like crazy. You'd better believe that seeing Canada on the schedule was a real buzzkill.

I actually preferred going to Iraq.

WWE started putting shows on for the troops in the early 2000s, and those shows were always looked forward to. They've continued to this day. We were told participation was completely voluntary and nobody was going to be forced to go but Rob Van Dam got huge heat when he refused. Vince was fucking pissed. I don't know why he told us it was voluntary if he was going to get pissed at someone for not volunteering. I thought that wasn't right. I don't know why Rob didn't want to go; that's his business. I was more than happy to volunteer. Every time we went, I wondered whether Linda, my high-school sweetheart, might be in the audience somewhere — and, if so, would she even recognize me?

I didn't ever feel in danger over there; they took good care of us. We had to have all the lights turned off in the plane when we were landing to keep from being detected. We had to wear military helmets and flak jackets as precautions to make sure we were safe. On one of the trips, all of the wrestlers were put up in one of Saddam's many palaces — it was unbelievable just how lavish it was.

The wrestling shows were great over there; the military audience was really into it. When they gave us plaques and medals at the end of one tour, the general told us that of all the acts brought in to raise morale, the troops wanted to see us more than anything else. More than the Dallas Cowboys cheerleaders, more than any country singer — above all, they wanted to see WWE. It was a great experience. These people are putting their lives on the line for our freedom, so going over there and giving them a great show is the least we can do.

I also loved doing the stuff for Make-A-Wish and the Special Olympics. Say what you will about WWE, they go out of their way to give those kids something to smile about. Going through all the locker-room politics and the never-ending travel was worth it for the look on those kids' faces when they saw us. Doing that superseded anything else I did. It was definitely a gratifying experience.

CHAPTER 33

CHRIS BENOIT

When people ask me about Chris Benoit now, I don't say anything. They ask because they know we were friends. It's an uncomfortable subject, but here are my thoughts, for what they're worth.

Chris Benoit was one of the nicest people I ever knew. We rode together, we worked out together, we were close. He loved his job and he loved his family. He was steady. Twenty-four hours a day, when he was around the other wrestlers, he never went up or down. To most people, he was like a brick wall, absolutely stone-faced. If you could make Chris Benoit laugh, you sure did something. He found the misfortune of others hilarious. That's not to say he was mean-spirited — it just tickled him. Everybody backstage liked and respected Chris. He was a man's man. He rarely had anything bad to say about anyone, but if he had something to say about you, he would say it to your face. He was a locker-room leader — how could he not be? If people came to him, he would offer advice, and if he knew you were serious about your craft, he would help in any way he could. Take MVP — he was a good guy who truly wanted it. Chris knew that he wasn't just another guy going through the motions because he kept asking questions, taking in everything Chris told him, and trying to apply it every night. Chris took him under his wing and mentored him. MVP found it hard to keep up sometimes and that was a little frustrating for Chris. He'd been one of the best wrestlers in the world for so long that everything was just second nature to him.

And make no mistake about it, Chris is up there with the best of all time. When he got in that ring, there was not one person who took his job more seriously than Chris Benoit. If you were in the ring, you'd better be on your game or he'd eat you alive. It meant a lot to him to be World Champion. In my eyes, for those few months he was champion, he was the perfect representative for the company. He was a consummate professional. He took his job seriously and he took the welfare of his family seriously.

When we had a house show in Mobile, he stayed at my house and got to meet Snickers, my giant schnauzer, and he was really impressed. Snickers was the best guard dog you could ever want. He sat right beside me and wouldn't take his eyes off Chris. I told him, "You can come over, he's fine," and Chris replied, "No, I'm going to stay over here . . . !" He was so impressed with the demeanor and stature of my dog that he just kept saying "wow" over and over. That was where he got the idea of getting a couple of dogs to protect Nancy and their son, Daniel. He ended up getting a couple of German shepherds.

In all the time we rode together, I didn't once see him get mad or worked up about anything. He was always polite. If somebody is rude to me, I'll be rude right back. Chris? He was nice to everyone, no matter how they acted. If he was ever brought the wrong order at a restaurant, he never got mad, no matter how tired or hurt he was. Whenever someone walked up to him, wanting an autograph or to talk, he was always polite. I never saw any anger in him. He got frustrated at times with his work or his home life but who doesn't? The frustration never seemed to turn into anger. He was balls-to-the-wall rough in the ring and got a lot of his frustrations out in there. That was one of his outlets. The other was alcohol. He'd sometimes grab a six-pack after a show and drink a couple in the car while I was driving us to the next town, but I never saw him drink more than two or three beers at a time. I know that he and Nancy liked to drink a lot when he got off the road though.

I liked Nancy. When she came with Chris to TV, I often wouldn't be working, so she and I would sit together and talk. She liked most of the boys but she despised Hunter. We both had the same view of him, that he was a backstabbing son of a bitch. She was a good woman but somebody you definitely did not want to piss off. I know that she and Chris had had problems for quite a while because Chris talked to me about it here and there. He never divulged too much regarding what they fought about, but he did say that both he and Nancy would get pretty volatile. He said that he would get worked up but it would never turn physical. If it was getting to be too much, Chris would leave for the apartment he had elsewhere in Atlanta and stay there for a couple of days. That was his way of calming down.

One thing I *did* know was that Nancy wanted him to take time off and he didn't feel he could. He was always one of the main guys and always in the middle of a storyline. The company had a lot of money invested in him. She wanted him home and he wanted time off but he didn't think the company would go for it. It got to the point where Nancy wanted him to quit but he wouldn't ever have done that. He loved wrestling too much. There were other stresses at home — Chris had two kids from a previous marriage so he had to pacify his ex-wife. He told me it was hardest when his kids came to stay for the summer. His son was fine and accepted Nancy as Chris's wife but his daughter wouldn't speak to her at all. She would live with them for the whole summer and not say a single word to Nancy, which caused a lot of tension. Chris didn't get to see his kids much, so he didn't want to scold his daughter for being rude, but he had to think about Nancy's feelings too. He felt like he was caught in the middle. He didn't elaborate hugely on things like this and I didn't push him. I don't ask those sorts of questions because it's none of my business. If he volunteered it, that was fine, but I wasn't going to push him. We didn't talk that much when we traveled — we both liked it that way. It might sound like a boring commute but everything else is such a whirlwind that you need that downtime. It was a chance for us to both decompress. I'd drive and he'd drink a couple of beers.

It turns out that a lot of Chris's close friends in wrestling had died. At the time, I didn't know he had lost so many friends. He never spoke about it. The only person I knew Chris was close to who died was Eddie, and he hardly spoke to me about that. I knew that Chris kept an action figure of Eddie in the passenger seat of his Humvee. Everywhere Chris went, that action figure of Eddie went too. I thought it was odd, but people grieve in different ways. I try to separate myself from grief because I don't want to let it affect my life. I figured Chris was handling it in the best way he knew. He was deeply religious, as was Eddie. They both carried a bible on the road and read it every day and night. They wanted to educate themselves about the whole religious thing. I guess that was their way of feeling closer to God. When Eddie died, it did something to Chris.

Chris was also upset when they moved him from *RAW* to ECW in 2007. He took that personally. I told him that I truly believed they needed star power on that show and were moving him so he could be the guy everything would be built around. He felt he was being phased out of WWE and being put out to pasture. He was concerned that he would make less money there, because *RAW* and *Smackdown* were the bigger shows.

During my recovery from elbow surgery, I found myself in Chris's neck of the woods in June because I had to go to Atlanta for a meeting with an attorney. Chris was getting off the road on Wednesday, so we had arranged for me to stop by his house. As I was driving back from my appointment, I figured that he probably wanted to have some time with his family because he'd only just got home. So I just went on home. I got a call from him that Friday, asking me why I hadn't stopped by or called. Chris chewed me out about it. I said, "You just got off the road, I know what it's like — I figured you'd want to spend time with Nancy and Daniel." He said, "That doesn't fucking matter, you're one of my best friends, you should have come over." I told him that I was off for at least a few more months, so I'd definitely come to see him. "Okay, you fucking better!" he replied, and then he told me he'd just been to see Dr. Astin and was heading home. I asked how everything was with him and Nancy and he told me, "She's acting like Hitler." I kind of laughed it off but he said, "No, really — she's acting like Hitler. I had to get out of the house." We talked a little bit more, then hung up.

I went about the rest of my day.

Chris went home and killed his wife.

The next day, he killed his son.

Then, on the Sunday, he killed himself.

Kevin Fertig was the one who told me. He was close to Chris too, and called to let me know that Chris had been found dead. I was in disbelief. Kevin told me that somebody had broken into their house and killed Chris, Nancy, and Daniel. I immediately knew that something wasn't right. Nobody was going to just walk into that house because they had two big dogs, not to mention that wolverine named Chris Benoit.

When I heard what had actually happened, I didn't want to believe it. How could someone do that to his own family? I have no idea what happened in Chris's head. I accept the facts but I just don't get how it could have happened. WWE immediately went about distancing themselves from the situation — it was necessary, self-preservation. I was glad I wasn't in the locker room at that point. I heard from a few of the boys but, for the most part, they were in their own world. When you're on the road, you're on the road. By the time I got back in the locker room, the whole thing was over.

I dealt with it the same way I dealt with Owen, Crash, and Eddie — I put it aside and didn't let it affect me. It was a real tragedy but I wasn't going to let what happened affect the rest of my life. I was close to both Eddie and Chris and just had to shut myself off. I would have been a mental wreck if I hadn't. I would have been bawling my eyes out 24 hours a day. I looked at it like, "That's life — it was that person's time to go." It might seem removed but it's how I cope. I accepted that it was Chris's time.

What *was* difficult for me to accept was that Chris killed his family. Because we traveled together and broke bread together, it's really hard for me to cast judgment on him. On the one hand, he was my friend. On the other hand, I wanted to say he was a sorry motherfucker for doing what he did, especially to a kid who had nothing to do with any of Chris's problems. Every time Chris brought Daniel to the show, you could see how much he loved that boy. Daniel would walk around with tape on his wrists like he was a wrestler. That's my memory of that child. It breaks my heart to think about how much Chris loved him and what he ended up doing.

I did think about why he killed Daniel. This is pure speculation, but I think maybe Chris and Nancy had been drinking — which I knew they liked to do — and got into a fight. He lost control and it got physical. It went too far and he ended up killing her without realizing what he was doing. Then it dawned on him — oh fuck, I just killed my wife. He had time to think about it and realized that Daniel was going to grow up knowing his mom was dead and his dad killed her and was in prison. He decided it was too much for that kid to grow up knowing, so he took matters into his own hands.

I have no idea what led to the argument that set everything off. There was some speculation about whether Chris was having an affair with one of the girls in the locker room, but I guarantee he wasn't. Just because one of the boys rides with one of the girls, it doesn't mean he's screwing her. One of the girls needed a ride and that was that. As strange as it sounds given what happened, Chris was 100 percent committed to his family.

In the investigation that followed the tragedy, it was reported that Chris had the brain of an Alzheimer's patient because of all the concussions. How could they say that when Chris never forgot a spot in that ring and always remembered every single thing you told him? With Alzheimer's, you forget everything. I got the feeling they were just trying to attach the blame to something, either steroids or concussions. I disagree — if the authorities were going to point the finger at anything, they should have pointed it at alcohol. The report mentioned that there were empty alcohol bottles in the house. By the time he killed himself, any alcohol Chris drank on the Friday would have been out of his system. He could have drunk a huge amount on the Friday and had a zero blood alcohol level on the Sunday. I genuinely believe that if not for alcohol, none of this would have happened.

You've got two people going head to head, both of them drinking; something's got to give. Alcohol mixes differently with different personalities. Some people get brave, some get mean, some get crazy, and some do stupid things. Nancy wasn't the sort of woman to back down and Chris snapped. He probably thought he was just going to shut her up and it all went downhill from there.

We've all made some strange decisions when drinking but different people have different temperaments. They say you've got to look out for the quiet ones. Chris was one of them. Long-term drinking affects the way a person thinks. It alters the mind and damages the ability to make good judgments. The people who claim the tragedy was caused by 'roid rage are looking for an easy target. Those people don't take steroids, so that is where they lay the blame; I bet those same people drink alcohol, and I guarantee that when they're lit, they've got a short fuse. Whichever way you look at it, as far as I can see, alcohol was far more to blame in that situation than steroids or concussions.

I felt a lot of guilt because I didn't go to visit Chris the Wednesday before this all went down. When I spoke to him on the day he killed Nancy, he was hot at me because I hadn't stopped by. He was adamant that he had wanted me to come to his house. That was uncharacteristic of him; looking back, I wonder if he'd been trying to reach out to me. I wondered for the longest time if I could have changed the course of events, if only I'd gone to see him. Would they all still be alive? It probably would have happened at some point regardless, but still, it's not a nice thing to carry around.

I think about Eddie and Chris from time to time, and what happened to them breaks my heart but I don't think too much on it. Death is part of life. Are you going to grieve forever or are you going to get to work? I cared a lot about both of them but there comes a point where you've got to put your grief behind you and move on.

PART 16: RELATIONSHIPS IN WRESTLING

It's difficult to maintain a relationship when you're in the wrestling business. When you meet somebody, you might explain to her the way the business works and she'll think she's all okay with it. After a while though, it gets old. She hasn't seen you in ages, so when you get home, she wants to go, go, go to make up for lost time, while all you want to do is rest because your body is beat up. It can go to hell in a hand basket pretty quickly. It's especially hard if you've got a kid. A lot of people think they can handle it but discover they can't. I should know — I've been divorced a couple of times. If the person you're with hasn't got the right mentality, you can forget it from the start.

To be honest, if you're in the wrestling business, it's probably not a good idea to be married. Most wrestlers' marriages end up in divorce. There is so much partying, drinking, drugs, women — that kind of stuff is all over wrestling. That was never me — I would go to my room after the show and stay there, and I still ended up divorced! Some guys go out drinking after the shows every night. Management doesn't put any pressure on you either way. They don't make it their business at all; they just want you to work.

Relationships with other people in wrestling don't work a lot of the time either. It's not something that will get you in trouble with the office, but it could compromise how you're seen by the company and by your peers. Melina and Batista had something going on when she was with John Morrison. John was an idiot for being okay with that; what man in his right mind would be okay with the girl he lives with messing around with another one of the boys? When he found out, he should have been a fucking man and whipped Batista's ass. John could have taken Batista in a fight for sure. He was just afraid he'd lose his job because Batista was one of the top guys and was living in Hunter's colon. I don't get why Morrison didn't just drop Melina. Nobody liked her anyway so he would have earned a lot more respect for walking away.

If you act like a pussy, you're going to lose everybody's respect. When Matt Hardy found out that Lita was fucking Edge, he went around telling everybody who would listen that when he came back, he was going to beat the shit out of Edge. He asked for my advice and I told him, "You're telling everybody you're going to do it, you've got to deliver." Everybody thought he was going to stiff Edge in their match. He even said to me, "Watch what I do," right before he went out. After the match, he came back and said, "Did you see what I did?" I said, "You didn't do a fucking thing!" I think that whole thing was a work anyway — Matt and Lita were finished so they tried to make an angle out of it and work the boys. If somebody was fucking the woman I was living with, I wouldn't have a conversation about what would go down in the ring. I would head straight over there and kick the crap out of him. Everybody lost a lot of respect for Matt after that. Edge kept his mouth shut, kept working hard, and ended up in the main events. I felt like they saw a platform to launch Edge to the next level, so they only brought Matt back as a stepping stone anyway.

CHAPTER 34

BETRAYAL

After I was cleared to come back following my latest — but not final — elbow surgery, Creative finally had a decent story for me. They brought me into a storyline as the hardened veteran who was going to test the new kid on the block. This wasn't my usual thing. I wasn't just going to be used for one match to put the new guy over, this was an ongoing program. They were going to use me to help the kid to develop his craft and understand how things work in a singles or a tag match. The kid in question was Cody Rhodes, son of the "American Dream" Dusty Rhodes. I was going to be his mentor, groom him, and help him get over.

We laid it out like this: in the first match, I would beat him. Then he would come back and ask for another match. I would beat him again. He'd keep coming back and I'd keep beating him. Each time, he would get closer to winning while trying to earn my respect. It was a good angle. From there, we built to a point where I started teaming with him and helping him onscreen because he had shown he was worth my time. He got to beat me in a one-on-one match at the end of the storyline, and we settled into a run as a regular tag team after that. I liked working with Cody. Because of his dad, I guess, he was old school and was quick to learn. I thought he was a good worker.

Cody earned my respect for his work and for his attitude too. Before our third singles match, we were going to do a segment backstage in which I would try to get him fired up. Vince came over to me early in the day and said, "Bob, this is TV. I want you to slap Cody. When I say I want you to slap him, I fucking want you to *slap* him." I said, "You ain't got to tell me but one time." We rehearsed the scene but not the slap. Cody wouldn't be able to take that twice. Vince came over and told Cody that we had to nail this because it was going to be played live in the arena. "Are you on board with this?" Vince asked. "Yes, sir, no problem," Cody responded. So they counted us down, we did our promo, and it came time for me to slap him. I fucking *cracked* him. I slapped the everlasting piss out of him. It sounded like a shotgun going off. You could hear the crowd in the arena going, "Whoa!" Cody sold it and whipped his head back around at me, and I could see that his eyes were sort of glazed over. We finished up, and as soon as the producer told us we were clear, Cody walked out of the room for a moment, shaking his head to clear the cobwebs. About five seconds later, he came back in. I asked him if he was okay, and he said he was fine. Vince was pleased, saying, "That's what I was talking about. Good job."

Our run as a team was fun, for the most part. We won the tag team titles from Lance Cade and Trevor Murdoch and held them for over six months. It didn't really mean a damn thing for me financially but I got a couple of pay-per-view checks out of it. Unfortunately, Cody wasn't getting over like the office thought he would. Any time we tagged on a house show, if I was on the apron the crowd would start chanting "Hardcore!" or "We want Holly!" no matter what Cody was doing in the ring. Even when he made the comeback, they still wanted me and not him. He just wasn't getting over. I don't know why. I'd tried my best to get him over and not be selfish with our TV time. He threw that back in my face in the end. Before one of our matches on *RAW*, his dad pulled him aside. I had no idea what was said and I couldn't figure out what was going on. I didn't think anything more of it, and we went to the ring. We had been given seven minutes, with the idea that I would start the match and then tag Cody. He would do some work, tag me back, I'd do some more, and then he would get the win. I wanted him to get the wins because he needed them more than I did. I worked about 40 seconds at the start of that match and tagged Cody in. Then I stood on the apron for another six minutes. He didn't tag me back and he got the win. I walked into the ring, got my hand raised, and said, "Thanks for tagging me back in — whatever happened to that?" He didn't say anything. When he got through the curtain, his dad walked right up to him, whispered something in his ear, and that was that. I knew they'd just pulled a fast one on me — it was their way of saying, "We'll show you because you're over and Cody isn't." After that, I didn't trust him anymore. I'd helped him along so much. It wasn't right that he treated me that way.

He wasn't the only guy back then who let me down. During the run with Cody, I had been working on *RAW* for the first time in years. Ken Kennedy had moved there earlier in 2007. I'd grown close to Ken on *Smackdown* in 2005 and we'd traveled together when I was on ECW because they filmed the *Smackdown* and ECW shows on the same night. On our days off, we'd talk on the phone too. We had one of those rare things in wrestling: a real friendship. I was going through a divorce at the time and he kept me sane. He always told me that if I got into an argument, I should just leave before I did anything stupid. He got me through a lot of stuff. And it went the other way too — when he got suspended for steroids in 2007, he had just bought a house, so he was worried about making his house note. I offered to pay it for him because I trusted that he would pay me back. I knew he was good for it, and I didn't want to see this young guy get behind on his mortgage. He said he was okay but if he needed some help, he'd call me. We vented to each other, confided in each other, we kept each other's head clear.

That's why I was so puzzled when he threw me under the bus.

My neck bothers me to this day. Everything changed because of my injury in that match with Brock back in 2002. My neck doesn't move the same way most people's necks do, so it puts stress on other joints. If I hadn't kept wrestling, I don't think I would have had any problems with my neck, but I wasn't about to quit. Maybe I should have. I was given a lot of pain medication during the recovery process but I stopped taking it after a couple of months. When I came back to wrestling in late 2003, I tried to work without medication, but after about six months, I started taking them again. It got out of hand. About a year after my comeback,

I realized I was taking them just for the hell of it, rather than to manage pain. I was taking Lortab and I was getting it legally, so my prescriptions were above board. Benoit had hooked me up with a doctor who was very liberal with writing prescriptions, so I was able to get quite a lot — far more than I needed. There was no one incident that made me think, "Hey, I'd better get off these." I just realized I was getting out of control. It was very hard but I got off them and stayed off for a long time. As the years went on, I took some pills when I needed them but I kept it under control.

In mid 2008, we were down at a show in Bakersfield, California. I needed some pain meds because my neck was hurting and I needed yet another elbow surgery, so I asked Ken if he had anything. He said sure and gave me some meds. He then said that if I needed any more later, I should just go in his bag and get them. That's normal. I can't tell you the number of times Ken came to me, saying, "Have you got anything?" and I told him, "Help yourself." Everybody in the locker room helps each other. It's an unwritten rule. The office knows it happens but they turn a blind eye. They know we need it sometimes.

Later that day in California, I needed some more meds. I finished doing my pre-tape interview and went into the locker room. About 15 people were in there. I grabbed another few pills from Ken's bag. He came in with Umaga moments later, so I told him I'd taken four pills and would replace them when I got my next prescription filled. He said that was fine and went about getting some pills for Umaga. I thought that was the end of it but then, a week or so later, a rumor started floating around that I'd gone into Ken's bag without permission. I called him at home to ask what was up and he assured me that everything was fine. Next time I saw him at tv, I talked to him about this rumor again and he said he didn't know anything about how it started. In the end, I got a call from Johnny Laurinaitis, asking me what was going on. I told him what had happened and he said that it wasn't what he'd heard.

I found out afterwards, through talking to John Cena and Shawn Michaels, the rumor had started when Umaga had told a couple people that I had gone into Ken's bag to get pills. Ken never told Umaga that he had said I could and, when the rumor started spreading, Ken could have stopped it by saying, "I told Bob it was okay" but he didn't. He'd been lying to me the whole time, claiming he didn't know what was going on and then not admitting that he hadn't squashed the rumour.

It was self-preservation for Ken. Word had spread that I'd taken stuff from Ken's bag and, when the rumor reached management, Ken could have got in trouble, so he stooged me out. You don't stooge the boys out and you always try to help each other. Everybody knows this. Maybe Ken didn't get the memo. All he needed to say was that it had all been a misunderstanding; he'd have got a talking-to and that would have been it. I guess Ken wanted to look like a victim. But if I was going to steal from him, why the hell would I go into his bag in plain sight in the locker room?

Ken really kicked me when I was down. I'd told him a lot of things that were going on with me, with my divorce and everything. I needed him to be a friend and instead his actions could have had serious implications for my career. As it was, I got a slap on the wrist from Johnny and that was that, but it could have been a lot worse. I confronted Ken and called him every name under the sun. I even tried to get him to come outside and settle it with me but he wouldn't. For years after that, I wanted to get even with Ken, but now all I want him to do is look me in the eye and give me an explanation about why he did what he did. I doubt I'll ever get one.

There ended up being a rumor that I got fired because of this whole deal with the pills. That is such bullshit. I had another surgery scheduled, so we finished off the storyline with Cody and they wrote me off TV. We did a switch: Cody turned heel on me and started teaming with Ted DiBiase. They ended up with the titles and I got my surgery. It bothered me that Cody didn't call to thank me for my help or to wish me well after my surgery. I taught that little bastard a lot, so his lack of gratitude bothered me. I hear he's using the Alabama Slam sometimes these days. I'd like to think that's a shout out to me but who knows? He hasn't beat anyone with it yet from what I heard, so I guess he's not doing it right!

Cody's heel turn was well done and got over, and it left the door open for me to return after my elbow had healed. After all, I was still under contract for the better part of a year. A few months later, I called Creative to discuss new ideas. Cody and Ted were getting a lot of heat, beating people in chickenshit ways, so I pitched the idea that I would come back to get revenge on them. We would do a cage match and they would beat me down, so I'd bring Billy Gunn in and the two of us would do a program with Cody and Ted: veterans against upstarts. They said they'd think about it but I didn't hear anything back. Then Johnny called to say that nothing was lined up for me. I told Johnny about my idea — he liked it and said he'd go talk to Creative for me. I got a call from him later just saying, "Sorry, Bob, they don't have anything for you." Johnny had been one of my main supporters over the years. He told me he'd gone to bat for me in meetings all the time and so had lots of the other agents. They knew how long I'd been loyal, how hard I worked, that I was always on time, that I stayed in great shape and did exactly what was asked of me. Yet it all came down to "We don't have anything for you." That was it — I was done. I told Johnny that I deserved more than coming back to sit in the locker room, doing absolutely nothing. So if Creative had nothing for me, they should just go ahead and send me my release.

In January 2009, 15 years after I'd started with the company, we parted ways. It would have been nice to get some acknowledgment for my hard work. I'm not talking about the Hall of Fame — that's just another way for the company to make money. The WWE Hall of Fame is the biggest crock on the planet. When you've got a guy like Drew Carey in there, a guy who has done nothing for the wrestling business, that tells me that if you're a television star, they might put you in the WWE Hall of Fame to get some publicity. The Rock and Roll Hall of Fame, the NFL Hall of Fame, the NBA Hall of Fame — people in there are recognized all over the world for their accomplishments and it's a big deal. You wouldn't see the NBA inducting Jack Nicholson into their Hall of Fame because he goes to watch the Lakers!

All I wanted was a good storyline that I could make some decent money with. That would have been my gold watch, so to speak. I look at guys like Mark Henry, who were utility guys year after year, and they are finally getting used. A lot of people say, "He's been here a while, he deserves that spot." Nobody ever said that about me. That does bother me — I deserved a better spot than I had. I put in so much time and enhanced so many people over the years. I was talented enough to carry a storyline. I'm not suggesting they should have used me in the main events, but I am saying they should have used me for *something*. I've seen them give chances to guys who "really deserved it" — I worked just as hard as them, put in just as much time, and did everything I was asked, but I don't think I got the run I deserved. It hurts that nobody seems to say, "He deserved better" about me.

Every single person who works for WWE goes there hoping to make a lot of money. To do that, you have to get to a point where you're used regularly in programs that draw money. Being made a singles champion means you'll make more money. The most-asked question in the locker room is "When is it going to be my time?" I guarantee the boys who are either used to get somebody else over — or simply not used — are all thinking, "My time is coming. I've just got to keep going." Not true — they'll use you when they want and not a minute sooner. God forbid you complain out loud. It does no good to complain. Crash used to do that a lot, asking, "Why aren't they doing this or that with me?" Albert used to do it too. As far as he was concerned, he should have been in main events and getting a good push. He was sure to let everybody know it. Both of those guys were let go in part because they were so vocal about their lack of push. WWE has a lot of guys sitting out on the porch, so to speak, but it's a very select few who get to come inside the house and sit at the table. If you complain, you get thrown off the porch.

The only time I really made a point about my standing in the company was some time in 2005. I remember being in catering and watching back the previous week's show. One of the commentators said something about me being "one of the toughest guys in the locker room." That got me thinking, and I ended up deciding to go and find Vince to talk about it. As it happens, I ran into both Stephanie and Vince in the hallway and said, "Hey, I have a question for you both — if the commentators are telling the whole world that I'm one of the toughest guys in the locker room, why am I losing all the time?" They both just stood there, staring blankly and searching for an answer. Eventually, Steph said, "You know, that's a good question." Vince said, "We'll get back to you on that." They didn't.

I only ever complained far away from the locker room. I wouldn't even complain in the car because you never knew who it might get back to. Of course it's frustrating when you've got the tools to go further and you're not being pushed. Don't get me wrong, I'm not saying I should have been

World Champion or anything but if they can make a main eventer out of Sheamus, who telegraphs so much of what he does and can't even do a decent headlock takeover, I think it's a fair thing to wonder why they never gave me at least a better spot than I had. Athletically, I was definitely good enough. I knew how to work an exciting, safe match, hit the time cues for TV, and tell a story. Granted, I wasn't good on the microphone to begin with, but my promos got better over the years. Hell, Jericho is the king of promos and he enjoyed my later stuff, so I must have been doing something right. . . . Go back and look at some of The Rock's earlier promos; he couldn't talk to save his life but look how he turned out with time and practice. I'm not bitter — I was happy doing what I was doing but I wasn't satisfied, if that makes sense. I just couldn't figure out why I wasn't getting used in programs that meant something.

Take Santino Marella — he's a funny gimmick and that's about it. They put the IC belt on him in his first week, and he's also been the US Champion since then. I'm a better wrestler, I look better . . . so I find myself wondering exactly what it was that stopped me getting used at the same level. I looked and performed like an athlete, and you can't tell me those facts were rendered completely irrelevant because I wasn't great at promos. Still, it's the only thing I can figure Santino has on me. I don't begrudge him his success but I would like to know why I never got a good opportunity to be more of a player. I want people to understand that, if they were in my shoes, they'd ask the same questions. It's like feeling you're being passed over for a promotion when you've been at the company longer than everybody else, and the guy who gets the promotion isn't anywhere near the worker you are. I think anybody would be annoyed by that.

In the end, after 15 years, I didn't even get a note or a phone call from Vince McMahon to thank me. You would think that he would thank each and every talent for busting their asses, putting their bodies through hell, keeping up with the schedule, and doing what they had to do to help make the product what it is. You'd think wrong though. Unless you're at the level of 'Taker, Triple H, or Shawn Michaels, you can forget about the company being grateful for your work. It's a thankless industry.

So why didn't I get further with WWE? I believe it was politics. Now, you're going to get politics in any company, but the situation is worse in WWE than in any other job I've seen. It doesn't matter how good somebody is. It's about being in the right place at the right time and knowing the right person. Look at Batista. Don't get me wrong, I like Dave but when they started his huge push, he was one of the worst wrestlers ever to step into the ring and couldn't talk either. He did improve with time because he learned from one of the very best in Hunter but, in the beginning, he was still too green for his spot and only got the big push due to his impressive look and Hunter bringing him into his inner circle.

And make no mistake — everything goes back to what Hunter wants. It's all a game to him. He wasn't satisfied just being in the business. He wanted a lot more and he set out to get it. This is just my perspective after seeing how everything played out backstage, mind you. Vince liked him, he ended up doing an angle in which he married the boss's daughter, and when she started to have real feelings for him, what do you think he was going to do? I'm sure he does genuinely love her now but I'm not sure how genuine he was with her at the very beginning. I think he was in love with the business and saw it as his way to the top of the industry. He's a smart fucker. He's both good and bad for business. He's a great wrestler who knows what to do in the ring. I recently watched one of my matches against him from back in the Attitude era and it reminded me of just how good he is. He was always very gracious to me in the ring, very unselfish, and that's because he understands how wrestling works, but he bases too many of his backstage decisions on how he feels about somebody. Vince bases his decisions on how much money he could make from a person or a situation; that's the difference.

I want to like the guy — I really do. He's great in the ring, nice to your face and fun to be around, but it's hard to like him when you know about all of his backstage maneuvering and how he's screwed with people's lives. Hunter has buried many a good worker just because he didn't like the guy. He nearly killed Cena right from the get-go. When you think that Cena has been the company's biggest cash cow for the last decade, it shows you how much Hunter knew about *that* deal. He always buried Jericho, he nearly got him fired. So many guys could have been a lot more than they ended up being. Kane, Booker, R.V.D. — all buried by Hunter. Rob Van Dam could have been huge. C.M. Punk is one of the top guys now but he could have been *the* guy. Even though Hunter never liked him, they had no choice but to go with Punk because he got over. You'll notice that Hunter made sure to go over on him though, to make sure everybody knew Punk wasn't on Hunter's level. Where's the sense in that? It just took away Punk's momentum when he was the hottest thing going. Punk could have made so much more money for the business if Hunter had had the balls to put him over.

It's got to be insecurity. It's strange, because he's such a great wrestler. He's got such a great mind for the business and he's actually a decent guy, as he showed when he took us all to that zoo in Australia. But when it comes to company politics, if he doesn't like you, he'll fuck you over, no matter how good you are. It's a crying shame.

Face to face, he acts like he's your best friend, but as soon as you turn away, out comes the knife. I'm not going to mention names because the people in question still work for the company, but I was told several times by several people that Hunter used to bury me directly to Vince in meetings. Once he was in power, I was going nowhere — especially after the incident with Duprée. I wish he'd had the balls to tell me what he really thought of me to my face. As far as I'm concerned, he's a coward for never giving me any indication there was something wrong between us.

Bret Hart hit the nail on the head when he said that Hunter tries to keep all of the money for his cronies. When they started up D-Generation X again in 2006, Billy, Road Dogg, and X-Pac wanted to come back in but Hunter put the kibosh on that. He wanted to keep it to just him and Shawn so that they could split the merchandise royalties two ways rather than five. Sure, they brought the others back for Raw 1000 but that's not the same as doing a proper run with everybody from D-X where they can all make money. Even then, at Raw 1000, they didn't bring Chyna back and she had been a big part of the group. I don't know why they didn't — and before anyone says it's because of her recent "career choices," didn't Waltman appear in one of those movies too? Bottom line is that everybody's got skeletons in their closet. Booker T and MVP had both served time, yet WWE still used them, so who gives a fuck? If they were going to do a D-X reunion, they should have brought them all back.

Consider this — in 2011, Hunter came back after a year out. His first match was the second biggest match at 'Mania, against Undertaker. Then he wrestled a couple of matches, buried Punk, got a main event against his buddy Nash — who has no business being in the ring anymore — and came back again just in time for another huge payday at 2012's 'Mania, against Undertaker again. His next match after that was the main event of SummerSlam against Brock Lesnar. Once again, a big money spot. Some of the other boys are struggling and could have used that money and the exposure of wrestling guys like 'Taker and Brock. Hunter doesn't need those paychecks, and the business doesn't gain from him being in those matches. He keeps people down so that they can't achieve success and make money for their families. It's a real shame he feels the need to do that.

It's no secret that I have my issues with the internet. I'm not the only one — a lot of wrestlers go nuts because so much of the so-called news isn't credible. Rumors go around and around until people believe what they've read. Anybody can say anything on the internet, and it seems that you don't need to be accurate anymore. Now, it's not like I go out of my way to find out what people have been saying about me but it tends to get back to me in one form or another.

Take my Wikipedia page, for example — I've had such trouble with that. At one point, it said I was born in Grants Pass. I was born in Glendale, California! But if you believe Wikipedia, I was born in Oregon, as well as having been married to Cathy "B.B." Dingman (I have no idea where the marriage rumor came from. I don't kiss and tell but I definitely wasn't married to her — you can check any marriage record anywhere!), and a whole bunch of other crap of questionable accuracy. I've had it changed back for me a number of times, but after a while, somebody else logs in and changes things again to reflect what they've heard and assume to be right. That's the internet for you; anybody can write anything and it gets legs and runs. Hell, at one point, my Wikipedia said that I was currently in a Pennsylvania jail, arrested for a bar fight. I read that when I was sitting in my den, watching TV. It worries me because kids use Wikipedia in school these days, so they could be learning things that aren't real facts. I've had to deal with the fallout of being painted as a bad guy by the internet. A lot of wrestling sites got all worked up about the Matt Cappotelli deal, so they labeled me a prick and a bully. When people meet me, they realize I'm nothing like how I'm often portrayed. I feel like I'm constantly trying to prove what the internet says about me is wrong. My job was to portray a vicious bastard and I was good at my job! Glen Jacobs is one of the nicest guys you'll ever meet. Kane is a homicidal maniac. Nobody confuses the two of them. I guess it's easier to believe my act because we all know people who are like that. Just because I played the role on TV doesn't mean that's who I am! If somebody dicks me over though, they're going to get what's coming to them. If people are decent to me, I treat them with respect.

FISHING DIAMOND LAKE, OREGON IN 2010. IT WAS FREEZING THAT DAY!

CHAPTER 35
FLIRTING WITH THE INDIES

After my release from WWE, I got a call from TNA. I knew they weren't going to pay me right, so we didn't even get that far. I just said no. I felt let down by wrestling and the people in the industry. I got a bunch of calls from various independent promoters too, looking to cash in on my years on TV. I wasn't interested. I just didn't care anymore and thought I'd had my last match. I didn't want to be one of those guys who stumbles through a match and bleeds like a stuck pig in the ring because they need the money. I think a lot of the boys need to know when to stop wrestling and just make appearances so they don't become a parody of themselves. I guess they need the money in some cases. I'm lucky in that I've got a trade, which many of the guys don't have, so if I ever need money, I'll go back to being a mechanic or a welder.

I was always smart with my money when I was with WWE, so I didn't need to go back to work unless I wanted to. I could have made good money on the indie circuit too — more than I was making with WWE at the end. The funny thing is that most people would read that and think, "How can you make more on the independent circuit than in the big leagues?" They think that if you're on TV with WWE, you must be making at least three or four grand a week. Let me tell you something: unless business is red-hot, when you're mid-card or undercard with WWE, you're lucky to walk away with a thousand dollars a week after expenses. You can make a good amount of money, sure — but you end up spending most of it in order to keep making that money.

For my last few years with the company, my downside guarantee was $175,000 and I didn't end up making any bonuses beyond that because I didn't get many PPV shows or any merchandise or real royalties. $175,000 looks nice on paper, sure, but from that, you're paying taxes, health insurance, and most of the expenses including rental cars, gas, hotels, and food on the road. The only thing WWE pays for is your flight. You can essentially work a regular job, end up with almost as much money, and sleep in your own bed every night. A regular job isn't going to break down your body the way wrestling does. You just can't keep wrestling beyond a certain age, so unless you work on top, you're going to have to be very smart to get out of the business with savings by the time your body is done.

So many of the younger guys act like they are superstars before they are making superstar money. When Muhammad Hassan came in, he was making huge money. He hadn't been in the company for six months, he had such an easy gimmick to get over, and he was working with Hogan, so he figured he'd keep making that money forever. He was staying in $300-a-night hotels, getting the most expensive rental cars . . . he thought he was untouchable. He got so much heat in the locker room because he had an ego like you wouldn't believe. Nobody went to bat for him when his character got cut, and he ended up homeless. Guys like that don't get that this is just a job that isn't going to last forever. They've got to think about the future.

I was lucky enough to be with the biggest wrestling company in the world when it was at its most popular. We all made so much money back then. One time, I got paid $4,500 for walking down to the ring with Crash on *RAW*. He was wrestling Bradshaw at the Georgia Dome and I just stood in the corner. I made nearly as much for that as I did for wrestling Brock Lesnar for the WWE title on PPV. Go figure. I was lucky to have a few good years with a $275,000 guarantee and the one year that I made $400,000, so I was able to put enough aside to retire comfortably. If I hadn't been part of the Attitude era, I wouldn't have been able to get out of the business. I don't understand how the mid-card guys these days can get by, given what they're earning.

In the end, I took a few bookings on the independent circuit. On the indie shows, the promoters paid for flights, transported me around, put me up, and then paid me per show, so with the limited expenses and by doing two or three shows at a time, I came back with a good chunk of money. In WWE, I was working underneath in a role that wasn't going to draw. On the indie circuit, a guy who had been in WWE for as long as I had was the featured talent, so I was in a better position to get paid.

I ended up doing a few shows for Henry Hubbard in the U.S. He does shows now and then for the military, so I'm happy to help. He always takes care of me. Billy Gunn asked me to go with him to work for a start-up group in Canada called WFX. The promoter, Mike Davidson, was a good guy and the production was very professional. It wasn't people throwing a show together at the last minute; they had writers and production people, and it was all organized. I ended up going up there once a month and making decent money. They paid for my hotel, rental car, gas, everything. WFX would have been a great TV program but somebody made some poor decisions somewhere and they ran out of money.

Bushwhacker Luke got me in touch with an Australian promoter named Sammy Russo who runs a promotion known as the AWE. He sounded like a goof on the phone and I almost backed out because I thought he wasn't legit but I'm glad I didn't — that guy took care of me better than anybody ever has. He flew me out to Australia and treated me as if I were a world champion. This guy went out of his way to make sure I had everything I needed. As soon as I got there, he gave me the money we'd agreed on and he actually went out of his way to get me more. I was supposed to do an interview with a rugby team, which I was going to be paid for, but the interview got canceled. Sammy still gave me that money. I told him not to, but he insisted and said he wanted me to have it. It was a first class operation all the way. Another first class guy is James Soubasis, who runs Legends of the Ring conventions and was involved in the documentary *Card Subject to Change*. He took very good care of me. I'll work for Henry, Mike, Sammy, or James in a heartbeat because I know they will take care of me and live up to their promises. They might be few and far between, but there *are* some decent people out there promoting wrestling.

Still, I've been fucked around by a few others. Billy put me in touch with a promotion in Atlanta and I ended up doing a show I didn't get paid properly for. I paid for my own hotel, which wasn't part of the deal, when the guy handed me my money, it was $300 short. He drove me back to the airport and I cussed that motherfucker from one end to the other. I was surprised he didn't just pull over and tell me to get out! There are a whole bunch of promoters out there who will fuck people over in a heartbeat just to make a little bit of money. It's sad.

The biggest disappointment for me on the independent circuit was the first group I worked with after I left WWE. Billy couldn't make his booking, so he asked me to fill in. I ended up becoming really good friends with the promoter and flew across every few months to do two or three shows at a time and to help train his students.

In the end, even though I thought we were good friends, he let me down. On the last tour I did for him, we got to the airport, and as I was just about to go through security, he told me, "I don't have all your money but I'll send you the rest next Friday." He still owed me over a grand but I trusted him and said that was fine. Friday came and went. And another Friday. And another. He kept saying there had been "miscommunications" and that his shows weren't drawing as well as he'd hoped. That doesn't matter. You should always make sure you've got the money before you agree to pay the talent. It's just basic decency. It turns out that not many promoters have that decency. I didn't like the lying. I didn't like the fact that he had waited until the last minute at the airport to tell me about not having the money. He still hasn't paid up what he owes me.

Although that relationship ended on a sour note, I enjoyed helping out and doing the training sessions. I would be happy to do more training seminars; I think I'm pretty good at it and have no problem getting in the ring with the trainees. I don't think you can really teach from the floor. I'd also like to do something else on TV — maybe some reality TV or hosting a show. Anything to do with NASCAR would be good!

But I won't go out of my way to wrestle anymore. It means a lot of stress, and dealing with people who let you down gets harder to take each time. If one of the four decent promoters I know asks me to help out, I might do something, but my body can't take the abuse any more. It takes me a lot longer to recover from matches now, so until further notice, I'll consider myself happily retired.

PART 19: THE STATE OF MODERN WRESTLING

Back in the day, wrestling had a mystique about it. Even if people thought it might be fake, nobody was sure. Nowadays, everybody knows that wrestling is entertainment so it's harder to get the fans to suspend their disbelief but that's not to say it can't be done. Things need to be kept simple. Back in the '80s, when Jake Roberts hit his opponents with the DDT, that was it. But as soon as people started kicking out of that maneuver, it stopped meaning anything. Now this move that used to be deadly is used as just one more maneuver that everybody does. When people are kicking out of finishers all the time, what do you do to top that? If everybody is Superman, where's the fun in that?

The main problem with wrestling these days, in my view, is that the talent pool is very weak. Many of the younger guys coming through have been pampered and can't take the travel, the schedule, or the roughness of being in the ring. They don't realize how good they've got it now because they for sure wouldn't have survived in the '90s. Look at the difference between Randy Orton and Matt Cappotelli, two guys I tested out within months of each other. Randy was born into the business as a third-generation guy; he knows what to expect, he's taken his knocks, he's hung in there, and he's now one of the biggest stars in the industry. Matt thought it would be cool to go on a reality show and be a star. One pretty tame ass-kicking later, he was reconsidering everything. Like I said earlier, it's a damn shame he got cancer but that doesn't change my point that the tough lifestyle of being a wrestler wasn't going to be for him.

A lot of the newer guys see wrestling on TV and say, "I want to do that," but there's nowhere for them to properly learn the business. Back in my day, you had to work hard to even find a trainer. These days, there are a lot of wrestling schools out there, but it's important to find one with a good reputation and experienced trainers. Although some of the schools are excellent, others are run by people who need more training themselves! And even if you turn out to be pretty good, the fact that there isn't a territory system anymore means that it's hard for new wrestlers to tour, pick up experience, and learn their craft. WWE has such a monopoly on the business that, until you get into WWE, you're likely going to be based in just one area. You might get some ring-time but you won't get the experience of being on the road and learning whether you're cut out for it. You won't get the experience of working in front of lots of different crowds and having to get yourself over from nothing every night.

WWE tried to reboot *Tough Enough* to create some new stars and put out another hour of television. I thought the show was fine for entertainment, but they're not going to find a top star that way. Bill DeMott, Booker T, and Steve Austin were all great trainers but it bothered me to see Trish Stratus there with them. Don't get me wrong, Trish is a good person and I like her but what does she know about training wrestlers? She needed to be one of the students! She didn't get in the ring to show them anything because that would have exposed her. That's why she just stood on the floor and pointed. Whenever I train new guys, I get in the ring and sweat my ass off with them, show them how it's done. I don't stand on the floor and direct traffic.

I feel most wrestlers these days don't take enough pride in their work. Up until the '80s, wrestlers believed in the characters they portrayed and took that part of the business seriously. Because *they* took it seriously, it was easier for the fans to suspend disbelief. A lot of the new guys treat it like a joke. Most of them don't even watch the rest of the shows they're on. It's important to keep watching for two reasons; one, you get a chance to learn what works and what doesn't from each wrestler on the card, and two, it gives you a chance to change your match if somebody else does a spot you have planned. If your finish is a superplex but someone uses that in the match before you, how are you going to know unless you're paying attention? Too many of the new generation sit in the dressing room, not caring what's going on. They should be paying attention and learning.

I don't like seeing guys come in and have a spot at the top handed to them. Look at Sheamus — because he was buddies with Triple H, he was the wwe Champion within six months. Are you kidding me? He'd only just arrived! It was like Lashley and Lesnar all over again, guys who got put on top before they'd earned the spot. I know Sheamus stuck around but what would have happened if he had left? They would have just sacrificed most of their roster for a guy who didn't deserve it. It makes me mad because they've got so many guys who *are* good and *do* deserve it, but it comes down to politics so much. In any other professional sport, you have your best guys in the best spots. In basketball, you play your best five guys. In baseball, you have your best nine guys. You play your best guys in the big game but the main event of *WrestleMania* in 2011 was John Cena vs The Miz and it was *horrible*. Despite the fact that John is pretty much the hardest-working man in wwe, he's not a good wrestler. Miz isn't much better — he's improved but he's nowhere near good enough to be wwe Champion and main-eventing the biggest show of the year. Meanwhile, you had Dolph Ziggler working underneath on that same card for about a minute. Miz couldn't even carry Dolph's bags. That goes to show you something is fucked up in that company. They really missed the boat with Dolph for such a long time. As I'm writing this, it looks like they might finally be giving him a run at the top but I can't believe they've been holding him back for so many years now. I bet Hunter told Vince that Dolph was too small to be believable. Well, you know what? Hunter's too much of a pussy to be believable as the tough guy he plays on TV, so what's the difference?

I don't go out of my way to watch wwe anymore but when I come across it, channel surfing, I give it a chance. I end up wanting to attack the TV. I don't like the storylines, I don't like who they're trying to push, and I feel bad for the guys they're doing nothing with. Guys like Ted DiBiase Jr. who end up doing jobs for every-body. That kid has it all and they do nothing but beat him on TV. They were pushing him and he was getting over; he's another Randy Orton and could really be big, but it seems like they're pun-ishing him. For what? It's wrecking his career and it's a waste of talent. The same goes for Drew McIntyre. He's got charisma, he's an interesting character, he looks good, and he can work. I have no idea why they stopped pushing him.

For the life of me, I can't figure out what they've been doing with some of their other guys. They built Daniel Bryan up as World Champion and then beat him in 18 seconds at *WrestleMania*. No champion should be beaten in 18 seconds! They're World Champion for a reason. It just goes to show how unimportant they thought Daniel Bryan was at the time, even though he can wrestle circles around Sheamus. I guess Hunter thought Daniel Bryan was too small to be "believable."

I also don't care for the fact that they make the boys do scripted promos these days. Nobody should know your character better than you. Cutting a promo in somebody else's words isn't going to work. The same guys are writing all of the promos, and every-body ends up sounding the same, as well as looking the same, and working the same. It's too cookie-cutter and very few of them have any flavor. It's not all bad though — there are some other guys who are great and have the potential to build the business up if they're used right. I'm glad to see C.M. Punk got there. He deserves it — he worked his ass off, gave his body to the company, and is super talented. He takes what he does seriously. Guys like that deserve to work on top. Randy Orton is top rank. He had so much potential when he started and he keeps getting better. Christian is one of the absolute best. He knows what he's doing three or four spots before you get to it; there are only a handful of guys who are that good. He was so smooth in that ring I could have worked with him every day of my life. I would have loved to see him go 30 minutes with Shawn Michaels. That would have been one of the best wrestling matches ever.

The wrestling world has lost so many of the great workers, though. Shawn is untouchable, and Bret Hart was right up there too. Flair was good in his day but he's a shell of himself now. Edge was good and now he's retired. Benoit was great. Eddie was one of the very best of all time. Even guys like Kurt Angle, Undertaker, Chris Jericho, Rey Mysterio, and Triple H (and despite what I think of him personally, Hunter *is* one of the best workers ever) are slowing down and won't be active for much longer. They just haven't groomed the next generation properly, so you end up with guys like The Miz and Wade Barrett, who are fine in the mid-card but can't get the job done at the top level. The company seems desperate for new stars. It's a great shame, especially when I see people like Dolph Ziggler busting their asses and being held down for years. I just hope they catch on and start using guys like Dolph and Daniel Bryan properly. These guys are good and they are over. The product would be a lot better if management just let these guys do what they are great at. There are also some older guys out there they could bring back and that would help. Look at Billy Gunn. He's hard working, he's got a couple of decades of experience, he looks great, and he can still go better than most of the locker room. He could teach the new guys so much about the business and be good for TV at the same time. He even seems to be in Hunter's good graces these days, so I don't get why they wouldn't use him. Bottom line is that, as this book is being written, the ratings are falling so what they're doing right now clearly isn't working and they need to try something else.

CHAPTER 36
HOW DO YOU LIKE ME NOW?

For over 20 years, I gave my life over to wrestling. Was it really worth it? I hadn't considered that properly until I began writing this book.

It was what it was . . . I liked the wrestling part of the job. Once that bell had rung to start the match, I enjoyed it. I didn't like the traveling, the physical wear and tear, the politics, and the frustration at always wondering when — or if — my time would come. I may not have won a World title; I didn't even win a secondary singles title. But I did work for the biggest wrestling company in the world for longer than almost anybody else and made enough money to retire long before I turned 50. That's no bad thing, but it came with sacrifices.

Because I was in wrestling for so long, I now live with physical pain every single day. It doesn't inhibit me but it does aggravate me. I have a bunch of nagging injuries — I've got absolutely no cartilage left in my elbows so I can't actually straighten my arms anymore, and whenever I get stressed out or worked up, my neck hurts like hell. The body wearing down is part of life — it just accelerates when you wrestle for a living.

People may understand that being a wrestler damages your body, but they don't consider the damage it can do to your personal reputation. For more than 10 years, I was told to go out there and be an unsmiling prick

— that was my job. I feel like I'm always trying to undo that reputation now. People seem genuinely surprised when they realize I'm not actually like I was on TV.

I don't feel like I made any lifelong friends in wrestling. It's the way the industry is — there are people you are friendly with and people who are good friends when you're in the business, but when you're out, your phone never rings. You learn pretty quickly in wrestling that nobody really gives a fuck about anybody but themselves, so you keep a wall up to protect yourself. There were a lot of people I really liked, and a lot of people who I would describe as a friend, but there isn't anyone I speak to regularly anymore. Billy Gunn is probably my best friend from wrestling and months will go by without us talking, sometimes years. If you do end up with a true friend out of wrestling, then you've got something special there.

I think I've missed out on some of the normal family stuff that a lot of people have. I do wish I'd reached out to my dad. When I last heard from him after I'd made it to the WWF, I was hurt because he had been out of my life for so long and had shown no interest in me until I had "made it big" on TV. I didn't want a relationship with him based on my fame. Still, the older I get, the more I wish I'd had some form of father-son relationship. It's a shame I didn't reach out sooner. I could have had a chance to know him at least a little.

I don't blame wrestling for the breakdown of any of my relationships. They just weren't the right relationships for me. It had nothing to do with wrestling. I missed a lot of milestones in Stephanie's life because I had to work. I'd spend as much time as I could with her when I was off the road, and I'd like to think my then-wife and I gave her a good home. It was hard to balance things because of my schedule. I almost missed Stephanie's high school graduation because I was wrestling. I made it just in time to see her walk up to receive her diploma. I was there just long enough to tell her I was proud of her and to apologize because I had to go straight to the airport to catch a flight for the next show. When I had days off, I would take her to the mall or we'd go out to eat, but that sometimes ended up becoming an ordeal for her. Back when the WWF was really taking off, people were constantly coming up and saying hi or asking for autographs. That upset her because it was taking away from her time with me and she wasn't getting 100 percent of my attention. It was really hard on her and I think she became a little resentful of wrestling. She didn't like having to share me. You can't blame a kid for not wanting to share her dad with everybody else.

I feel like both wrestling and life in general have jaded me. The older I get, the more cynical I seem to get. I've helped so many people out, yet those same people have turned around and stabbed me in the back. Nowadays, I can usually figure out whether a person is decent or not after five minutes of conversation. It's something I've learned from being around so many shady people in the wrestling business. I still get blindsided now and then, but nowhere near as often or as badly as I used to. Still, as jaded and cautious as I have become, I'm still polite, trusting, and hopeful. If somebody earns my love and trust, I will love and trust them completely.

On Labor Day in 2009, my brother and I were at our mom's house. We were watching a DVD from his high school reunion and I asked whether anyone had heard from Linda or knew what she was doing. I didn't really expect him to know anything. I figured he'd already have told me if he did. "Yeah, I talk to her on Facebook," he said. I asked, "Facebook? What the

hell is that?" I had no idea. The social media thing had passed me by but he showed me how to open an account and told me what her last name was now. I looked her up, and sure enough, there she was. It had been so long. I didn't know what to do. I sat there for ages, just looking at her profile and thinking, "Holy jeez!" Finally, I wrote her a message: "Is this the girl who broke my heart 30 years ago?" I gave her a brief overview of what I'd been doing since we last saw each other and said I'd love to know how she was doing. I sent the message and waited. All those years, I'd always wondered what had become of her. I had no idea where she was but I'd think of her every time I heard a Bob Seger song. I hoped she would write back.

The reply came later that day. She was happy to have heard from me. She told me a little about what she'd done since we last saw each other, and that's how we got to talking again. My brother had told her what I had been up to. She always knew I'd been enamored with wrestling when I was a teenager but was surprised to find out that I actually ended up wrestling for a living. We wrote messages to each other and started speaking on the phone a lot. The more we found out about each other's lives, the more we realized how ironic our situation was.

After she had been stationed in Texas, Linda left for a tour in Spain. She was there for five years, then she went to Pope AFB/Fort Bragg in Fayetteville, North Carolina. At one point or another, she was stationed in both Minneapolis, Minnesota, and Sacramento, California for special duty. I can't count the number of times I wrestled at the Target Center and Arco Arena! She was no more than a stone's throw from me and I never knew. The biggest irony was that she was stationed in Montgomery, Alabama, for six years and I was living a two-and-a-half-hour drive away in Mobile. My high school sweetheart had only been two and a half hours down the road! She used to visit Mobile to go to the beaches and Dauphin Island all the time — I sometimes wonder how many times we might have just missed each other.

Back then though, I was married and traveling the world as a wrestler. She was married and traveling the world in the Air Force. In 2009, however, there were no complications. I had been divorced for just over a year and she'd been widowed for four years. To me, it all happened the way it was supposed to happen. She was still the same person she'd been in high school: very goofy, very funny, and very clumsy. She's Lucille Ball all over again. She'll trip over a blade of grass in a second. After a month or so of talking on the phone and sending messages, we decided we wanted to see each other, so I got in my car, drove up to Dubuque, Iowa, and never left. We got married on June 28, 2010. That's when my "happily ever after" started.

I might have stopped wrestling full time but I'm still very active. Despite the pain I live with daily, I work out five days a week. I'm always mountain- and road-biking. It's great having somebody to share these things with. Linda matches me every step of the way. We go camping a lot. I love being out in the woods; if I could live in a tent in the woods forever, I'd do it! When this book hits the stores, I'll likely be in training to do a

Tough Mudder event in Chicago, which is an obstacle course designed by the British Special Forces. It's hardcore, just like me!

When I'm at home, I'm always at work on my Jeep and my other vehicles. I still love everything to do with bikes and cars. I'll spend a lot of time iRacing, which is an interactive virtual racing simulator. A lot of the NASCAR guys race on there, and it's pretty damn cool. On top of all of that, in late 2011, we brought home Abby, an Australian shepherd puppy, and she keeps me plenty busy!

After all the things that have been written about me — some fairly, some unfairly — at least now I've had the chance to tell "the hardcore truth." Now, when people make their minds up about me, they'll have had a chance to get to know Bob Howard, the man, and not just "Bob Holly the wrestler, as presented by WWE." People can like me or not, I'm not going to lose sleep over it. I just prefer that they make their judgment in possession of all the facts. At least then, the conclusion they come to is properly thought through.

So, how do *you* like me now?

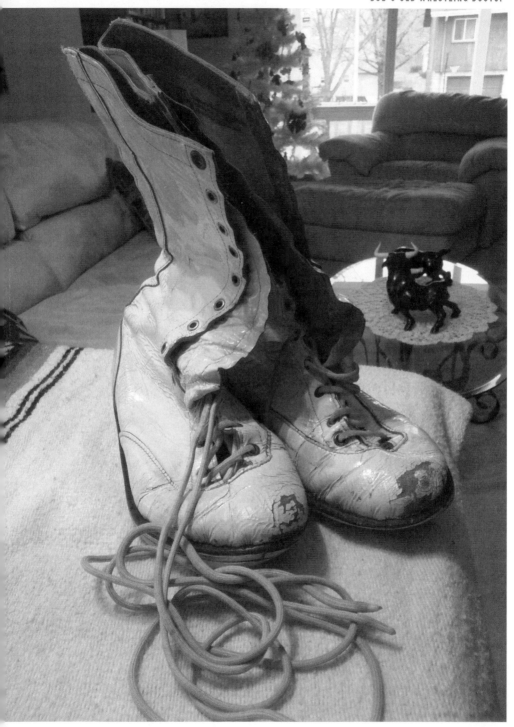

ACKNOWLEDGMENTS

Both Bob and Ross would like to thank ECW Press and Michael Holmes for giving us this platform and their belief in this project.

BOB HOWARD

I am grateful to everyone who has been a part of my life — family, friends, colleagues, and fans.

A special thank-you to:
My mom, Judy, for always doing the best she could for my brother and me. Aunt 'Laine, for always being a ray of sunshine in my life. My first wife, Terri, who cared for my daughter while I was on the road. My wife, Linda, for her unwavering support and unconditional love, as well as playing an integral part in the process of writing this book.

Ross Williams, for his tireless dedication to this project, ability to capture my personality with his words, and the finesse with which he has told my story. His partner, Victoria Welton, for her contributions and sacrifices while Ross was meeting our deadlines.

Both Lenny Hawkins and Paul Bearer, for believing in me and my abilities as a wrestler; your support was instrumental in giving me the opportunity to become a WWE wrestler.

Vince McMahon, for the many years of work. I may not have achieved all that I wanted, but I always appreciated the opportunity.

Ann Russo-Gordon and Nicole Dorazio in the WWE office, for always making my road-life easier.

All the commentators (especially Michael Cole and Taz) who made me seem like the toughest man on the planet, the referees, and everybody involved in the WWE production.

All my travel partners over the years for keeping me sane, particularly Paul Wight and Sid Eudy for being so gracious and generous to me.

Bradshaw for all the ass-whippings — I always looked forward to our matches!

To everybody who ever put me over and helped make me who I was — the guys who have the thankless job of putting others over are the backbone of the industry. No wrestler could become a star without the help of guys who work just as hard but get a lot less in return.

Finally, I want to thank each and every wrestling fan. Sports entertainment would not exist if it weren't for your loyal support and it was truly a privilege to entertain you all.

ROSS WILLIAMS

Firstly, to Bob, thank you for trusting me to tell your story — it has been an honor to do so. Thanks for years of entertainment, your wrestling advice, and even those dozen or so chops. I told you they would make a good story one day! Linda, thank you for your endless contributions to this project, and thank you *both* for your friendship.

Thank you to my "better half," Victoria Welton, for a legion of things, not in the least your patience, understanding, and support during this project. Iain Burnside, your feedback on the numerous drafts of this book has been invaluable — thanks for being my "go-to guy" for well over a decade now!

Thanks also to Katie Carpenter and Donna-Marie Constable who, respectively, encouraged me throughout my wrestling training and "career," and to Chris Bartlett, David Bloxham, and Dan Evans for their ongoing support.

Above all else, to my wonderful family — Mum, Dad, Anna, and Gus — thanks always for your unconditional love and long-held belief that my ability to put words onto paper might come in handy one day.

GET THE eBOOK FREE

At ECW Press, we want you to enjoy this book in whatever format you like, whenever you like. Leave your print book at home and take the eBook to go! Purchase the print edition and receive the eBook free. Just send an email to ebook@ecwpress.com and include:

- the book title
- the name of the store where you purchased it
- your receipt number
- your preference of file type: PDF or ePub?

A real person will respond to your email with your eBook attached. And thanks for supporting an independently owned publisher with your purchase!